Words and the Poet

Characteristic Techniques of Style
in Vergil's *Aeneid*

R. O. A. M. LYNE

CLARENDON PRESS · OXFORD

1989

Oxford University Press, Walton Street, Oxford OX2 6DP

Oxford New York Toronto
Delhi Bombay Calcutta Madras Karachi
Petaling Jaya Singapore Hong Kong Tokyo
Nairobi Dar es Salaam Cape Town
Melbourne Auckland

and associated companies in
Berlin Ibadan

Oxford is a trade mark of Oxford University Press

Published in the United States
by Oxford University Press, New York

British Library Cataloguing in Publication Data

Lyne, R. O. A. M. (Richard Oliver Allen Marcus), 1944–
Words and the poet : characteristic techniques of
style in Vergil's Aeneid.
1. Epic poetry in Latin. Virgil. Aeneid. Critical
studies
I. Title
873.3'01
ISBN 0-19-814896-8

Library of Congress Cataloging in Publication Data
Lyne, R. O. A. M.
Words and the poet : characteristic techniques of style in
Vergil's Aeneid / R.O.A.M. Lyne.
Bibliography: p.
Includes Indexes.
1. Virgil. Aeneid. 2. Virgil—Style. 3. Latin language—Style.
I. Title.
PA6825.L97   1989   883'.01—dc19   89-3086
ISBN 0-19-814896-8

Set by H. Charlesworth & Co. Ltd, Huddersfield
Printed in Great Britain
by Bookcraft (Bath) Ltd, Midsomer Norton

Acknowledgements

My special thanks are due to Dr D. P. Fowler. I profit constantly from this fine scholar's knowledge, ideas, and criticism.

I have other large debts to acknowledge. Mr J. Griffin read portions of this book at an early stage, and subjected them to his usual acute and constructive criticism. Dr G. O. Hutchinson as well as Dr D. P. Fowler read the entire book in a penultimate draft, effecting numerous improvements, and saving me from many mistakes. To all these scholars I am most grateful. If errors of fact or judgement persist, they are due to my own stubbornness.

R.O.A.M.L.

Oxford
May 1989

Contents

I

Vergil's Diction: Context and Definitions

1. The setting. 'Ordinary words' and 'combination': theorists

'Every revolution in poetry is apt to be, and sometimes to announce itself as, a return to common speech' (T. S. Eliot).[1] Much, perhaps most, poetry delights in a poetic diction, language strange to ordinary speech and evocative of experience other than our own.[2] Equally it will sense a need to retain contact with the real language of those with whom it wishes to communicate. This latter consideration, as Eliot says, periodically seems paramount, both to practitioners and to theorists. Then the problem presents itself, consciously or unconsciously: how is poetry substantially composed in the language of everyday men to *be* poetry? The problem presents itself, if less acutely, to those who champion the paramountcy of poetic diction. If I (no poet) string together words exclusively restricted to poetical usage, I will not produce everyday language; but neither will I produce the genuine article. But the problem is perhaps more acute and visible when ordinary language is the material favoured. In all cases, however, it is there: how to make the words poetry? Poets are practitioners of the answer. Critics must try to understand and analyse the process.

The ancient world periodically provides its theorists who champion or recognize the importance of ordinary language in poetry, and poets who promote it in practice. Euripides was one

---

[1] T. S. Eliot, *The Music of Poetry* (Glasgow 1942), 16, reprinted in *On Poetry and Poets* (London 1957), 31 (quoted by L. P. Wilkinson at the start of his excellent article 'The Language of Virgil and Horace'; for 'as' the reprint has 'to be').

[2] There must be substantial agreement among us all on what is meant by 'poetic diction' and other such quasi-technical terms (among which I include 'ordinary speech / language'); but of course our opinions, perhaps rather our ways of articulating our understanding, start to differ considerably when we proceed to detail. For the moment I rely on the assumed substantial agreement. I shall define more closely what I mean by the terminology in sections 3 and 4.

such poet, and was seen as such by Aristotle (*Rhet.* 1404b. 18–25):

... wherefore it is necessary for a poet [A. is thinking at this point particularly of dramatic poets] to conceal his art ... The beguilement[3] is well effected if he picks and combines words from ordinary language: which is what Euripides does, and he was the first to show the way.[4]

'Longinus' makes a similar point about Euripides and others in 'On Sublimity' 40.2:

Many poets ... who use in general common and everyday words which carry with them no special effect, nevertheless acquire magnificence and splendour, and avoid being thought low or mean, solely by the way in which they combine and fit together their words. Philistus, Aristophanes sometimes, Euripides generally, are among the many examples.[5]

And he quotes in illustration Euripides' Heracles who, after the killing of his children, says (*Her.* 1245):

γέμω κακῶν δὴ κοὐκέτ' ἔσθ' ὅπῃ τεθῇ

I'm laden with troubles, and there's no room left for more.'

And among other theorists' statements[6] we must cite famous lines of Horace, wearing his critic's hat in the *Ars Poetica*,[7] 46–9 and 240–3:[8]

> in uerbis etiam tenuis cautusque serendis (46)
> hoc amet, hoc spernat, promissi carminis auctor. (45)[9]
> dixeris egregie notum si callida uerbum
> reddiderit iunctura nouum.

---

[3] κλέπτεται: see next note.

[4] διὸ δεῖ λανθάνειν ποιοῦντας ... κλέπτεται δ'εὖ, ἐάν τις ἐκ τῆς εἰωθυίας διαλέκτου ἐκλέγων συντιθῇ· ὅπερ Εὐριπίδης ποιεῖ καὶ ὑπέδειξε πρῶτος. κλέπτω, translated 'beguile', refers to the deception effected by art, the 'illusion'. For the use of the verb cf. Pindar *Nem.* 7.23 σοφία δὲ κλέπτει παράγοισα μύθοις.

[5] πολλοὶ ... ποιητῶν ... κοινοῖς καὶ δημώδεσι τοῖς ὀνόμασι καὶ οὐδὲν ἐπαγομένοις περιττὸν ὡς τὰ πολλὰ συγχρώμενοι, διὰ μόνου τοῦ συνθεῖναι καὶ ἁρμόσαι ταῦτα ... ὄγκον καὶ διάστημα καὶ τὸ μὴ ταπεινοὶ δοκεῖν εἶναι περιεβάλοντο, καθάπερ ἄλλοι τε πολλοὶ καὶ Φίλιστος, Ἀριστοφάνης ἔν τισιν, ἐν τοῖς πλείστοις Εὐριπίδης.

[6] For some others see Wilkinson, 'Language', 182 f.

[7] Horace presents a different picture of the diction suited to poetry in *Epist.* 2.2. The shift in the *Ars* is I think explicable.

[8] Note that this second passage particularly concerns Satyric drama. On the difference in purpose and emphasis see Brink's note on *Ars* 240–3.

[9] The transposition was made in an edition of 1516 and sustained by Bentley. For its justification see Brink ad loc.

In the joining[10] of his words the aspiring author of a poem[11] should be delicate[12] and cautious, fancying one word and rejecting another. Your style will have excellence if expert[13] combination makes a familiar word new.

> ex noto fictum carmen sequar, ut sibi quiuis
> speret idem, sudet multum frustraque laboret
> ausus idem: tantum series iuncturaque pollet,
> tantum de medio sumptis accedit honoris.

I will aim at a poem created out of the familiar, such that anyone might hope to emulate it, but sweat much and toil in vain if he ventured to; such is the power of connection and combination, such the dignity that can accrue to words taken from the common stock.

There are keynotes here. Each talks in one way or another of 'ordinary words' (more on this in a moment), and each talks of their 'combination'. The Greek for 'combine', common to both Aristotle and 'Longinus' is συντίθημι; and Horace's repeated word is 'iunctura'. In the 'combination' clearly resides the mystery: this is the magic process that renders ordinary words poetic. Now Aristotle is not I think implying anything special in his use of the word συντίθημι: he is referring simply to the fact that Euripides does put together ordinary words and that the result is poetry: he is implying nothing as to what happens or how in 'combination', he is implying no explanation of the mystery. 'Longinus' on the other hand, if one reads on past the above quotation, seems to be referring to 'combination', σύν-θεσις, in the rhetorical sense of the euphonious arrangement of words (40.3). He is therefore implying an explanation for the metamorphosis. Harmonious sound is produced by the skilful ordering of words, and this is the secret of poetic combination. D. A. Russell in his commentary ad loc. respects what 'Longinus's' text says, thinking the thesis not without justification. But

[10] On the use of 'sero', by no means obvious in its collocation, and of 'series' in the next quotation, see Brink on *Ars* 46, and below n. 24. I think that Horace wishes to suggest a metaphor from carpentry.

[11] This is Wilkinson's translation ('Language', 186) of 'promissi carminis auctor'. There is probably some pun in 'auctor': see Brink ad loc.

[12] 'Tenuis' is a difficult word to translate here; it conveys λέπτος; see Brink ad loc. Wilkinson 'Language', 186 translates it 'subtle'.

[13] On the implications of 'callidus' see the discussion of 'callet' at Hor. *Carm.* 4.9.49 in section 2 below.

surely the clue to Euripides' poetry in the quoted line resides not
in sound but in sense, in the *semantic* effect of the combination.
What is remarkable (I merely point in what I think to be the right
direction) is the effect of combining γέμω with κακῶν, which
makes *metaphor* (the metaphor is from the loading of a ship),[14]
and of then combining this expressive phrase with the (colloquial?)[15] simplicity of κοὐκέτ' ἔσθ' ὅπη τεθῇ; this combination,
and the rest of the context, makes these intrinsically common-
place words pregnant with horror. Wilkinson following O. Im-
misch[16] thinks in fact that wires have got crossed here and that
'Longinus' is quoting from and misinterpreting a source in which
the effect of σύνθεσις from the semantic point of view was
precisely the point at issue. However this may be, the ability of
combination semantically to enhance words is certainly what
Horace has in mind in the quoted passages, as Brink, Wilkinson,
and many others have seen.[17] How else (we might ask) but in
semantic terms can a 'familiar word' be 'made new'? If he had
been asked about the line of Euripides quoted by 'Longinus',
Horace would have said that 'combination', *iunctura*, makes the
relatively 'familiar word' γέμω 'new'—by making it metaphorical, and in this particular way; and it makes the 'familiar words'
κοὐκέτ' ἔσθ' ὅπη τεθῇ 'new' by making them pregnant with
horror. And, saying this, he would have been right.

2. Horace in this setting

Greek literature provided its Euripides (among others) who
favoured ordinary words and rendered them poetic by combination. And Latin literature provides us with the lyric poet Horace,
true to the theory expounded in the *Ars*. Axelson has shown that
Horace eschews poetic diction in the Odes to a remarkable
degree, and not only favours a predominance of ordinary words,
he employs a high degree of words identifiably *prosaic*[18] (all

---

[14] See Bond ad loc.
[15] Cf. Wilkinson, 'Language', 182.
[16] Wilkinson, 'Language', 182
[17] See Brink on Horace, *Ars Poetica* 47–8 and 242, Wilkinson, 'Language', 186.
[18] Axelson, 98–113; cf. Wilkinson, 'Language', 188. Since I shall criticize Axelson
within seconds on a particular point, I should perhaps stress that I regard his book as
seminal, indeed epoch-making. His general position has been criticized by Williams,
TORP, 743–50, productively criticized by Ernout, 'Review', and reassessed by Watson.

these terms will, as I say, be exactly defined below). But, a fact which Axelson grossly underestimated, Horace does indeed 'combine' them (by syntactical agreement, by simple proximity, or by both) in such a way as to 'make them new', imparting overtones and ambiguities of sense to them through their collocation. In a spectacular couple of pages Wilkinson points to metaphors, puns, oxymora, and so on[19], produced by Horace's combinations, which do in a real sense render the constituent words 'new'. I would like to refer to one other passage, since it is picked out by Axelson and sternly castigated as merely and culpably prose,[20] *Carm.* 4.9.45 ff.:

> non possidentem multa uocaueris
> recte beatum; rectius occupat
>   nomen beati, qui deorum
>   muneribus sapienter uti
>
> duramque callet pauperiem pati
> peiusque leto flagitium timet,
>   non ille pro caris amicis
>   aut patria timidus perire.

You would not call a man who owns many things correctly happy; the name of happy man is more correctly appropriated by him who knows how to use the gifts of the gods wisely and to suffer harsh poverty, and fears disgrace as something worse than death: not fearful he to perish for dear friends or for his country.

Here more than one combination is effective (I regret that my translation is indeed merely prose: I cannot reproduce Horace's combinations). First, note 'beatum'—an ordinary enough word. Horace contrasts the genuinely happy man with the man whose 'happiness' is material prosperity; he is making 'beatum', by its conjunction on the one hand with 'uocaueris recte' and on the other with 'possidentem multa', yield its sense 'happy, blessed' and its sense 'materially wealthy',[21] the former prospective and dominant (because of the adjacent 'u. recte'), the latter retrospective. (The ambiguity, established in 'beatum', will then be remembered in 'beati', and this in turn will activate a somewhat similar but subliminal ambiguity in 'muneribus'.) In Horace's text, 'beatus' is renovated.

[19] Wilkinson, 'Language', 188–90.
[20] Axelson, 111–12.
[21] See *OLD* s.v. 'beatus'.

'Flagitium' is a common word for 'disgrace', 'outrage', frequent in prose but eschewed by most of the poets.[22] Its natural habitat is in everyday moral, political and legal contexts; this everyday usage will have been the reason why the poets generally felt it to be unuseful to them (cf. below pp. 10 f.). But Horace has a task for it—and 'renders it new'. He combines it with a word of poetic diction, 'letum'. 'Letum', the evocative word of fearful, fabled death, is said by Horace *not* to be as fearful in the estimation of the wise man as regular, familiar old disgrace. That should make us look at 'disgrace' with new eyes, think about it, search it for a significance to which through familiarity we have become desensitized.

Finally 'callet'. He uses the verb 'callet' instead of say 'nouit'[23] because (for one thing) it possesses a distinct nuance of sense that he can profitably activate. 'Calleo' is at root a very physical word: it derives from 'callum', a callus. 'Calleo' comes to mean 'be knowledgeable', because practical experience gives one calloused hands and it is through such experience that one becomes knowledgeable. Cf. Cicero on the cognate adjective 'callidus': *N. D.* 3.25 'uersutos eos appello quorum celeriter mens uersatur, callidos autem quorum tamquam manus opere sic animus usu concalluit', 'I call those whose minds move nimbly "adroit"; those whose minds have become calloused with experience as the hand is calloused by work I call "knowledgeable" (*or* "expert", 'callidus')'. 'Calleo' therefore most naturally suits a *practical* intelligence, the intelligence say of a Cato: Liv. 39.40.5 'urbanas rusticasque res pariter callebat (sc. Cato)', 'Cato was knowledgeable in the business of town and country'. By combining 'callet' with 'dura', 'pati', and indeed 'pauperiem', all of which are words of potentially physical import, Horace reminds one of this

---

[22] See Axelson, 111. *TLL* s.v.: 'saepe apud Plaut., Ter.; imprimis usurpatur per totam latinitatem ab oratoribus et historicis praeter Caes.; raro legitur apud poetas excepta prisca latinitate.' Some figures: Enn. 1 (341J = 395V), the glorious 'flagiti principium est nudare inter ciuis corpora'), Lucr. 0, Catull. 1 (67.42), Prop. 0, Tib. 0, Hor. 3 (*Serm.* 2.4.82, *Carm.* 3.5.26, 4.9.50), Verg. 0, Ov. 0, Luc. 0, Val. 0.

[23] Axelson, 111, acknowledges 'callet' as an effort 'to lift the diction above the everyday' ('die Diktion über die Alltagssprache zu erheben'), but calls its poetic value 'questionable'. I doubt whether it 'lifts'. I would hazard the guess that the word is nearer colloquial than poetical, but surviving instances make its tone very hard to estimate. Whatever its stylistic register was, Horace is presumably using this as well as the semantic nuance I point to. If it *was* colloquial this would reinforce the down-to-earth effect I describe.

physical root and brings it, and the practical orientation of the word, right to the fore. In this way he brings his philosophizing down to earth in a satisfyingly Roman fashion, and 'calleo' is freshened, rendered new, by its combination—like 'beatus' and 'flagitium'.[24]

Latin literature provides us with Horace as a poet who favours ordinary language to a remarkable degree; and it provides us with Vergil. But before I proceed to Vergil I shall seek to define my terms a little more precisely. First, that term 'ordinary language' vel sim.

3. Ordinary words: the categories. Prosaism, colloquialism, neutral words

All our theorists in section 1 talk in one way or another of 'ordinary (current, standard) language or words'. Aristotle at *Rhet.* 1404b. 24 has ἡ εἰωθυῖα διάλεκτος. He talks too of τὸ κύριον (ὄνομα etc.) in various places, which Horace translates as 'dominantia (nomina uerbaque)' at *Ars* 234 f.[25] 'Longinus' 40.2 has τὰ ὀνόματα κοινὰ καὶ δημώδη, and Horace at *Ars* 243 'de medio sumpta'; and Horace's 'notum uerbum' at *Ars* 47 seems to me not significantly (*pace* Brink ad loc.) distinct from these. And there are other ways of referring to the concept.[26] Thus our theorists. It will be helpful to us to introduce categories. And I must now acknowledge a particular emphasis. Others things besides simple choice of words contribute to whether language may be basically termed 'ordinary' or not, and to what category of the 'ordinary' it may be assigned: morphology, accidence,

[24] In the words of the *Ars*, the collocation of 'dura', 'pati', 'pauperiem' and 'callet' is 'callida iunctura'. It may now be evident that Horace effects a 'callida iunctura' in 'callida iunctura' itself. The conjunction of 'serendis', 'callida', and 'iunctura', all potentially physical in import, brings that physical import to the fore, and suggests, I think, a metaphor of carpentry. In this respect it is significant that neither 'sero' nor 'iunctura' are familiar, and thus rendered inert, in the verbal metaphors that Horace gives to them: see Brink on *Ars* 46 and 47–8. Cf. Caes. *Gall.* 4.17.6 for 'iunctura' of a joint between beams.

[25] Aristotle *Rhet.* 1404b. 5–6, 31–2, 34–5, *Poet.* 1457b. 1. Brink on *Ars* 234: 'As Bywater says, Ar. *Poet.* 21, 1457 b 1 n., κύριον in Ar. is (a) "the established and familiar name for a thing", as distinct from glosses, metaphors, and any other "strange use" of language, and (b) more specifically, the literal term distinct from the metaphorical'. In, say, Arist. *Rhet.* 1404b. 31–2 and *Poet.* 1457b. 1 (and 3) as well as Hor. *Ars.* 234 it seems to me that sense (a) is dominant.

[26] See Brink on *Ars* 47.

syntax. But I concentrate on the manageable question of word-selection. It is in fact a matter of great consequence that a poet chooses this word and not that, and one that seems to me to be undervalued in discussions of the Latin poets.

We may name three groups of words which are involved in or implied by the umbrella term 'ordinary words': *prosaic, colloquial, neutral.*[27]

First we should try to distinguish the *prosaic*[28] and the *colloquial:*[29] i.e. diction that is characteristic of the most ordinary literature and diction that is confined to ordinary speech. Often, perhaps usually, prosaic words will *also* be used naturally in speech (e.g. 'panis' below; contrast 'osculum'; this is a point I shall not trouble to reiterate); by colloquial I mean words that are *restricted* to, or much more typical of, the spoken tongue (e.g. 'basium').

I shall try to use these terms in a strictly generic way. It is a statistical fact that some words are confined to certain basic genres written in prose; they may have a currency visible or to be assumed in the spoken tongue, but they are otherwise more or less exclusively confined to the prose genres.[30] It is also a statistical fact that other words are confined more or less exclusively to the genres agreed by scholars most to reflect the spoken tongue. It is to such facts that I am referring when I call diction prosaic or colloquial. But I shall attempt the next stage, which is to try to determine *why* diction is thus limited, to determine what qualities of sense or habits of usage have

---

[27] The 'ordinary language' of the ancient theorists and my three groups of words will not necessarily coincide exactly. For example, some 'colloquialisms' might have seemed unordinary to our theorists.

[28] Antiquity has ways of designating 'prose', e.g. Aristotle's simple λόγος at *Rhet.* 1404b. 5 or his ψιλοὶ λόγοι at 1404b. 14; or 'oratio soluta' (as opposed to 'uersus') at e.g. Varro *Rust.* 1.1.9 or 'prosa oratio' (as opposed to 'carmen') at Sen *Epist.* 94.27; but antiquity does not so far as I know define the idea of a prosaic diction in the sense above.

[29] Antiquity has terms that coincide with English 'colloquial language', the 'spoken tongue', sim.: cf. Aristotle's διάλεκτος (in its context) at *Rhet.* 1404a. 34, Horace's 'sermo' at *Serm.* 1.4.42, *Rhet. Her.* 3.23 'sermo est oratio remissa et finitima cotidianae locutioni', etc.

[30] Identifying many of these was the great achievement of Axelson. Williams, *TORP*, 745 writes: 'there is no real lexicographical boundary in Latin between prose and poetry.' There may be a good deal of No Man's Land, but Prose and Poetry do indeed possess some territory that is distinctly their own.

restricted a word's use in these ways.[31] This is the most interesting, but, especially with a dead language, the most difficult stage, given that our knowledge of nuances, particularly the nuances of the spoken tongue, is so tiny. Often our efforts will be no more than informed or inspired guesses.

When gathering statistics to define prosaic diction, there are precautions to be taken. First (and this is true of all categories of diction), we should so far as possible take account of lapses of time and changes in taste.[32] If a word is prosaic in (and, according to statistics, only in) the Silver Age, this should certainly not shape our view of the word in Vergil's time: Tacitus, for example, takes much diction poetical in Vergil's time from Vergil himself. He is precisely trying to adapt poetical vocabulary to the writing of history.

In general it is sensible, when gathering statistics to define a basic prose diction, to be wary of prose works which (like Tacitus) are known to be receptive to diction otherwise largely poetical, and to favour those that are demonstrably more austere. We should thus favour Caesar,[33] Varro, and other technical writers (cautiously)[34] over not only Tacitus but e.g. Livy, especially in his first decade; or, to put it another way, we should distinguish between what we might call *business* prose (Caesar, etc.) and *imaginative* prose (pre-eminently rhetorical

---

[31] Here Axelson is deficient. An assumption I make is that there must ultimately be a reason why a word becomes the particular property of (say) prose.

[32] A point made by Williams, *TORP*, 744 in his critique of Axelson.

[33] We remember that the *Commentarii* were intended as a plain, factual narrative, raw material that another professional historian would then turn into artistic history. Cf. Cic. *Brutus*, 262 'ualde ... probandos (sc. Caesar's *Commentarii*); nudi enim sunt, recti et uenusti, omni ornatu orationis tamquam ueste detracta. sed dum uoluit alios habere parata, unde sumerent qui uellent scribere historiam, ineptis gratum fortasse fecit, qui illa uolent calamistris inurere: sanos quidem homines a scribendo deterruit; nihil est enim in historia pura et inlustri breuitate dulcius.' The excellence of the *Commentarii* as they stand may have deterred the professionals, but this does not change the fact that they are essentially a plain and soldierly narrative, and naturally eschew more colourful, poetical diction that a rhetorical historiographer might tolerate. Such an attitude to diction would be enhanced by Caesar's beliefs as an 'Analogist': cf. Leeman, i. 157, 174 f., noting especially this dictum from Caesar's *De Analogia* (Gellius 1.10.4): 'tamquam scopulum, sic fugias inauditum atque insolens uerbum'.

[34] Varro (*Rust.*) and Vitruvius, in most respects eminently 'business' prose writers (for the term see below), do display some colloquial tendencies: Löfstedt, *Syntactica*, ii. 337 f.

historiography),[35] favouring the former over the latter as our criterion for the prosaic. When defining the prosaic we should also be considered in our use of those prose works known to be hospitable to colloquial diction (e.g. Cic. *Letters*, Petronius). On the other hand, we should not be surprised into changing our categorization if diction otherwise statistically prosaic occurs in verse genres that can be shown to accommodate prosaic (as well as colloquial) diction (e.g. Horace's and others' Satires, Hor. *Epist.*).

On each occasion when I identify a word as prosaic I shall (as I say) make efforts to explain or guess why its use was restricted in this way. But some general suggestions may be offered in advance; I consider why a word should be prosaic as opposed to poetical.

(1) Prosaic words are often, I think, denotative rather than connotative: steady and limited in their designation rather than generous and suggestive. Poetry, a suggestive medium, naturally inclines to words that are rich with implications. The task of many prose writers, especially 'business' prose writers, urges upon them *precision*.[36] They therefore favour words of exacter definition. Words that have become generically prosaic may owe their status to this quality. They have become prosaic because they offer exacter definition, a precise denotation; and because they do not offer suggestiveness. We know exactly what we are talking about with the word 'gladius': it denotes the weapon of Roman regular army issue; and therefore a writer like Caesar uses it. We know what we are not talking about with the word 'ensis': the sword of Roman regular army issue. It is limited to no such denotation, offering instead the suggestive and inexact connotations of the blades of epic heroes. And so the poets generally prefer it.[37]

(2) At a given time some kinds of subject-matter may be deemed more suited to (certain types of) prose than to poetry.[38] In the Augustan age, for example, some everyday subjects, e.g.

---

[35] I avoid the normally useful term *Kunstprosa* because I am loath to deny that title to Caesar. Oratory has both its 'business' and its 'imaginative' moments.

[36] Tränkle makes cognate remarks about prose's pursuit of *clarity*: he talks (7) of 'die um gedankliche Klarheit bemühte Sprache der Kunstprosa' (I would not use the term *Kunstprosa* in this connection).

[37] On 'gladius' and 'ensis' see ch. V.1.i.

[38] In this connection cf. the comments of G. Williams, *TORP*, 748.

mercantile affairs, bodily needs, and medical conditions, are more naturally dealt with in prose genres than in poetry. Now this is not to say that any subject-matter is absolutely untreatable in poetry at a given time. It is to say that words too directly or actively associated with such matter will be avoided by the poets, but accepted by certain prose writers; and poets wishing to refer to the topic will find other words. Thus prose writers will be happy to talk of money, 'pecunia', but poets will usually prefer to broach the topic by a more roundabout and glamorous route (e.g. 'aurum', 'opes').[39] A Cato, Celsus or Pliny (a 'business' prose writer) happily and exactly talks of the bread we eat, 'panis'; poets prefer to talk not exactly of the bread we eat, and favour the resonating, indirect metonymy 'Ceres'.[40] Pregnancy can be adumbrated in the highest of genres without offence (e.g. 'grauis' at *Aen.* 1.274), but it takes prose with direct needs (Cicero in *Div.*, Varro in *Rust.*) to use the word 'praegnans', unless some exceptional effect is being pursued.[41] Sometimes the words disfavoured by poetry are denotative, and denoting too fixedly the topic in question, without other and camouflaging connotations; i.e. point (1) may coincide with point (2): this is the situation I think with the words just mentioned. Sometimes the word has plenty of connotations, but all of them belong in the area felt to be unpoetic: this I think may be the case with 'flagitium', above p. 6, which suggests many types of scandal and disgrace, but all of them belong to an everyday world which the poets did not think their business.

(3) We should note that the process of becoming generically prosaic is probably self-reinforcing. Once prose has exhibited a particular interest in a word (for, say, reason 1 or 2), that interest in itself may become (another) reason why poetry avoids it.

When we turn to identify words typical of the spoken tongue, we find ourselves operating with the greatest difficulties. The conversational language, even that of the cultivated and literate

---

[39] Axelson, 108. Cf. the situation with the word 'merces': Lyne, *Further Voices*, 52, 59.

[40] Cato *Rust.* has 7 examples of 'panis'. (Varr. *Rust.* 4). *TLL* 'panis': 'legitur inde a Plauto, Catone; saepissime in script. sacr., cum antea pauci sint, qui frequentent, sc. praecipue Cels. et Plin. *Nat.*; in carminum genere grandiore substituitur uox q.e. "Ceres" … itaque "panis" omnino deest Lucr., Verg., Hor. *Carm.* (septies in *Sat.* et *Epist.*), Tib., Prop. [etc]'. Cf. the situation with 'cena': figures at Axelson, 107.

[41] Cf. Lyne, *Further Voices*, 53, 59 f.

classes,[42] is the province where our knowledge is most acutely defective. We are dependent on written documents, indeed literary works, which seem to reflect the spoken tongue, but to a greater or lesser extent inevitably refract it. Such writers and genres, most likely to be evidence for the spoken tongue, are: Plautus, especially in his *senarii*,[43] other comedy, Catullus' casual poems, Cicero's *Letters*, Horace's and others' *Satires*, Horace's *Epistles*, Petronius. Sometimes the persistence of a word in the romance languages can be used to confirm or to argue for its colloquial status in classical Latin.[44] It will be noticed that we are driven to scrutinize authors widely separated in time, and the fact that tastes and attitudes to language shift over the generations must here be especially borne in mind. A large incidence of a word in, say, Plautus is not much evidence for the colloquial status of a word in Vergil's time, without corroborating witnesses: it might well have become obsolete by then. But it remains a possibility, and *faute de mieux* we sometimes have to consider possibilities.

What factors lead to a word's becoming statistically colloquial? We may advance one explanation in line with the second explanation offered for prosaism above. Literature has ways of treating any kind of subject-matter. But words too directly or actively associated with subjects that contemporary taste from time to time deems not well suited to literary expression—e.g. the intimate feelings, objects and actions of everyday private life — will be avoided.[45] Thus late republican literature is happy to

---

[42] On the spoken tongue see Hofmann, but note the criticisms of his use of comedy as a source in Happ 73 ff. Löfstedt rightly stresses the gradations within colloquialism, *Syntactica*, ii. 354 ff.; likewise Happ 64. On colloquialism see too e.g. Marouzeau, *Traité*, 181 ff.

[43] On the use of Plautus as a source, see Happ esp. 79 ff.

[44] See Löfstedt, *Syntactica*, ii. 317 ff., esp. 320 ff. 'Basium' I take to be a case in point. Löfstedt shows us that we should be prepared for the phenomenon of (so to call it) the 'classical gap'. Often a colloquial word will be attested in early Latin, late Latin, and the romance languages, but be unattested in surviving witnesses to the Latin of (say) the 1st century BC. This is due to the high degree of squeamishness of the surviving Latin of that period, not to a temporary and inexplicable period of obsolescence.

[45] The Elder Seneca (*Contr.* 7 *praef.* 3 f.) criticized the orator Albucius for not displaying sufficient discrimination in the face of the everyday: 'res dicebat omnium sordidissimas, acetum et puleium et lanternas et spongias: nihil putabat esse quod dici in declamatione non posset. erat autem illa causa: timebat ne scholasticus uideretur ...' Seneca's taste is notably and perhaps idiosyncratically abstemious, but

talk of 'oscula', but 'sauia' or 'basia', too directly evoking the
action of everyday, are eschewed except by genres reflecting
speech.[46] People can groan, 'gemo', in literature, but (as I shall
argue, ch. V.2) 'congemo' actively brings to mind the inglorious
action of everyday, and was therefore avoided (normally) in the
higher classes of literature.

The third category I would identify among 'ordinary words' is
one we may call 'neutral words'. By 'neutral words' I mean
words which may occur in any or all of the genres of prose, in the
spoken tongue, and too in poetry, but which belong particularly
to none of these and bear the stamp of none of them. I mean
words like 'sol', 'uir', 'herba'.

4. Poetical words and poetic diction

The term 'poeti*cal*' and how I shall use it must also be
defined.[47] It too I shall use primarily in a generic sense: it will
mean essentially that a word is statistically confined to the poets.
But there are complicatory factors to note, and precautions to be
taken.

We must, for example, again take acount of lapses of time and

his criticism arises from a principle that all conventional orators would have
supported. We should however observe that his remark contains one confusion. He
should have said 'uerba' not 'res'. There is nothing conclusively objectionable about
the 'res' 'lanterna' (for example), even to a Seneca, as long as it is adumbrated by
other 'uerba'. Cf. how the elevated poet Vergil, some steps further up the ladder of
linguistic sensitivity, conveys the 'res' 'lucerna' (i.e. a 'res' comparable to a
'lanterna'): *Georg.* 1.391 'testa ... ardente', *Aen.* 1.726 'lychni'. Propertius incidentally
is happy with the 'uerbum' 'lucerna' (2.15.3, 4.8.43), and so is Horace (3 examples in
Carm., 3 in *Serm.*). Quint. *Inst.* 8.2.2 criticized excessive scrupulousness (like
Seneca's?) in matters of diction: 'et obscena uitabimus et sordida et humilia. sunt
autem humilia infra dignitatem rerum aut ordinis. in quo uitio cauendo non
mediocriter errare quidam solent, qui omnia quae sunt in usu, etiamsi causae
necessitas postulet, reformidant; ut ille qui in actione Hibericas herbas se solo
nequiquam intellegente dicebat, nisi irridens hanc uanitatem Cassius Seuerus spar-
tum dicere eum uelle indicasset.' I am indebted for these references to Tränkle 109,
who provides other material on the topic. For other factors which might lead to a
word's colloquial status, see Löfstedt, *Syntactica*, ii. 350–1.

[46] Cf. Axelson, 35, Tränkle, 126. 'Basium' seems to have displaced 'sauium' as the
favoured word of the spoken tongue at some point in the late republic.

[47] I shall henceforth almost entirely restrict the word 'poetic' to the technical
phrase *poetic diction*, to be defined shortly (hitherto I have allowed myself to use this
word in a general and suggestive way).

changes in taste. And here there is a special factor: Vergil (and what I say about Vergil could also be said about Ovid). If Vergil, Valerius, Silius, and Statius all use a word, we must not simply count hands unchronologically and infer that it was a conventional poet's tool. Valerius and co. often use a word simply because Vergil did. Vergil sets precedents, legitimizes much diction that was in fact *un*poetical in his day.[48] This 'legitimizing' effect I have remarked on elsewhere,[49] and will have occasion to do so again. Sometimes very amusing examples can be cited.[50]

To make statistics on poetical words subtler we should also be aware of the *hierarchy of genres*.[51] Some genres regard themselves as grander than others and favour elevated poetic diction in consequence; others border on, or affect to border on, ordinary speech and are receptive to, indeed evidence for, the categories of ordinary diction, prosaism and colloquialism. We have already touched on this in other contexts (Section 3): it is clear, for example, that we should not regard occurrences in Plautus, especially his *senarii*, as reason in itself to label a word poetical. But I develop the topic slightly for my present purpose. Horace identifies his Satires as 'sermoni propiora' (*Serm.* 1.4.42) and entitled them *Sermones*.[52] Even if he is not entirely serious in so doing, we should expect a different attitude to diction in these from that in the Odes, the poems which he hopes will merit his insertion into the canon of Greek lyric poets (*Carm.* 1.1.35). And we find it: we find, for example, more colloquialisms. We should expect Ennius' epic to differ in attitude to diction from his Satires, Catullus' poem 64 to differ from his insulting epigrams, Vergil's *Aeneid* to differ from his *Bucolics*, and Ovid's *Metamorphoses* from his love elegies.[53] These and similar expectations are

---

[48] Cf. Williams, *TORP*, 744.

[49] 'Diction and Poetry', 71 ('excutio').

[50] Vergil *Aen.* 6.513 f. 'ut supremam falsa inter gaudia noctem / egerimus, nosti' legitimizes a phrase 'noctem / diem egero' for the wretched Valerius (5.298, 8.454) who did not realize 'egerimus' was the perfect subjunctive of 'ago' (Leumann, 138 n. 43 = Lunelli, 168 n. 43); contrast Sen. *Epist.* 59.17 f., correctly understanding the passage. For other such misunderstandings in Valerius see Courtney, 151 f.

[51] That there is a hierarchy of genres is an assumption of Axelson's which I think his book justifies. The assumption was challenged by Williams, *TORP*, 746 ff., but supported by Watson.

[52] Cf. *Epist.* 1.4.1, 2.1.250, 2.2.60.

[53] Note the contrast Ovid himself draws between Elegy and Tragedy, *Am.* 3.1. esp. 39 f.; see further Tränkle 17 f.

natural, and are indeed frequently borne out by statistical facts. This is not to say there is a *rigid* hierarchy. Long before the Augustan age, there had been designed interaction between the genres,[54] and we should also expect poets creatively to depart from norms which they may still feel: these factors are particularly evident in, say, the lyric Horace and (as we shall see) the epic Vergil. But in assessing diction we must nevertheless be aware that some hierarchy still existed. And so if the only poets to show a word are Lucilius, Horace in his Satires, and Juvenal, this is not much (if any) compromise of an otherwise prosaic or colloquial profile; if Ennius shows it in the *Annales* or Vergil in the *Aeneid*, it may be.[55]

What factors contribute to a word's becoming statistically poetical? I have already suggested above (section 3) that poetry inclines to suggestive vocabulary, to words that are connotative rather than denotative. Many, probably most, poetical words are suggestive in a definable way, one which would clearly encourage their adoption by poetry, and discourage their adoption by prose. We may call these words *poetic diction*. I now offer an initial definition of what I mean by poetic diction; I have tailored the term to my own particular circumstances.[56] By poetic diction I mean words that are able to introduce into a poet's text resonances or connotations unavailable in the categories of ordinary language but available in another source. To proceed beyond generalities, we will consider the two main components of Latin poetic diction, archaism and grecism. Ancient and modern discussions of these are curiously unhelpful, particularly as regards their function.[57]

---

[54] See Kroll, 207–24 on the 'Kreuzung der Gattungen'.

[55] A simple illustration of generic hierarchy is afforded by the prosaic and spoken word 'panis'. Cf. the description of the word above p. 11 and n. 40, noting its occurrence in Horace's *Sermones* and *Epistles*; note too that it occurs twelve times in Juvenal. Tränkle, 18 examines expressions for the inception and cessation of love in Augustan Elegy, Catullus' longer poems, and the *Aeneid*, and neatly thereby indicates some hierarchical differences.

[56] My approach is lexically-oriented (cf. p. 7), and I have confined my use and definition of the term accordingly. The studies of Kroll ('Die Dichtersprache'), Leumann, and Jannsen are more general. The focus of Bell's *The Latin Dual and Poetic Diction* is even more different from mine, but his book is stimulating and useful. I have also profited much by the books of Tillotson and Barfield, though their field is English literature. The best ancient comments on the topic are Aristotle's. See n 57.

[57] Cf., as well as the items in n. 56 above, Löfstedt, *Syntactica*, ii. 406 ff., Ernout, *Aspects*, 72–96, esp. 86 ff., and on Vergilian archaism in particular Cordier, 6 ff.,

What a Latin poet is doing when he archaizes is, as a rule, drawing an obsolete term from a *literary* source or tradition.[58] Vergil archaizes by using the language of, for example, Ennius. The diction thus revived brings with it the connotations which it had in that tradition: that is why it is revived. This is true with the meanest of examples. 'Infit' in Vergil does not mean the same as 'incipit': its sense of 'begin (to speak)' has epic resonance; 'olli', 'ollis' are dative forms of a pronoun that refers to epic characters, not to Everyman. You and I have never seen and can never see the 'clipeus' of the archaizing poets: it is the defence of heroes from the epic tradition, of men who are not such as ourselves.[59] Words such as these refer to objects and actions of a fabled world, a world *other* than our own. That is why they are chosen: to suggest such 'otherness'.[60]

Similar things can be said about grecizing. Vergil and, much more noticeably, Ennius, finding the native Latin tradition insufficient to meet their need for diction with heroic connotations, for 'otherness' of sense, turned to Greek literary tradition and sought to import such connotations. Ennius borrowed Greek, usually Homeric words, made calques of others (e.g. 'marmor' for the sea),[61] constructed compound adjectives in the Homeric manner, and so on: all to help the texture of his poetry

---

Norden on Aeneid 6, Anhang 1, Wilkinson 'Language', 181 ff., esp. 185, R. D. Williams on *Aen.* 3.354 (and the indexes to the other commentaries of R. D. Williams and Austin), and, on Vergilian Grecism, Cordier, 174 ff., Wilkinson, *loc. cit.*, Austin on 2.377, R. D. Williams on 3.705, 5.352 and 452, Austin on 6.141. Ancient discussions of, or allusions to, archaism and grecism are to be found at: Hor. *Serm.* 1.10.20 ff., *Epist.* 2.2.115 ff., *Ars* 52 ff., Cic. *De Orat.* 3.152 ff., Quint. 1.5.65–70, 1.6.39, 12.10.33 (an interestingly curious remark).

Note, however, Aristotle's perceptive comments on ξεν(ικ)ός *sim.* language: *Poetics* 1458a. 22 ff., *Rhet.* 1404b. 10 ff., also 1405a. 8 ff., 1406a. 15.

[58] The existence of the word in literature is vital. The revival of a purely obsolete word would be quite different in impact, and is not what is at issue. (For a very special effect Vergil once revives an archaism devoid of literary life, 'obnubo' at *Aen.* 11.77: see ch. VII.7.)

[59] On 'clipeus' see V.1.i; my careful phrasing ('the 'clipeus' *of the archaizing poets*') is designed to allow for the fact that 'clipeus' can be used non-poetically to denote a particular type and shape of archaic shield, i.e. a 'real' and unheroic one: e.g. Liv. 1.43.4, ch. V p. 104. On 'infit' see Enn. *Ann.* 385 with Skutsch's note, Verg. *Aen.* 5.708 etc.; on 'olli', 'ollis' see Skutsch's *Ennius*, intro. pp. 64–6.

[60] What I mean by such 'otherness' and what Aristotle talks of in connection with ξενικός language are similar. See above n. 57.

[61] Enn. *Ann.* 377Sk. = 384V; cf. Homer *Iliad* 14.273 ἄλα μαρμαρέην. Vergil supplies the more exact Homericism, 'marmoreus': see *Aen.* 6.729 with Austin ad loc.

suggest *another* time and order, distinct from the mundane present: Homer's time and order. Vergil grecised similarly but, having a richer Latin tradition at his disposal, less stridently.[62]

So we can in fact see a single purpose behind Vergil's (and other poets') grecizing and archaizing: the introduction of suggestive sense that has accrued in a literary tradition, in particular the epic tradition. Vergil brings in words from Ennius or Homer to suggest actions, people, things distinct from ordinary experience. And this gives us our fuller definition of poetic diction in general - whose main and typical components in Latin are archaism and grecism. It adds 'otherness', it introduces connotations (in fact, sense) unavailable in the categories of ordinary language, connotations that have accrued in a literary tradition.[63]

5. Vergil, and the subject of this book

Horace makes poetry out of 'ordinary words' to a remarkable degree, and is perhaps most striking for his use of prosaisms. Investigators of Vergil's vocabulary[64] have likewise established that in spite of being 'amantissimus uetustatis' (Quint. 1.7.18) Vergil relies remarkably little, considering his genre, on archaism and other poetic diction; like Horace he favours the use of 'iunctura', 'combination', to produce poetry from 'ordinary words';[65] and like Horace he is receptive to prosaic diction in particular and to the effects that can be gained with it. Some characteristic Vergilian techniques of combination, operating for the most part with 'ordinary words', are illustrated in this book.

It seems to me that Vergil's procedures with language are often more extreme than Horace's. Vergil uses combinations not only

---

[62] Such literary grecizing is to be distinguished from Greek borrowings made in the spoken tongue. These are the work of sailors, businessmen, artisans, and so on, people exposed to everyday Greek influence, and are obviously quite different in impact. See Jannsen 28 = Lunelli 114 (Lunelli provides updated bibliography).

[63] Some words derive from and are confined to the literary tradition—they are in short poetic diction—but they are difficult to label as archaism, or whatever, e.g. the word 'ensis' (see Ch. V.1.i). But since the purpose of poetic diction has been established as fundamentally single, and a word like 'ensis' shares this purpose, the matter is not great.

[64] Cordier, Wilkinson, 'Language', 185 f.

[65] See the under-read chapter in Jackson Knight, 225 ff., 'Language, Verse and Style', and Quinn, 384 ff.

as Horace to 'make a familiar word new', to freshen it, but to extort novelty of sense, to wrest from a word some quite unexpected meaning. Horace can put prosaic (or colloquial) words to work in spite of their unpromising familiarity; Vergil can more vigorously exploit them. Because of the more extreme nature of such techniques, I adopt assertive, even violent metaphors to describe them: 'extortion', 'exploitation'.

But not all Vergil's methods merit such descriptions. His use of the traditional simile is characterized rather by discretion and guile. Discreetly and guilefully 'narrative through imagery' accompanies more forceful methods of making poetry, on key occasions linking up with them. Guilefully, too, Vergil may use (say) one of his exploitations as an incitement to us to pursue a sequence of related effects; and he may discreetly persuade a neutral word to acquire some special sense over a stretch of text.

The total result is dense, teasing, often puzzling. Vergil can seem, and has seemed even in antiquity, elusive or obscure. So it seemed to M. Vipranius, if that be his name.[66] While I illustrate some of Vergil's characteristic techniques in this book, it may be that I shall lighten some obscurities.

The detailed information and statistics which I provide on diction derive in the first place from the *Thesaurus Linguae Latinae*, and from the special indexes and concordances to individual authors. Latterly (Summer 1988) some computer-searchable Latin texts have become available in the Bodleian Library on IBYCUS (PHI Demonstration CD. Rom #1), and I have used these so far as possible to check and supplement

---

[66] The Donatan Life of Vergil ch. 44 records that 'M.Vipranius a Maecenate eum suppositum appellabat nouae cacozeliae repertorem, non tumidae nec exilis, sed ex communibus uerbis, atque ideo latentis'. In the face of Jocelyn's massive and daunting article '*Vergilius Cacozelus*' I am loath to make confident assertions about who is saying what about which work of Vergil. But I am still fairly persuaded that the remark concerns the *Aeneid*, and that what 'M.Vipranius' critically calls 'noua cacozelia ex communibus uerbis' Horace would have called 'iunctura' of the 'notum uerbum'. And one of the positive things that emerge from Jocelyn's article is that 'cacozelia' is frequently associated with obscurity: pp. 78 and 108. Wilkinson 'Language', has a good discussion of the Donatan passage (183–5), but I think Jocelyn has shown that it is wrong to emend the text to Vipsanius and to identify him with Agrippa. Görler also attributes the remark to Agrippa, but his discussion of 'cacozelia' is useful, and he suggests passages in Vergil which might have attracted the censure: see esp. 179 ff.

statistics already gathered. Of those texts on the disk which might have been useful to me, only the following seemed to me to be reliable (some of the texts that I should like to have used had I think been machine-read and not subsequently checked): Lucretius, Catullus, Propertius, Tibullus (and the *Corp. Tib.*),[67] Horace, Vergil, Ovid (minus the exile poetry),[68] Lucan, Valerius; Caesar (*Gall.*[69] and *Civ.*), Cicero, Livy, Sallust (*Jug.* and *Cat.*), Tacitus.

[67] Figures I give for Tibull. do not include the *Corp. Tib.*; if needed, figures for the latter are given separately.

[68] But figures I give for Ovid of course include the exile poetry.

[69] The Ibycus text includes Book 8 (Hirtius); the figures that I give for Caesar *Gall.* include this book too.

II

Extortion

1. taenia

Vergil contrives local collocations and larger contexts which wrest surprising senses from words. Compared with Horace's combinations, Vergil's can be extortionate (I.5). To illustrate the point, we will observe first how he extorts sense from an apparently poetical word: 'taenia'. 'Taenia' is a Latin borrowing of the Greek word ταινία, which basically means 'ribbon', 'headband'. More information will be given on this word in a moment. For now we observe that the denotative value of 'taenia' seems the same as that of the Latin 'uitta'; 'taenia' seems therefore (and has been judged to be) simply a poetical variant, a grecism, for 'uitta'.

The Fury Allecto flings a snake at Amata in order to inflame her. It ranges over and into her, becoming in its progress items in her apparel. Vergil's description includes these phrases (7.351 ff.):

> fit tortile collo
> aurum ingens coluber, fit longae taenia uittae
> innectitque comas et membris lubricus errat.

The huge serpent becomes the twisted gold necklace on her neck, it becomes the ribbon of her long headband, and binds her hair, and ranges slippery over her limbs.

The serpent, Vergil tells us, 'becomes' her necklace, 'tortile' (a poetical variation for 'torques'), and it 'becomes' the matronly ribbon in her hair, 'taenia uittae' (an apparent periphrasis). We have a vivid picture of items in Amata's dress actually turning into the invading snake. The scene can be visualized with particular facility and concreteness because 'torques', 'twisted necklaces', are intrinsically and often explicitly serpentine in form.[1] The picture we have, therefore, is of Amata's golden necklace *coming alive*. It is a nasty but vivid picture.

---

[1] Heyne ad loc. makes this point. See the pictures in Daremberg–Saglio s.v. 'torques'. Manilius 5.584 uses the word 'torques' of the coils of a sea-serpent.

A question remains to be asked. What is the point of the periphrasis 'taenia uittae'? We have said that the denotative value of the two words is or seems the same. Of course the Latin word 'uitta' can impart a Roman matronly connotation which the Greek word cannot. But if that is what is wanted, why not just say 'uitta'? Servius ad loc. tries to distinguish the denotative meaning of the two words. He tells us that 'taenia' denotes the *end* of the ribbon forming the 'uitta'.[2] This convenient distinction has proved popular,[3] but it has no foundation. Servius has seen a problem but is guessing at the solution. The denotative equivalence of 'uitta' and 'taenia' (= ribbon) is proved by Vergil's one other use of 'taenia' (5.269), by other Latin uses (see below), and by uses of the Greek ταινία. Why anyway should the snake just turn into the *tip* of Amata's ribbon? Horsfall in his commentary on the line[4] acknowledges an equivalence in the two words, and explains the superfluity involved by saying that Vergil is constructing a periphrasis in the manner of 'litoris ora', 'formae species' (*genitiuus inhaerentiae*). But only one parallel for such a construction is cited by Horsfall (or L–H–S) in Vergil himself, and in this ('litoris ora' at 3.396 and *Georg.* 2.44) some point seems to me identifiable in the combination of the two words.[5] Our phrase seems to me pleonastic in a way uncharacteristic of Vergil—unless there is more to it.

We must look more closely at 'taenia'. In its sense 'ribbon' it is fair to categorize 'taenia', as others have done, as rare poetic diction, a grecism: a grecism for 'uitta'. Ennius used it once in his *Alexander, Sc.* 67J = 51V; it occurs once more in the Tragic fragments (Accius), and twice in the Comic fragments (Caecilius). But it does not then occur at all in Lucr., Catull., Hor., Prop., or Tibull. Nor does Vergil's excavation of the word inspire his successors, which is quite surprising (no examples in Ov., Val., Stat., Sil.). A precedent set by Vergil usually catches

---

[2] Servius on 7.352: 'taenia est uittarum extremitas'.
[3] See e.g Conington–Nettleship or Fordyce ad loc.
[4] *Aeneid vii; notes on selected passages*, unpublished Oxford D. Phil thesis, 1971.
[5] The *edge* of the shore is being stressed in the phrase 'litoris ora'. On the *genitiuus inhaerentiae*, also called the synonymous genitive, see further Leumann–Hofmann–Szantyr, 63 f. Other examples quoted include Furius Antias fr. 2M 'omnia noctescunt *tenebris caliginis* atrae', where the two nouns are surely not synonymous. The construction becomes much commoner and more prone to combine real synonyms in Late Latin.

on.[6] Perhaps the reason why it did not catch on was the infection of another main sense. In this other main sense the word is a 'business' prosaism, indeed a technical term. It is used in Latin as well as Greek to mean 'tape-worm': Galen 14.755K, Cato *Rust.* 126 *al.*, Plin. *Nat.* 11.113 *al.*, etc.

Now I think we can see Vergil's purpose. Context extorts this second and horrid sense. We remember that the snake 'becomes' Amata's necklace in a way we can visualize: the snake-shaped necklace comes alive. Now we can see that the same thing is happening with her 'tape–ribbon', 'taenia uittae': it too *comes alive*. The picture is even more concrete than we thought: snake-shape becomes snake and tape becomes tape-worm, as this versatile serpent proceeds about its business of turning itself into items of Amata's apparel before invading her vitals: a nasty and effective picture. Vergil includes the word 'taenia' in the periphrasis because it has this desirable second sense. 'Combination', in particular the parallel description of what happens to the snake-necklace, then forces this sense to the fore. Vergil extorts a sense which one does not much expect to find in an epic.

We can now, too, see a point in the emphasis 'ingens'. The great serpent metamorphoses itself into this small writhing creature—as well as ranging over Amata's limbs, etc.: such is its versatility.

2. ardeo

I shall now show Vergil extorting sense from what I think should be called a neutral word (above p. 13): 'ardeo'. Sometimes Vergil uses this verb in an essentially literal sense = 'burn' (e.g. 5.525 'in nubibus arsit harundo', 11.77 'arsurasque comas'); often he uses it in a metaphorical sense (e.g. 9.198 'ardentem adfatur amicum'). Other examples are more teasing.

First, an introductory point which concerns another verb. At 11.195, during the great scenes of cremation and lamentation which open this book, spoils including chariot wheels are thrown onto a funeral pyre, to be consumed in the flames:

> spolia ...
> coniciunt igni, galeas ensisque decoros
> frenaque feruentisque rotas.

[6] Cf. the phenomenon of the 'legitimizing' effect, I.4 *init.*

They cast spoils on the fire, helmets and glorious swords, reins and burning wheels.

As Servius saw,[7] 'feruentis' is designed to recall a general characteristic of chariot wheels, their heat in vigorous use (cf. *Georg.* 3.107 'uolat ui feruidus axis', Hor. *Odes* 1.1.4 f. 'feruidis ... rotis'); this is confirmed by 'decoros' which performs a similar function for 'enses'. In the immediate vicinity of 'igni', however, 'feruentis' must also bring to mind their imminent literal burning on the pyre (cf. e.g. Prop. 2.8.32 'feruere ... Dorica castra face').[8] It intimates therefore both past vigour and present annihilation, and so contains within itself the sort of contrast which it is a main intention of this part of the poem to convey. So 'feruentis' is strikingly 'rendered new'—though some critics, puzzled or offended by the effect (M. Vipranius might have been among them),[9] have not wanted to see the sense thus extorted.[10]

This combination ('iunctura') then prepares the way for another and perhaps more startling one. Four lines later (11.199 f.) we read:

> tum litore toto
> ardentis spectant socios.

Over the whole shore they behold their blazing companions.

The Trojans, we are told, watch their companions burn, on the pyre. But, having seen that 'feruentis' is suggestive first of past vigour and second of present annihilation, we should be jogged into realizing that 'ardentis' suggestive of present annihilation also intimates past vigour: their burning companions were once those who 'blazed' in the frequent metaphorical manner of the *Aeneid* (e.g. 'ardentem amicum' above). This, a rather grimly ironic effect, and not perhaps to everybody's taste,[11] is irremovably there: context extorts it. In addition we may infer a contrast

---

[7] 'Nimio scilicet cursu', and he compares the two passages that I cite.

[8] Cf. too *Aen.* 4.567 'iam feruere litora flammis', though this phrase is not unambiguous.

[9] See I.5

[10] Cf Conington ad loc. He felt compelled to choose one sense, accepting Servius' interpretation with the following comment: 'But the epithet is an awkward one here, as they were so soon to glow from another cause.'

[11] It will have been to Ovid's taste. He contrives a similar effect, though he spells it out more patently, at *Fast.* 3.545 f.: 'arserat Aeneae Dido miserabilis igne, / arserat exstructis in sua fata rogis.' I.e. Dido burning on her pyre once blazed in another way.

between the ugliness of the 'blazing companions' and the beauty
of the 'blazing stars', 'stellis ardentibus' (202),[12] and between the
mortality of the one and the immortality of the other—I think it
is effective.[13] With 11.200 we might compare 2.311 f. 'iam
proximus ardet / Ucalegon'. Vergil's substitution of Ucalegon's
name for his house enables us to find a similar effect: Ucalegon
burns in flames who once burnt with the emotions of life.

3. concepit furias

At the decisive moment when Dido determines to die, she is
described thus (4.474):

> ergo ubi concepit furias euicta dolore
> decreuitque mori ...

So when, conquered by anguish, she conceived fury and decided to die
...

The phrase which I wish to concentrate on is the one which
signifies Dido's contraction or assumption of madness, 'concepit
furias'. It comprises what may probably be termed neutral
words.[14] But extortion operates.

Two similar-sounding phrases may be adduced and considered, Catull. 64.92 (Ariadne) 'cuncto concepit corpore flamm-
mam' and Cic. *Ver.* 5.73 'furore ex maleficiis concepto'. The
former is Catullus' striking metaphorical application of what
had come to be an ordinary enough phrase designating literal
'catching fire', 'flammam concipere';[15] it was the phrase you
might use of, say, a match catching fire. Catullus applied it
metaphorically to Ariadne and her love, and his example had
followers: see *TLL* IV.57.70 ff., 58.5 ff. Cicero's 'furore ... concepto' is an example of a frequent, more loosely metaphorical
use of 'concipio' to mean 'contract' diseases, moral stains etc.,[16]
and 'furor' itself is commonly an object: *TLL* IV.61.16 ff., esp.

---

[12] On the stars' proverbial beauty see Fränkel, 49 f.

[13] But Mynors in his app. crit. to 202 mentions the variant 'fulgentibus' with the comment, '*propter* ardentis (*u.* 200) *non male*'.

[14] One may wonder how much currency in the spoken tongue 'furia' / 'Furia' had. It is e.g. absent in Plautus and Terence, but is used thrice in Horace's Satires.

[15] But is it *in origin* metaphorical, derived from the sense 'conceive', 'become pregnant with' (exemplified below)? Lucretius vivifies such a connotation at 2.545.

[16] In some instances it is clear that they derive from the sense 'conceive'; cf. the preceding note.

23 ff., also *OLD* s.v. 'concipio' 8. Both these uses are clearly relevant to ours. We might be tempted to think them sufficient explanatory material, especially the latter, and to be contented with a translation 'contracted fury' *vel sim.* ('furiae' can be in effect a common noun); and we would I suppose interpret the fury to be the fury of her resolve to die: 'decreuitque mori'. But Vergil's combination and context in fact extort quite another, additional sense for the phrase 'concepit furias' and another implication to Dido's fury.

'Furias' we must grant to be at least ambiguous. We may on occasions understand the word simply to mean 'fury', but a sense 'Furies' must as it were be *excluded* by context if it is not to obtrude (for that is its most essential meaning),[17] and our context performs the reverse of this service. Immediately adjacent to these 'furiae' ('Furiae'), in the line before (473), are certainly personified Furies under their appellation 'Dirae'. Given this we are bound to think of 'Furias' before 'furias' in 474. Dido's Furies are thus potentially animate. This suggestion then works powerfully with, and is reinforced by, the verb 'concepit'. A potentially animate object with 'concipio' must bring to mind generation, female conception as the verb's sense: this is indeed one of the verb's basic and commanding senses: *TLL* IV.55.81 ff., e.g. *Aen.* 5.38, 8.139.[18] The activation of this sense in turn confirms the animation of 'Furias'. The result is powerful, the combination disturbingly productive. Dido, Vergil's extorted intimation is, has *conceived Furies in her womb.*[19]

There are analogies for the idea of 'pregnancy with Furies'; and it can be shown that Vergil integrates it constructively into his text. First, as analogies we may observe Hecuba and Venus *pregnant with torches / fire* (in actuality so, not in dream, according to Vergil's Juno), 7.319 ff.: 'nec face tantum / Cisseis praegnas ignis enixa iugalis; / quin idem Veneri ...'. We may observe too Clytemnestra, who dreamed that she gave birth to a serpent

---

[17] On the ambiguity of 'furiae / Furiae' in Latin (and perception of it), and on other uses of the word in the *Aeneid*, see section 3a. The section also suggests a source behind Vergil's 'concepit furias' which supports the interpretation given above.

[18] For the verb in this sense constructed in the active with an object, cf. e.g. Cic. *Cluent.* 33, Ov. *Met.* 4.611 'quem pluuio Danae conceperat auro' (very commonly it is constructed passively of the conceived, or absolutely in the active).

[19] Austin's gloss is a quarter there: 'when she had quickened the seed of madness within her ...'. DServius misses the point completely, glossing 'furore completa est'.

(Aesch. *Cho.* 527). More indefinitely but still suggestively we might think about Amata 'loved' and perhaps impregnated by her demon-lover, the Fury Allecto, 7.343 ff.;[20] likewise we might think of Propertius' Tarpeia who slept with Furies (4.4.67 f.);[21] cf too [Sen.] *H. O.* 243 f. 'conceptum ferens / Maenas Lyaeum' and some interesting passages cited by Nisbet and Hubbard on Hor. *Carm.* 2.19.6. Vergil's type of suggestion is striking but not entirely without parallel.

Now let me show how Vergil makes this suggestion contribute to his context. The poem has already raised the question of Dido's conceiving, in a literal context. 4.327–30:

> saltem si qua mihi de te suscepta fuisset
> ante fugam suboles, si quis mihi paruulus aula
> luderet Aeneas, qui te tamen ore referret,
> non equidem omnino capta ac deserta uiderer.

At least if some offspring had been gotten by me from you before your flight, if in my hall a tiny Aeneas were now playing, who might bring you back by his face, I would not now feel so utterly captured and desolated.

Dido bewails the fact that Aeneas leaves her without his child. This specific reference helps us to pick up the dark suggestion in line 474. We can also begin to see how that suggestion integrates into the story. Note 'capta ac deserta' in 330. Vergil makes Dido say that, because she has got no child by Aeneas, she feels 'captured and desolated'. She speaks of herself in military imagery: the phrase is in fact evocative of a defeated city.[22] Vergil himself then suggests that in this defeated state, perhaps *because* of this defeated state ('euicta', 474), she *conceived Furies*. A point is emerging. Love in the tragic love story of Dido turns to hate, generous and positive impulses become perverted and twisted. Vergil has a variety of ways of making this point. One is to show simply how the fire, 'ignis', of her love turns into the fire of her hate and revenge (4.2 'carpitur igni' ... 384 'sequar atris

[20] Cf. Lyne, *Further Voices*, 13 ff. for Amata 'loved' by Allecto. On top of this, it seems to me hard to exclude the ideas of sexual penetration and impregnation from Vergil's description of the assault by snake in 7.346 ff. Of course this means that we have to attribute considerable sexual versatility to Allecto. But she is a demon, after all.

[21] Cf. Lyne, *Hermes*, 99 (1971), 376–7.

[22] See Austin ad loc. The phrase fits into the 'siege' to 'sack' sequence of imagery: see Lyne, *Further Voices*, 18 ff.

ignibus').[23] Another is to suggest that her impulse to be a mother to Aeneas' child turns into the desire to conceive, indeed the act of conceiving, Furies. And the Furies are, we learn, to punish and pursue him. (A desire to pursue and punish is the further and important implication of her fury in 474.)

The punishing Furies of Dido's conception are already in Dido's mind when she promises to pursue Aeneas with 'dark fires' at 4.384 (just mentioned, 'sequar atris ignibus'): these are evocative of, and Dido has in mind, Furies' torches.[24] The topic is then taken up most clearly—dark suggestions become patent —at 625. This is the climax to Dido's great curse upon Aeneas and his descendants which starts at 607 ff. At 625 f. Dido says:

> exoriare aliquis nostris ex ossibus ultor
> qui face Dardanios ferroque sequare colonos ...

Arise, some avenger, from our bones, to pursue the Dardan settlers with torch and iron.

Dido prays for an avenger, but in notable language. In particular, the choice of 'exorior' is notable. One can talk in Latin as in English of avengers *sim.* 'arising', 'springing up' ('exorior'), with no very distinct image in mind: *TLL* V.2.1573.68 ff. But the combination with 'ossibus' extorts a very distinct image and sense for the verb. Dido uses 'ossa' to refer to her dead self.[25] 'Ossa' in fact is much more evocative of the dead than 'bones' in English because, I suppose, Rome was a cremating society and bones were the obvious residue of the dead, evident to all. 'Ossa' is so frequent on tombstones that it elicited compendia: see *TLL* IX.2.1093.10 ff., also 1097.29 ff.; and 'ossa' is often effectively a metonymy for the dead: IX.2.1098.36 ff. Now there is an area of use in the verb 'exorior' which so jars with this connotation, is so paradoxical in conjunction with it, that it must be activated. The words work together, activate each other, like words in oxymoron. A sense is extorted, poetical but well established for 'exorior', namely 'arise' in the sense of *be born*: e.g. Lucr. 1.5, 23, *TLL* V.2.1575.8 ff. Dido intends a grim paradox (we might call it an oxymoron) in this part of her curse, 'be *born* some avenger from my *bones*—and pursue the Dardan settlers with the *torch*'.

---

[23] See Lyne, *Further Voices*, 121 n.31.

[24] Cf. Pöschl, 113.

[25] But does Vergil also have in mind (as a subliminal suggestion) 'ossa' as the seat of love? See *TLL* IX.2.1095.20 ff., 1099.72 ff., Lyne on *Ciris* 164, *Aen.* 1.660, 4.101.

Now it was Furies who were avengers *par excellence*, and there is a hint of Fury in the 'fax' with which Dido equips her avenger (cf. above). So: Vergil said that Dido conceived Furies. Dido confirms,[26] illuminates, and extends the idea by expressing her wish that an avenger-Fury should be *born* from her, from her bones.

But how might all this happen? In the way that it did. The Furies intimated in Dido's prophesy in 4.384 actualized, the Furies conceived in 474 indeed found birth, as she prayed in 625. Hannibal was her avenging Fury (inescapably brought to any Roman's mind by line 625).[27] Hannibal was the eventual flesh of the Furies conceived by the Queen of Carthage.

3a. The ambiguity of 'furiae' / 'Furiae', and perception of it; other uses in the Aeneid

The potential ambiguity of 'furiae' / 'Furiae' (ἐ- and Ἐρινύς, etc.) was keenly felt in the ancient world. Cf. e.g. the rhetorical *topos* that sinners' 'Furiae' should actually be seen as 'furiae': Cic. *Pis.* 46 'nolite enim ita putare, patres conscripti, ut in scaena uidetis, homines consceleratos impulsu deorum terreri furialibus taedis ardentibus. sua quemque fraus, suum facinus, suum scelus, sua audacia de sanitate ac mente deturbat; hae sunt impiorum furiae, hae flammae, hae faces.' Nisbet ad loc. parallels the *topos* at Aeschines *Tim.* 190–1 (Ποιναί), Cic. *Sext. Rosc.* 67 and elsewhere. The orators in these passages ask us (in effect) to make a decision between small and capital letter, rejecting the latter for the former; but in so doing they recognize and exploit the potential ambiguity. At *Aen.* 3.331 'scelerum furiis agitatus Orestes', Vergil is striking a balancing act between the Tragic and the orators' view of madness consequent upon crime: 'agitatus' makes in the Tragic direction, 'scelerum' in the orators', and 'furiae' can be interpreted both as objective Furies and as a reference to Orestes' state of mind. (R. D. Williams' note ad loc. is helpful, though he urges a choice between the alternative interpretations which Vergil's language in fact excludes.) At Soph. *Antig.* 603 φρενῶν ἐρινύς (and other Greek passages)

---

[26] Dido's 'exoriare' confirms a sense 'conceive' in 'concepit'. Note the collocation of 'concipitur' and 'exortum' in Lucr. 1.5.

[27] Servius ad loc.: 'et ostendit Hannibalem.' Cf. further Pease ad loc.

ambiguity should likewise be respected; modern editions illuminatingly disagree as to whether ὲ or ’E should be printed.

At Apoll. Rhod. 4.385 f. (Medea to Jason) ἐκ δέ σε πάτρης / αὐτίκ’ ἐμαὶ ἐλάσειαν ’Ερινύες, the capital ’E seems, if we are to choose, preferable. This is of consequence for the interpretation of ‘concepit furias’ given above, for Apollonius’ imprecating Medea is clearly a major source for Vergil’s scorned Dido.

I now comment on other uses of ‘furiae’ / ‘Furiae’ in the *Aeneid*. In three of his uses Vergil is certainly referring to full animate Furies. At 3.252 ‘Furiarum ego maxima’ is Celaeno; at 6.605 ‘Furiarum maxima’ is the Fury who administers the tantalizing feast in the Underworld; and at 8.669 Catiline in the Underworld trembles at the ‘Furiarum ora’. In one or two it seems that context excludes the capital ‘F’; perhaps e.g. at 10.694 ‘rupes ... obuia uentorum furiis’.[28] In others we should certainly savour the uncertainty. Ambiguity is clearly and cleverly constructed at 3.331 (above). Note too e.g. 7.392 ‘furiisque accensas pectore matres’ (in the context of the Fury Allecto’s assault), 12.101 ‘his agitur furiis’ (of Turnus who has been assaulted by Allecto). And what of Aeneas, ‘furiis accensus et ira / terribilis’ at 12.946?[29] Cf the ‘matres’ just quoted. Cf. too Dido’s exclamation at 4.376 ‘heu furiis incensa feror!’—assessment of that might affect our account of Dido and Furies above.

4. bibebat amorem

longumque bibebat amorem.

Dido ‘drank in a long [draught of] love’. Thus Vergil’s description of Dido (1.749), as she begins to question Aeneas about his experiences. The words themselves are neutral, but the metaphor (if that is the right term) produced by their combination is by no means obvious, or copiously paralleled, and requires attention. Austin ad loc. compares Plaut. *Aul.* 279 ‘malum maerore metuo ne mixtum bibam’; DServius comments, tantalizingly, ‘sic Anacreon ἔρωτα πίνων’ (= Anacreon 105 (*PMG* 450) Page, 131 Gentili), the context of which is unknown to us. It is most obvious

---

[28] I suppose that Hardie might well disagree, possibly rightly: cf. his account of storms and gigantomachy, 90 ff.

[29] In this connection Renger, 96–8 on the *Erinys Pallantis* is interesting to ponder.

to assume that behind Vergil's metaphor lies the idea of a love potion: this seems clearly the case in Plautus' image at *Truc.* 43 f. 'si semel amoris poculum accepit meri / eaque intra pectus se penetrauit potio' (a 'real' love 'poculum' is talked of by Horace at *Epod.* 5.38). In addition (besides frequent allegorical uses of 'bibo')[30] we should recall metaphorical uses of the verb with 'auribus' (*TLL* II.1966.35 ff., e.g. Prop. 3.6.8), and infer, I think, that Dido falls in love *as she listens* (1.748 f. 'uario noctem sermone trahebat / infelix Dido longumque ...'), captivated by Aeneas' words.

But there is a factor that makes that idea of a potion alarmingly actual. Context heightens our awareness of the literal value of 'bibo'—extorts it, I should say. It becomes difficult in the end to see 'bibebat amorem' as a mere metaphor. We remember that the scene is a banquet, and the company including Dido herself are actually drinking (1.736–9):

> dixit et in mensam laticum libauit honorem
> primaque, libato, summo tenus attigit ore;
> tum Bitiae dedit increpitans; ille impiger hausit
> spumantem pateram ...

With these words she poured a libation on to the table, and was the first to touch her lips to the wine; then chiding him she gave it to Bitias; he briskly drained the foaming cup ...'

Dido drinks (or rather, sips) as she 'drinks' love. This must make us wonder how merely metaphorical the 'drinking' is. If Dido drinks as she 'drinks', can we dissociate the two?[31] Must we not think of the latter as involved in the former, happening in the process of the former, due to the former? Must we not think of a potion? I think the choice of 'metaphor' in this context compels such a thought. But what may we imagine happening? We should recall that one of Cupid's two weapons referred to by Venus at 1.688 was 'uenenum'. This may take literal as well as metaphorical form. If so, what better way to administer it than in the sip of wine that Dido takes?[32] This may be why Dido 'drinks'

---

[30] *TLL* II.1965.30 ff., e.g. Prop. 3.1.6.

[31] Servius on 1.749 'bibebat amorem' comments interestingly but enigmatically 'adlusit ad conuiuium'.

[32] A favourite method of poisoners: Cic. *Cluent.* 166, etc. Being a god Cupid could presumably ensure that Dido's sip was poisoned, while the draught taken by Bitias was not.

love while she drinks: she is sipping a divine love potion. There may thus be a sense in which she literally 'drinks love', in that she drinks from a poisoned love chalice. Such thoughts should at least occur (I make no stronger claim), extorted by the choice of 'metaphor', by the combination and context.

5. amor deceptam morte

> postquam primus amor deceptam morte fefellit

After my first love cheated me deceived by death ...

Thus Dido at 4.17. Once again the words themselves are neutral.

A moving idiom, almost exclusively confined in our sources to inscriptions, refers to the 'deceptions' of death, using the word 'decipio'. The idiom takes two forms: the bereaved are said to be cheated by the death of a loved one, and the dead persons themselves are said to have been cheated by death: e.g. *CIL* 9.5412 '... coniux decepta cum filis posuerunt,' 5.7962 'filiae ... quae immatura morte decepta uixit annos XIIII', *TLL* V.1.178.66–9 and 75–8, *OLD* s.v. 'decipio' 3. Such tombstones (there are many of them) attest an image that appealed to popular sentiment, and still strikes a chord. Vergil has put it (in the first version) at the heart of Dido's reference to her bereavement in 4.17. Dido feels cheated by death. Her sense of being cheated by death may seem to be reinforced by 'fefellit'.

Dido feels cheated by the death, 'morte', of Sychaeus. The interpretation so far is legitimate. But Vergil (Dido) actually makes her 'first love' the subject of 'fefellit' and 'morte' an ablative of means with that verb (as well as with 'deceptam'; it is impossible to divorce 'morte' from either). And 'deceptam' may legitimately be seen as reinforcing the action in 'fefellit': 'deceptam fefellit' = 'decepit atque fefellit'.[33] Vergil therefore says that Dido's first love, i.e. Sychaeus,[34] deceived and cheated her.

Seen this way, the phraseology takes on a quite different complexion; a whole new area of thought is extorted. Lovers conventionally 'cheat' and 'deceive' in love, 'fallunt' and 'decipiunt'. Cf. Prop. 1.13.5 'deceptis ... puellis', 2.21.11 'Colchida sic hospes quondam decepit Iason', Ov. *Her.* 2.63 ff. 'fallere creden-

---

[33] DServius, 'fefellit me et decepit', Servius, 'morte sua decepit me et fefellit'.
[34] On 'primus amor' see the parallels cited by Pease.

tem non est operosa puellam / gloria ... sum decepta tuis ... uerbis', etc. etc. This sort of passage, referring to unfaithfulness, may seem unwelcomely compared. But it is impossible, certainly wrong, to close one's ears to the kind of idea and expression. Dido has used this kind of expression. Nor should it be difficult to see what is behind it, what is fuelling it. She feels deceived by death, but simultaneously she feels *betrayed by Sychaeus*.[35] By his death Sychaeus has cheated her as surely as, much more surely than he would have by leaving her for another woman. Such unfair (and perhaps largely unconscious) resentment in the face of bereavement is something that I think we can all understand. Certainly Dido feels it, and Vergil's language extorts it for her.[36]

6. petit ore cruento

Pallas dies at 10.488–9:

> corruit in uulnus (sonitum super arma dedere)
> et terram hostilem moriens petit ore cruento.

He fell headlong onto his wound; his armour clashed over him; and dying he sought the enemy land with his bloody mouth.

I am concerned with the phrase 'petit ore cruento'. The first two are neutral words; 'cruentus' occurs commonly and happily in much prose and poetry, but one suspects that it had very little currency in the spoken tongue.[37]

Our probable first inference from the phrase is that Pallas 'bites the dust', a Homeric as well as Hollywood motif. Vergil employs it specifically at 11.418:

> procubuit moriens et humum semel ore momordit.

... has fallen in death, and bitten the earth once and for all.

---

[35] Cf. the resentment expressed by Euryalus' mother, 9.482 f. 'potuisti linquere solam, crudelis?' I take it that she means a reference to his leaving her *by dying*.

[36] Williams ad loc. translates fairly, but makes nothing of it. Austin translates very misleadingly, in a way that seems designed to avoid the implications of Vergil's phraseology: 'cut short my hopes, and slipped away from me in death.' Pease misses the significance. Fairclough's translation is interesting: 'since my first love, turning traitor, cheated me by death.' (Dryden, 'since Sychaeus was untimely slain'.)

[37] Note its absence in Comedy. *TLL* s.v.: 'legitur inde ab Ennio ... frequentant: Cic. Verg. Ov. Liv. Luc. [alii], deest praeter alios: Plaut. Ter. Catull. Caes. [aliis].'

Cf. Homer *Iliad* 2.418 ὀδὰξ λαζοίατο γαῖαν, 11.749 ὀδὰξ ἕλον οὖδας, 19.61, 22.17, *Od.* 22.269. Conington–Nettleship however, on *Aen.* 10.489, profess doubt as to whether Vergil intends this motif or simply the idea of Pallas' falling on his face: cf. *Od.* 22.94 δούπησεν δὲ πεσών (cf. 10.488), χϑόνα δ' ἤλασε παντὶ μετώπῳ ('he struck the earth with his whole forehead'); 'the latter', they say, 'is perhaps more probable'.

Vergil's cautious mode of expression admits ambiguity and forces no decision. In fact I think it forces us to consider and include another possibility. 'Petere ore' is coterminous neither with ὀδὰξ ἑλεῖν nor with μετώπῳ ἐλάσαι, nor indeed is its canny generality exhausted by their sum. Once we are stimulated to recall Homeric motifs, we should consider a third allusion, which is just as easily conveyed by 'petere ore' as the other two. Cf. *Od.* 5.463 κύσε δὲ ζείδωρον ἄρουραν, 'he kissed the life-giving earth', and 13.354 χαίρων ᾗ γαίη, κύσε δὲ ζείδωρον ἄρουραν, 'rejoicing in his homeland, he kissed the life-giving earth'. (Cf. *Aen.* 8.615 'amplexus nati Cytherea petiuit', Catull. 45.12 'ore suauiata', etc.). Odysseus kisses his life-giving homeland in grateful welcome, Pallas 'kisses' the land of enemies in death—a dreadful and powerfully ironic allusion. The potential positive charge of this allusion is so productively and effectively negated by 'hostilem', and by 'cruento' too, that I would say these words help to extort it: the oxymoron effect again.[38]

7. tela

Juno at 10.90–3:

> quae causa fuit consurgere in arma
> Europamque Asiamque et foedera soluere furto?
> me duce Dardanius Spartam expugnauit adulter,
> aut ego tela dedi fouiue Cupidine bella?

What caused Europe and Asia to rise up to arms and to dissolve pacts in theft? Was it under my leadership that the Dardan adulterer (i.e. Paris) took Sparta by storm? Did I provide the weapons or nurture war with Desire?

Thus Juno, in her angry retort to Venus before the council of gods. By each rhetorical question she means that the responsible

---

[38] See above p. 27.

person was *not* herself, but *was* ultimately Venus, Venus with her erotic machinations (she has a point: Venus had bribed Paris with the promise of Helen in the famous beauty contest).

On 'expugnauit' Williams ad loc. says: '"laid siege to", rhetorically exaggerating the deeds of Paris.' In fact Juno means 'take by storm', and she is using the language of 'militia amoris':[39] this should be clear straightaway from her choice of subject for the verb, 'adulter'. In the language of 'militia amoris' lovers 'lay siege' to their beloveds or their beloveds' houses, while pimps or husbands or the woman's own obduracy (depending on the situation) fuel the resistance, and successful lovers carry their siege by storm: cf. Ov. *Ars* 2.526 'quid nostras obsidet iste fores', Prop. 3.13.9 'haec etiam clausas expugnant arma (sc. luxuries) pudicas', Hor. *Odes* 3.15.8 f. 'filia rectius / expugnat iuuenum domos', and the motif is frequent in comedy.[40] Paris was a successful lover: he got the girl, the Spartan Helen. In terms of the imagery she is employing Juno can thus legitimately say that he took Sparta by storm. And Juno will have enjoyed the fact that, whereas in literal truth the Greeks took Troy by storm, there was a sense in which (so she could claim) a Trojan 'took' Sparta.

An additional point to be noted is that 'expugno' is, in spite of the few verse passages I am able to quote above, prosaic.[41] This will be due, I assume,[42] to its strong association with contemporary warfare, an area of experience deemed properly the province of prose; 'storming' in heroic warfare is given more suggestive language, language more redolent of 'otherness':[43] e.g. *Aen.*

---

[39] On 'militia amoris' see Lyne, *The Latin Love Poets*, 71–8. Servius takes 'expugnauit' literally, employing inventiveness to do so: 'cum sollicitata Helena Parin sequi noluisset, egressus ille ciuitatem obsedit. qua euersa Helenam rapuit ...'

[40] Cf. Ter. *Eun.* 771 ff., Plaut. *Pseud.* 586 ff., 766, *Truc.* 170 f. Vergil makes use of the motif at 7.343 also: see Lyne, *Further Voices* ..., 18 ff.

[41] Here are some figures for 'expugno' in the poets—it is notably infrequent: Enn. 0, Acc. 1 (= *trag.* 503 [by plausible emendation]), Lucr. 2, Cic. *poet.* 0, Catull. 0, Prop. 1 (= 3.13.9, quoted above), Tib. 0, Vergil 2 (= 9.532, 10.92), Hor. 3 (*Carm.* 3.15.9 quoted above, *Serm.* 1.9.55, 2.5.74), Ov. 1 (= *Met.* 9.619, an interesting use allied to 'militia amoris'), Luc. 3, Val. 0, Sil. 3, Stat. 4. By contrast, the 'business' military writer Caesar has 24 in *Civ.* and *Gall.*, and Livy has 118. For prose uses see further *TLL* V.2.1807.70 ff. The low incidence not only in the epic writers (the Flavians' interest is commensurate with Vergil's) but in the Elegists too is remarkable, given their fondness for 'militia amoris' imagery.

[42] Cf. my remarks above pp. 10 f.

[43] Cf. my remarks pp. 15 f.

2.4 f., 603, 611 f. In Vergil's poem therefore 'expugno' is eye-catching;[44] and we note that once again Juno is prepared to exploit diction that is unexpectedly down to earth,[45] though as I have shown she does enhance it by using it figuratively. Propertius' and Horace's uses quoted above are for the same reason more striking than they first appear.

Juno exploits other amatory language in this speech besides her 'militia amoris' use of 'expugno'; it serves her purpose which is to imply that responsibility for the Trojan war lies with Venus and her erotic machinations. The commentaries wax solemn on what 'foedera' existed between Greece and Troy, to be dissolved (as Juno implies) by Paris.[46] At one level Juno may mean the 'laws of hospitality', but equally or primarily she has in mind the *marriage* 'pact' between Helen and Menelaus which Paris did indeed temporarily dissolve. This is in origin a Catullan-amatory use of 'foedus',[47] and the Catullan nuance is helped to the fore by the resonant Catullan reminiscence in 'Europamque Asiamque' (cf. Catull. 68.89) as well as by the surrounding amatory language—among which note in particular the adjacent 'furto'.[48] In this context too 'bella' must take on a double meaning—especially with 'Cupidine' (or 'cupidine') immediately adjacent. Saying that it was not she that nurtured the war, the Trojan war, Juno glances at the erotic 'war', Venus' business, that lay behind it.[49]

With a context established like this of amatory language, in particular military amatory language, it is impossible not to reflect on 'tela' (in general a neutral word). If Vergil intended no double meaning here, he wrote badly. In fact the combination of 'tela' with other 'militia amoris' language extorts a double meaning. Juno coarsely means (on one level) that it was not she

---

[44] For the 'eye-catching' nature of prosaic diction in a poem, see III.1. *init.*

[45] Cf. Lyne, *Further Voices*, 52 f.

[46] Conington–Nettleship: 'The "foedera" are doubtless the laws of hospitality, which Paris broke [thus Williams] ... That there was any formal treaty between Greece and Troy does not appear from Homer ...' Servius: 'legitur in historiis quod Troiani cum Graecis foedus habuerunt. tunc etiam Paris est susceptus hospitio ...'

[47] See Lyne, *The Latin Love Poets*, 34–8.

[48] *OLD* 'furtum' has a separate subsection (2b) for 'furtum' = 'secret love, stolen pleasures'. See further Pichon, 158.

[49] Cf. Prop. 2.1.45, 3.8.32, *Aen.* 11.736 quoted below. It should be noted that 'foui' does not necessarily increase the erotic nuance: cf. Liv. 42.11.5 'Persea ... bellum ... alere ac fouere omnibus consiliis'.

who provided Paris with his sexual equipment. (Nor of course, on a literal level, did Venus. But she encouraged and assisted the employment of such equipment, and that is enough for Juno.) Latin, like many languages, is partial to violent imagery for the male sex organ: on 'telum' itself see Adams 17, 19 ('the sexual symbolism of weapons was instantly recognisable in ancient society'),[50] 20. For other coarse talk by Juno see Lyne, *Further Voices* ... 53, 59 f.

At 11.735–40 Tarchon uses the image and language of 'militia amoris' to taunt his soldiers for their lack of relish for real 'bellum' (his sarcasm carries extra point and weight in that, as Tarchon says (734), their adversary is a woman, Camilla):[51]

> quo ferrum quidue haec gerimus tela inrita dextris?
> at non in Venerem segnes nocturnaque bella,
> aut ubi curua choros indixit tibia Bacchi.
> exspectate dapes et plenae pocula mensae
> (hic amor, hoc studium) dum sacra secundus haruspex
> nuntiet ac lucos uocet hostia pinguis in altos!

To what purpose our swords? Why are we carrying these weapons vainly? But you aren't slow for Venus and the wars of night, nor when the curving pipe has announced Bacchus's dances. Wait for your feasts and goblets at a full table—this is your love, this your desire—until the diviner at the hour of success proclaims the religious rites and the fat victim summons you into deep groves!

'Nocturnaque bella' is explicitly 'militia amoris'. In this context it is hard not to see some allusion in Tarchon's use of 'tela'. In full his message would be something like this: 'You carry your weapons of war to no effect. But you aren't slow for Venus and the wars of night, nor slow to use your "weapons" of love.'

---

[50] Adams also tells us that 'it was not unusual in ancient humour for epic verses and situations to be deliberately misinterpreted in a sexual sense.' In that sort of climate Vergil must have known what he was doing! Among other examples, Adams refers to Suet. *Vesp.* 23.1, which tells us that Vespasian, on seeing a well-endowed man, quoted the Homeric verse (*Il.* 7.213) μακρὰ βιβάς, κραδάων δολιχόσκιον ἔγχος. Ausonius of course, in the *Cento Nuptialis*, found exploitable *double entendre* in Vergil's own uses of 'telum', *sim.* (though not the actual lines I discuss above): cf. 92, p. 215 P., 120, p.217 P., Adams, 19 f., Fowler, 'Virgins', 196.

[51] Servius on 736 'at non in Venerem segnes' makes what I think is a legitimate point: 'latenter hoc dicit: fugitis mulierem, quia armata est; alias primi ad hunc curritis sexum.'

Context again extorts a sense which we do not expect to find in an Augustan epic.

Then, interestingly (with an effect which I find hard to pin down), Vergil turns Tarchon's imagery on its head. Tarchon had used military language of love: Vergil uses amatory imagery of war. Tarchon promptly rides against the suggestively named 'Venulus' (742), 'embraces' his foe ('complectitur hostem'), and bears him off 'gremium ante suum'. Some might like to make something of 'gremium'[52]—and indeed much other detail in this section of text. I leave it like this, with the point made: Vergil turns Tarchon's imagery round, ironically[53] using amatorily suggestive words of war.[54]

[52] Cf. Adams, 77, 92, 220.
[53] But 'not only is sex like battle: battle is like sex' (Fowler, 'Virgins', 187). That might be a profitable thought to apply.
[54] There is no other use of 'complector', 'amplector', or cognates in combat in Vergil; but cf. (for ironic uses) *Aen.* 2.214 and 218 of Laocoon's serpent, 8.260 of Hercules serpent-like grip on Cacus, also 8.488 'complexu in misero' of the wretched form of death to which Mezentius condemned his victims.

III

Exploitation: I

Horace, I said above (I.2), is prepared to make use of prosaic diction, in spite of the fact that it will often appear unpromisingly familiar. For example, wishing to focus our attention on the dangers of 'money' or the pleasures of an ordinary 'dinner', he uses words that denote these everyday things directly, even in the Odes: 'pecunia', 'cena'. Most poets, deeming such things to be more the province of prose, prefer to gloss and cover them with other and glamorous connotations: they use the words 'aurum', 'opes', 'dapes', and 'epulae'—gold, wealth and feasts. But, Horace would say, if you are moralizing about real money, it is pointless to glamorize, camouflage or in any way to deflect attention from the real, everyday thing. Likewise if it is your attention to laud plain, old dinner.[1]

Horace makes use of prosaic words; and, too, colloquialisms. Vergil I think more vigorously exploits such diction. This is what I shall begin to demonstrate now. But I should mention a preliminary point. I suggested in I.3 a couple of factors which might induce a word to become generically prosaic, or colloquial. We should now note that, when a word has become prosaic or colloquial, it possesses another quality simply by virtue of that fact. In a poem it is 'eye-catching': it is unexpected. So a prosaic word catches the eye, and then directs the attention to an exact and limited meaning, or to an area of experience not normally associated with poetry; or it may do both of these things simultaneously. And colloquialism catches the eye, and directs the attention to one of its particular provinces of experience. In both cases Vergil then exploits this package of qualities.

[1] 'Cena': Horace *Carm.* 3.29.15, Axelson, 106–7, with useful comparative figures but unsympathetic interpretation of Horace; 'pecunia': Horace; *Carm.* 3.16.17, 24.61, 4.9.38, Axelson, 108, again with figures but unsympathetic interpretation.

Before I proceed I should like to point the difference between what I mean by extortion and exploitation. In certain combinations Vergil employs, typically, neutral words, and extorts from them, by means of his combination, a sense which we did not expect. In other combinations he operates with the obvious and expected sense of a word, usually indeed a familiar and everyday sense, for he typically operates on these occasions with prosaic or colloquial words; but in his combination he manages to exploit this expected sense.

1. conlabor

'Conlabor' is a verb that is more definitely characterized than the dictionaries suggest—though *TLL* ('coll-') conveniently provides all the information necessary for such a characterization. It is the typical, indeed we should probably say technical, verb for the 'collapse' of buildings and erected structures. It is used in innumerable and widespread inscriptions recording the collapse of houses, walls, temples, amphitheatres, and so on; Livy and later prose writers use it in the same particular way. Cf. Liv. 22.18.7 'conlapsa ruinis pars moenium erat', 29.18.17, etc.; for examples of inscriptions see *TLL* III.1573.46 ff. ('sescenties'), e.g. *CIL* X 1640 'opus pilarum ui maris conlapsum', X 1406 (AD 76, Herculaneum) 'templum matris deum terrae motu conlapsum', X 6565 (Velitrae) 'amphitheatrum', XIV 2919 (Praeneste) 'publica aedificia in ruinam conlapsa', XI 6224 (Fanum Fortunae, beginning of 1st. cent. AD) 'bassis'. We should infer from all this that the word not only had this technical sense in the time of the quoted evidence, but had had it for a considerable period. Such a widespread use does not spring up over night. We may conclude therefore that in Vergil's time 'conlabor' was a technical term to refer to the collapse of erected structures. We may also infer that in Vergil's time this was a pretty exclusive use: for while this use is patent, scarcely any other is even traceable for that time.[2] And *qua* technical term it was probably prosaic, even 'business' prosaic.

---

[2] The only example cited in *TLL* before Vergil and Livy (and later Augustans, inscriptions, etc.) is Plaut. *Truc.* 671; I am not sure what precise sense Plautus intends. The *TLL* location is III.1573.17 ff., 'translate, i.q. incidere in, deerrare'.

TLL attests no use between Plautus (*Truc.* 671, see n. 2) and Vergil, Livy (and later Augustans, inscriptions etc.) at all. When Vergil has given the lead, other poets follow suit, more or less enthusiastically (Verg. 8, Ov. 7 (all *Met.*), Luc. 2, Val. 3, Stat. 4, Sil. 7), sometimes showing obvious Vergilian influence:[3] the 'legitimizing effect' (I.4 *init.*). Vergil exploits it. He exploits the fact that, *qua* (probably) prosaic, it is eye-catching in his text; and he exploits its limited and technical sense.

His use is a surprise. On most of the occasions on which he uses it, he transfers it to the collapse of *people*, or to parts of people's bodies. According to the surviving evidence he is the first so to transfer it.[4]

In 9.708 the effect achieved is notable, but easily comprehensible. A gigantic[5] warrior Bitias falls:

> conlapsa ruunt immania membra,
> dat tellus gemitum et clipeum super intonat ingens.

His vast limbs collapse and fall headlong. The earth groans and the huge shield thunders over him.

That Bitias' vast limbs should merit a word distinctly suited to the collapse of buildings seems simply right. Vergil exploits this eye-catching word with its distinct sense to make an implicit comparison. 'Ruunt' too contributes to this implicit comparison (cf. *OLD* 'ruo' 3, *CIL* XIV 2919 'publica aedificia in ruinam collapsa', etc).

Implicit comparison is the right term: Vergil is talking of the collapse of Bitias in terms of the collapse of a building. He then makes explicit the implicit in the succeeding simile, which compares Bitias' fall to that of a pillar or pier (710 ff.)

> talis in Euboico Baiarum litore quondam
> saxea pila cadit...

So on the Euboeic shore of Baiae sometimes falls a stone pier ...

We could indeed see 'conlapsa' as a metaphorical anticipation of the simile: the word used of Bitias in the narrative is one which

---

[3] Cf. e.g. Ov. *Met.* 10.186, Stat. *Theb.* 11.643, Sil. 5.549.

[4] Others quickly follow suit: *TLL* III.1572.62 ff.

[5] Bitias is not only explicitly and physically huge, but also, as Hardie shows (145, cf. too 287), associated with the mythical Giant Typhoeus.

would most naturally suit the edifice in the simile.[6] Or we could say that simile language has as it were trespassed into the narrative. David West might call this 'transfusion of metaphor'; in Michael Silk's terms (adapted from I. A. Richards), we can see it as an instance of 'vehicle' language in the 'tenor'.[7] However we wish to phrase what is happening, the reason for the choice of 'conlapsa' becomes perspicuous, and the effect when seen satisfying. Huge Bitias collapses like a building.

Less obvious is the use of the same word for the dying Dido at 4.664:[8]

> atque illam media inter talia ferro
> conlapsam aspiciunt comites

And her companions see her in the midst of such words collapsed on the sword.

—which is, we could say, anticipated by Dido's faint at 4.391, 'conlapsaque membra'. Dido has no vast limbs like Bitias. Why the choice of verb normally reserved for the description of collapsing buildings?

At 4.664 we are just five lines from the simile that compares the lamentation at Dido's death to that which might attend the sack of her city (669 ff.). Lamentation rises to the heavens ...

> non aliter quam si immissis ruat hostibus omnis
> Karthago aut antiqua Tyros ...

even as if all Carthage were falling headlong, or ancient Tyre ...

---

[6] The edifice is a 'pila'. Cf. most immediately *CIL* X 1640 quoted above.

[7] See D. West (1969) 48 f., (1970) 265; he associates the phenomenon particularly with the second half of the *Aeneid*; Silk 9 ff., 235 f. 'Vehicle' language in the 'tenor' is a reasonable use of Silk's terms (I have consulted the author), but not in fact how Silk himself chooses to call the particular phenomenon to which I am referring. With great fineness of discrimination he calls it (235 f.) 'Metaphor as ground term to simile', perhaps a slight ellipsis for what might be in full 'metaphor in place of what would be the ground term ...' Excellent examples are cited by Silk from both Greek and English literature. This is a topic to which I return in IV.5, preferring the appellation 'trespass'.

We might note that, just as 'conlapsa' metaphorically anticipates the simile, so from one point of view does 'ruunt' ('ruo' as I say above can be used of edifices), especially given the use of 'ruina' in the simile (9.712).

[8] The surprising aspect of Vergil's phraseology is emphasized if we compare and contrast a model, Soph. *Ajax* 899 νεοσφαγὴς / κεῖται, κρυφαίῳ φασγάνῳ περιπτυχής. Vergil replaces περιπτυχής with 'collapsam'.

Vergil suggests by this simile an equivalence between Dido's death and the fall of her city: she is Carthage's Hector.[9] Note that he does indeed talk of the destruction of Carthage in terms of its physical fall, its headlong collapse, 'ruina': 'ruat' (669).[10] Vergil is I think anticipating, foreshadowing this suggestion of equivalence when he uses, to record decisive stages in Dido's collapse and death, a verb reminiscent of the collapse of an edifice. What this is is a subtler metaphorical exploitation of the value of 'conlabor' than happened with Bitias. Bitias' fall is like the collapse of an edifice because he is so physically vast. Dido's collapse may be compared implicitly to the collapse of an edifice because her death and fall has the *significance* of the fall and destruction of her city. Again we might see 'conlapsa' as an example of metaphorical anticipation of simile ('conlapsa' antici- pates 'ruat'), or of simile language trespassing into the narrative, or transfusion of metaphor, or vehicle language in the tenor. (We might note in addition that the 'collapse' of Dido works effec- tively with—perhaps sadly offsets—her claim (at 4.655) 'urbem praeclaram statui, mea moenia uidi'.)

There may be unexpected confirmation of this line of interpre- tation in what looks to be rather an odd use of 'conlabor'. The lolling head of the dead Euryalus is described thus, 9.433–4:

> pulchrosque per artus
> it cruor inque umeros ceruix conlapsa recumbit...

Gore runs over his beautiful limbs, and his neck collapsing sinks back onto his shoulder.

Is it not strange to describe the pretty hero's slumped neck with a term that suits a collapsed building? We note that Vergil's loyal plagiarizer, the author of the *Ciris*, censors this particular detail (*Cir.* 449): 'et caput inflexa lentum ceruice recumbit'. What Vergil is doing is I think imitating an ambivalence which he saw in his Homeric source. The model for 9.434 is *Iliad* 8.308, the death of Gorgythion:

> ὣς ἑτέρωσ' ἤμυσε κάρη πήληκι βαρυνθέν

So did his head bow to one side, weighed down with his helmet.

---

[9] See Lyne, *Further Voices*, 20. The point is later emphasized by Anna, 4.682 f., 'exstinxti te meque, soror, populumque patresque / Sidonios urbemque tuam.'
[10] Cf. the comments on 'ruo' above p. 40 and n. 7.

The word ἠμύω means literally 'bow' or 'bend'. But Homer uses the word twice metaphorically of the fall of a city, *Iliad* 2.373 and 4.290:

τῷ κε τάχ᾽ ἠμύσειε πόλις Πριάμοιο ἄνακτος

Then would the city of king Priam soon bow ...

Vergil seems in consequence to have felt an ambiguity at 8.308: he saw Homer using a word of a lolling head that could also be used of a falling city. And his 'conlapsa' is designed to reflect what he saw. Of course the ambiguity he provides is a kind of mirror-image of the supposed ambiguity in Homer: Homer's ἠμύω, literally suited to the bending of necks, might metaphorically refer to the fall of a city; 'conlabor', suited to falling edifices, is *metaphorically* applied to a bending neck. Nevertheless, Vergil's design is I think to reflect the putative Homeric ambivalence. Why he should have wished to reproduce it (in mirror-image) I am not fully sure. But I think we should now realize that he is using 'conlabor' *metaphorically* at 9.434. We should also accept that he sees 'conlabor' as a possible substitute for ἠμύω, thus as a word suited to the area of sense 'a city falls'. In this there is unexpected support for the point I made above about Dido's collapse and Vergil's wish to foreshadow in the verb 'conlabor' the equivalence of her fall to the fall of her city.

Other Vergilian uses of 'conlabor', more or less explicable in the light of what I have said above, are: *Georg.* 3.485, *Aen.* 6.226, 8.584, 9.753. Particularly explicable are 6.226 and 9.753; particularly interesting is 8.584.

2. uxorius

For my next observation, I should say a little about the word 'uxor'. Axelson, 57 f. pointed to its partly unpoetical status: he showed that it was in particular avoided by epic, including Ovid's *Met.*, in favour of 'coniunx' or periphrases (no examples of 'uxor' in Verg. *Aen*, Ov. *Met.*, Val., and Sil., and only one, 3.353 in Lucan). We may go a little further. First, some more statistics; to give a rough and ready context I compare occurrences of 'uxor' simply with those of fem. 'coniunx'.[11]

[11] Cf. also the figures and discussion of Watson, 431–2.

'Uxor' is common in Ovid's elegiac works (over 50 examples, including 5 in *Fast*.); but so is fem. 'coniunx'. Plautus has a truly vast number of examples of 'uxor',[12] but (outside two in the *Argumenta* appended to his plays) only one of 'coniunx', fem.: *Amphit*. 475, where Mercury refers to Alcumena thus (and high diction would in context patently be fitting). Terence similarly uses 'uxor' very frequently (130), but has no example of 'coniunx' at all. Tibullus has 4 examples of 'uxor', 2 of fem. 'coniunx'; Propertius 7 of 'uxor', 7 of fem. 'coniunx'. Horace, *Carm*. 'uxor' 7, 'coniunx' fem. 8; *Serm*. 'uxor' 9, 'coniunx' 2 (*Epod*. 1 / 0, *Epist*. 3 / 1). Cicero, *Speeches* 'uxor' 84, 'coniunx' fem. 29; *Epistles* 'uxor' 18,[13] 'coniunx' fem. 7. Cato *Rust*. 'uxor' 1 (143.1 of the 'uilicus''s wife), 'coniunx' fem. 0. Varro *Rust*. 'uxor' 3 (all referring to Varro's own wife), 'coniunx' fem. 0. Caesar *Gall*. and *Civ*. 'uxor' 11, 'coniunx' fem. 1. Livy 'uxor' 57, 'coniunx' fem. 97. Tacitus 'uxor' 100, 'coniunx' fem. 71.

'Uxor' we may conclude is the strictly prosaic word, the word preferred by the writers of 'business' prose (Cato, Varro, Caesar); it will also have been the regular word of the spoken tongue: this is reflected in the almost total preference of comedy; note too the preponderance in Cicero's letters and Horace's Satires. To generate these generic statistics 'uxor' must have denoted the ordinary wife of everyday experience, the wife one talks about casually and the real wife a 'business' writer would want to convey directly. Given such a sense, it is comprehensible that the love Elegists should not shy excessively at the word. Real wives have their part to play in the world of Augustan love. In addition (and rather differently) Catullus had promoted the concept of the everyday wife into an ideal, and thus suggested a possible new resonance in the word 'uxor' for those in tune with his ideal. (But Catullus' own use of the *word* 'uxor' suggests he felt *it* as merely ordinary. He confirms its spoken status and mundane denotation.)[14] Horace's affection for 'uxor' in the

[12] There are 104 examples in the ten plays on IBYCUS (Am., As., Aul., Bac., Cap., Ps., Rud., St., Trin., Truc.)

[13] This figure includes 'uxoris' restored in *Att*. 6.1.25 by Schütz and accepted by Shackleton Bailey.

[14] On Catullus' promotion of the concept wife, see Lyne, *The Latin Love Poets*, 34–8, 56–7. But, as I say, Catullus himself makes nothing much of the *word* 'uxor'. He uses it in the romantic epithalamium (61.185); but his other two uses are emphatically mundane, confirming the basic denotation I argue for above ('the wife

Odes tunes with his well attested penchant for ordinary diction even in that lyric genre,[15] and in some of his uses we can see a special effect being sought.[16]

'Coniunx' fem. was the word of more elevated literature, almost exclusively preferred by epic, useful as well as 'uxor' to the Elegists,[17] and playing a substantial role in grand, imaginative prose, particularly that of Livy. It was clearly a more resonant appellation than 'uxor', the word (it is almost a periphrasis) to suggest consorts and helpmeets of a higher plain. It conveys the affective connotations of English 'wife', while excluding mundane associations: it lends itself to an emotive formula with 'liberi', which accounts for a very large proportion of both Cicero's and Livy's uses—and this is how Caesar's single use appears.[18]

So, 'uxor' was a prosaic word, used also in the spoken tongue, denoting the ordinary wife of everyday experience; 'coniunx' fem. had the connotations that many poets deemed appropriate. The adjective 'uxorius', meaning 'belonging to a wife' or 'to do with a wife' (the English 'uxorious' *sim.* should be avoided as a translation),[19] has a mundane sense in line with 'uxor', is prosaic in line with 'uxor' (though overall very rare), and it too probably had a currency in the spoken tongue.

The prosaic status of 'uxorius' is shown by (besides the expectations created by 'uxor') (a) its avoidance in the poets (see below) and (b) its use on a few significant occasions in 'business'

one talks about casually'): 59.2., 74.4. Catullus has 'coniunx' fem. four times, 23.6, 64. 298, 329, 78.1. The first and the last of these show no respect for the elevated tone I argue for in 'coniunx', but that is not unexpected in a satirical Catullus. (Quite interestingly Catullus uses 'coniunx' masc. 11 times, all in the 'high' longer poems 61, 62, 64, and 64, showing respect for the elevated word in its masculine form.)

[15] See I.2.

[16] 'Uxor' at *Carm.* 1.17.7, 2.14.22, 18.28, 3.3.67, 15.1, 27.21, 73. At 3.3.67, for example, 'ter uxor / capta uirum puerosque ploret', the ordinary tone of 'uxor' is confirmed by 'ploret', a colloquialism (cf. French 'pleurer') exploited by Elegy as well as Horace: Axelson, 28 f.

[17] See appendix below.

[18] Caes. *Gall.* 7.14.10 'liberos, coniuges in seruitutem abstrahi.' At this point Caesar is reporting a speech (in *oratio obliqua*), and making some effort to reflect a dignified emotion. Hence the elevated and affective 'coniunx'.

[19] Dictionaries (*OLD*, *LS*) and translators (e.g. Winterbottom in the Loeb of Sen. *Contr.* 1.6.7) attribute to 'uxorius' a sense 'devoted to, in love with, one's wife' *sim.* (i.e. 'uxorious'). But the uses of the word that I cite above suggest that, at least in Vergil's time, its application to a man will have implied that he *belonged* to his wife, not just was very fond of her.

prose. Cicero uses 'uxorius' three times. At both *Off.* 3.61 and
Topica 66 'rei uxoriae' refers to a wife's property, in situations of
legal dispute over it. At *Amic.* 34 'uxoriae condicionis' is used of
a marriage match or contract. A few more prose examples can be
seen in *OLD.* s.v. Cicero's examples, particularly the first two,
suggest to me that in certain contexts 'uxorius' was a 'business'
mot juste.

Comedy makes a couple of constructive uses of the word.
Plautus talks of 'sumptu uxorio' in a fr. (1) of the *Aul.*, blunt
phrasing for what is clearly a sore point[20] (and the *Argumentum*
to the *As.* (line 2) talks of 'sub imperio ... uxorio'). Ter. *Andria*
829 uses 'res uxoria' as a way of saying marriage:
'adulescentulo / in alio occupato amore, abhorrenti ab re uxoria'. Cf. Cic. *Amic.* 34 above, but Terence's words are functional
in context. As the young man is occupied 'alio amore', Chremes
pointedly avoids saying simply 'marriage' and stresses that it is a
matter of a *wife*. Then Ovid at *Ars* 2.155 formulates the cutting
and emphatic comment 'dos est uxoria lites'—at this point he is
not in favour of wives. These examples (*a*) suggest that 'uxorius'
had a spoken currency (note the examples in comedy in particular) and (*b*) confirm that it had a basic denotation as mundane
as, or more mundane than, that of 'uxor'; and (*c*) since these are
in fact the only examples (besides the two I shall promptly quote)
to be found in a very large range of verse,[21] we have confirmation of the prosaic status of the word.

In Vergil's time, therefore, the occasional pointed use had been
made of a word whose other uses were dull and/or technical.
Vergil had another idea, involving an inventiveness of quite a
different order.

Mercury finds Aeneas building Carthage for Dido, dressed in
Tyrian clothes supplied by Dido.[22] He is prompted angrily to
exclaim, 4.265 ff.:

> tu nunc Karthaginis altae
> fundamenta locas pulchramque uxorius urbem
> extruis? heu, regni rerumque oblite tuarum!

Are you now laying the foundations of lofty Carthage and, as the

---

[20] 'pro illis corcotis, strophiis, sumptu uxorio. / ut admemordit hominem!'
[21] Enn., Lucr., Catull., Cic. *poet.*, Prop., Tib. (and *Corp. Tib.*), Hor., Verg., Ov.,
Luc., Sen. *trag.*, Val., Sil., Stat.
[22] On these clothes see VIII.3.

property of your wife, building up its fair city? Alas, forgetful of your own kingdom and fortunes!

We can perceive various reasons why Mercury is angry. In particular, he is offended by the fact that Aeneas is 'oblitus regni rerumque suarum', and he is offended by two other points. He packs two insults into the lines to correspond to these two points.

We could sum up Mercury's underlying ground for offence (besides Aeneas' forgetfulness of his kingdom) by saying that the hero seems to him to be behaving like an Elegiac lover: he is happy to serve the beloved in order to win her favour; he is displaying 'obsequium'.[23] Now 'obsequium' (or the proclamation of 'obsequium') shocked public, moral opinion because it involved free men serving what were probably disreputable women: women thus had all the appearance of *owning* free men. The Elegiac lover himself of course gloried in this fact, professing himself indeed the woman's *slave*.[24]

This leads us to one of the two points which specifically offend Mercury: Aeneas appears to be *owned* by Dido. Mercury conveys his opinion that this is so in the eye-catching and in context insulting word 'uxorius': Aeneas 'belongs to his wife'. But of course there is a *second* insult contained in 'uxorius', reflecting the second point which offends Mercury: Aeneas belongs to his *wife*. Propertius might glory in the thought that he not only served Cynthia, but she might be deemed his wife.[25] But Aeneas not only has no business serving anyone except Fate, he has no business considering anyone his wife, or letting anyone consider herself his wife, until he meets his fated wife in Italy (2.783 f.). But of course, as we know, Mercury's jibe, the second as well as the first, has point. Aeneas has let someone—Dido—gain the impression that she is his wife. This is the topic on which he is going to have to defend himself, standing on the letter of the law, in what some of us regard as not his finest hour (4.333 ff.). So Mercury, caustically observing that he 'belongs to his wife', is being doubly insulting and with some justification: not only is Aeneas in the pocket of a woman, but this woman considers

---

[23] Cf. Ov. *Ars* 2.177 ff. (the text-book account), Tibull. 1.4.40 ff. ('obsequium' to a beloved boy), etc.; Propertius' complaint in 1.1 is in effect that he has displayed 'obsequium' but still not won Cynthia's favours.
[24] See Lyne, *The Latin Love Poets*, 80–1.
[25] Ibid.

herself and appears to be his wife. I said above that Mercury packs two insults into the quoted lines. In fact they are packed into the single word 'uxorius'.

Mercury uses a mundane and ordinary word—and by his choice of diction is we might say characterized.[26] Vergil and Mercury exploit a prosaic word, and not just for its eye-catching quality. We can see that the denotative, distinct, and ordinary value of 'uxorius' is vital to them. A cognate of, say, 'coniunx' would have been vastly inferior. Mercury has every reason to focus Aeneas on the everyday reality 'wife' in the bluntest possible way; and every reason not to overlay the denotation with elevated and suggestive resonances that might obscure the everyday reality.

Horace at *Carm.* 1.2.19 f. 'uagus et sinistra / labitur ripa Ioue non probante u- / xorius amnis' essays an effect which I must leave others fully to interpret. But we must I think say that Horace is being patronizing, even derisory of the vengeful Tiber who is 'in the pocket of his wife'—which is interesting.[27]

This is the other poetical example of 'uxorius' that I mentioned above. Several times Vergil and Horace in the Odes can be observed making parallel experiments with language. This is due, I think, to pre-publication collaboration (see further p. 54).

3. mutabile femina

At 4.266 Mercury employed a prosaic word, and insulted Aeneas bluntly; and in part at least his jibe was untrue: Dido was not actually his wife. At 4.569 in his eagerness to get Aeneas on his way Mercury delivers the opinion that

> uarium et mutabile semper
> femina

A woman is an inconstant and changeable thing.

As a basic generalization this may strike us as at least debatable. Applied to Dido, as Mercury intends it, it is flatly untrue and meant to strike us as such. And it concludes a speech by the god which is centred on a lie ('illa dolos dirumque nefas ...',

---

[26] For other examples of diction characterizing see V.2 and 3.
[27] Nisbet and Hubbard observe that 'the picture of the doting Tiber [is] frivolous'.

563 ff.).[28] Mercury, we begin to realize, is not an honourable or pleasant character.

There are refinements of unpleasantness in the phrasing 'uarium et mutabile semper / femina'. To begin with, we should notice the contemptuous neuter case 'mutabile': a woman is a changeable *thing*.[29] The contemptuousness of this neuter is reinforced by the word 'mutabilis' itself, admirably exploited by Mercury.

I shall attempt a description of the stylistic register and semantic nuances of 'mutabilis', although surviving instances are not such as to make this easy ('-bilis' words in general, of which Vergil is fond, admit of no single characterization).[30] Before Vergil a substantial proportion of surviving examples occurs in Cicero, who has 11 examples in all (*Phil.* 10,[31] *Epist.* 1). In Vergil's time it looks as if it was a mainly prosaic if not a Ciceronian word;[32] and it is naturally used of the changeability of insensate things (substances, circumstances, etc.). Cf. e.g. Cic. *N.D* 1.34 'sensuque deum priuat et eius formam mutabilem esse uult', 3.30[33] 'si omnia e quibus cuncta constant mutabilia sunt, nullum corpus esse potest non mutabile; mutabilia autem sunt illa ex quibus omnia constant ...', *Att.* 7.11.5 'ea uelim scribas ad me, et quidem, quoniam mutabilia sunt, quam saepissime', *Rep.* 2.43 'ea autem forma ciuitatis mutabilis maxime est'. In Livy (6 in all) we find its use extended to include men's characters, sim., e.g. 2.7.5 'ut sunt mutabiles uolgi animi', 29.23.6 'memor ... quam uana et mutabilia barbarorum ingenia essent'. The subjects in these two ('uulgus', 'barbari') might support a deduction that the transference of the word from the inanimate to the animate would not be flattering to its animate recipients. It is patronizing and dismissive: these people are changeable like events, circumstances, and substances.

---

[28] Cf. Austin on 4.569 'But Mercury is lying, as he lied in 563 ...'. Lines 592 ff. esp. 595 ff. give the lie to 563 ff.

[29] See Pease ad loc.

[30] See R. D. Williams on 3.39 and 5.591 and a useful discussion in Leumann–Hofmann–Szantyr, i. 348–9. Adjectives in '-bilis' were obviously metrically useful to a dactylic poet.

[31] Three of these bunch at *ND* 3.30 quoted below.

[32] Note too 'mutabiliter' at Varr. *Men.* 78.

[33] The text is disputed but the examples of 'mutabilis' are secure.

The few uses that can be cited from a large range of verse[34] do not undermine, they rather confirm, the prosaic profile I suggest for the word, especially in Vergil's time; and they do not argue against the semantic nuance I have just proposed. Horace provides two[35] examples, but both occur in the *Epistles*, poems hospitable to prosaic diction: *Epist.* 2.1.101, 'quid placet aut odio est quod non mutabile credas?',[36] and 2.2.189 'Genius ... naturae deus humanae ... uultu mutabilis'; in the latter I think that Horace means (ultimately) to be rather unflattering to human nature. Vergil himself uses it again at 11.425 (see below). In Ovid we find four examples, in the first of which at least he is influenced by Vergil: *Her.* 7.51 (see below), and *Met.* 2.145 and *Fast.* 4.601 'mutabile pectus', with which cf. *Trist.* 5.13.19 'neque enim mutabile robur ... pectoris'. There is too one example in the *Corp. Tib.* (3.4.63), and a few in the Flavians (Val. 1, Stat. 1, Sil. 5). A continuing prosaic status for the word in Seneca's time is quite vividly suggested by the fact that Seneca uses it fifteen times in his prose works and never in his tragedies. Cicero's and Seneca's uses might suggest it had a rather dry, scientific tone.

The examples in the *Aeneid* are therefore eye-catching by virtue of the fact that they are prosaisms in a poetical text. And at 4.569 f. we can now see that Mercury is given several tricks to reinforce his contemptuous utterance in respect of women. (1) The neuter phrasing: woman is a changeable thing. (2) This first insinuation is reinforced by 'mutabilis': the adjective is normally applied to inanimate things. *TLL* lists Vergil *Aen.* 4.569 as the first example of 'mutabilis' transferred directly to 'homines' (and we might compare Livy above). I would rather say that Vergil has not really transferred it. Rather, *vice versa*: he has transferred the 'homo' in question. Mercury's 'homo', woman, is not worthy to be graced with the name 'homo'; she is a mere 'thing'. This is what the diction is designed to emphasize, both the neuter case and the word 'mutabilis'. (3) Mercury's third trick is to exploit a prosaic word. It is eye-catching. If it was a dry and scientific

---

[34] Enn., Lucr., Catull., Cic. *poet.*, Prop., Tib. (and *Corp. Tib.*), Hor., Verg., Ov., Luc., Sen. *trag.*, Val., Sil., Stat.

[35] Two, if *Epist.* 2.1.101 is sound, one if it is not: see next note.

[36] This line is deleted by Haberfeldt, rightly in the opinion of C. O. Brink, transposed by others: see the app. crit. of Shackleton Bailey, who inclines to transposition.

word (as suggested above: note the use in philosophy, Cic. and Sen.), this too will have contributed to Mercury's tone of contempt.

Mercury concludes his apophthegm with the word 'femina', which I translated 'woman'—not quite correctly. The use of 'femina' is ironic; indeed 'femina' makes a kind of oxymoron with 'mutabile'. 'Femina' is the grand, respectful term for a woman ('lady' rather than 'woman'), the word in fact usually preferred by Augustan poetry,[37] but preferred because it is grand, respectful, noble.

It is pleasant that Ovid makes Dido throw the word 'mutabilis' back at Aeneas, *Her.* 7.51:

> tu quoque cum uentis utinam mutabilis esses!

Oh that you too had been changeable with the winds!

Dido is changeable, says Vergil's Mercury. Oh that Aeneas had been so despicable! respond Dido and Ovid.

At 11.425, where Vergil's other example of 'mutabilis' occurs, Turnus philosophizes thus:

> multa dies uariique labor mutabilis aeui
> rettulit in melius ...

The passage of days and the changeable toil of inconstant time have often returned things for the better ...

and Turnus continues further in this vein. I think that Vergil selects 'mutabilis' because it suits Turnus' uncharacteristically philosophizing mood: note the distribution of occurrences in Cicero and Seneca above.

4. edax

When 'edax' came into Vergil's hands, it seems to have been confined to the literal sense 'greedy', 'gluttonous' (the root is 'edo', eat), i.e. it referred to a human and animal reaction to

---

[37] See Axelson, 53–7, a fine discussion. On 'mulier' and 'femina' in Propertius, see Tränkle 121. Some more light on 'mulier' / 'femina' is now shed by the *TLL* article 'mulier'; see especially *init.* where there are excellent statistics. It should however be noted that when *TLL* says that 'mulier' is not well suited to dactyls, it omits to mention that 'femina' is more or less in the same position. Neither word is amenable in the oblique cases.

food. The evidence is small, but suggests I think that we should term the word colloquial; this status will be due to the fact that it denoted a very everyday, even vulgar experience ('auidus' is a more literary word). 'Edax' occurs once in Plautus, three times in Terence, twice in Cicero's letters (*Fam.* 9.20.2, 23.1; and Cic. has 'edacitas' literally at *Q. Fr.* 3.7.9), and once in one of his speeches (*Flacc.* 41). These, all literal, are the only pre-Augustan[38] uses surviving at all.

Only literal uses then are attested in pre-Augustan Latin, and for the most part they occur in colloquial genres. If we now follow this *literal* use of 'edax' down into later Latin, we shall find our picture not seriously gainsaid: it seems a word better suited to the vigorous world of the spoken tongue; non-colloquial writers who employ it are making special use of a particularly vigorous or immediate word for 'greedy'. Here are the instances (of *literal* 'edax') in Augustan[39] Latin; it is important of course for an estimation of the word's stylistic register to note those authors (e.g. Livy) who do not use it (Livy does not use the word at all).[40] Horace has *Epist.* 2.1.173 'aspice Plautus ... / quantus sit Dossenus edacibus in parasitis' (cf. 'parasitus edax' also at Ter. *Eun.* 38, *Heaut.* 38; it seems a typical parasite's epithet), *Serm.* 2.2.92, and *Epod.* 2.34 'turdis'; Horace thus uses it in more conversational genres and moods.[41] Ovid has three examples, all consonant with the utilization of a colloquialism: at *Am.* 2.6.33 and *Trist.* 1.6.11 he applies it to a 'uultur',[42] at *Rem.* 209 to a 'piscis'.[43] That is all.

[38] For the purposes of this section I include all Horace's works under the 'Augustan' label. I apologize for this historical inelegance. For some purposes (e.g. political-historical purposes) the Satires and Epodes must of course be regarded as belonging to a different period from the Odes. On other occasions the distinction introduces unnecessary complications (and I find the catch-all 'Triumviral and Augustan' repellently clumsy). The problem does not present itself again in this book.

[39] See n. 38.

[40] Bömer 15 gives incorrect information on occurrences of 'edax'.

[41] *Serm.* and *Epist.* are genres more hospitable to colloquial diction. In *Epod.* 2 'faenerator Alfius, iam iam futurus rusticus' is speaking. His diction in general is very ordinary, in tune both with his present occupation and his apparent aspiration: note in particular 'mulier' (39, cf. p. 51), 'uxor' (42, cf. pp. 43–5), 'pecunia' (69, cf. p. 38). His one venture into high diction, 'dapes' (48, cf. p. 38), is designed to produce a special effect: it makes an oxymoron 'dapes inemptas'.

[42] The 'edax uultur' at *Am.* 2.6.33 is designed forcefully to contrast with the delicate and human-like 'psittacus', 'illa loquax humanae uocis imago'.

[43] Ovid here accumulates a pile of voracious words, among them 'edax', to build the fish up to a monstrous status—for comic effect, to contrast with the line that

The first century AD (after Augustus) shows only a very few authors using the word in its literal sense, only Colum. 6.2.14 ('boues'), Sen. *Epist.* 60.3 ('animalia'), Plin. *Nat.* 11.67 ('apes'), Val. 6.420 (a hunting dog). The limitation to animals suggests a coarseness in the word, consonant with a presumed colloquial status. On the other hand, the fact that the word is not used at all by Persius, Petronius, and Juvenal argues against any wide currency in the spoken tongue in the first century.

I return to Vergil's time, and sum up. Evidence suggests that he found in 'edax' a word with the very blunt and everyday sense of literally 'greedy', and the word was in consequence of this sense colloquial; it was not necessarily common in the spoken tongue, but it was a spoken rather than a literary word. In addition, it seems that, when Vergil wrote, it had developed no metaphorical life. (But this last claim involves one assumption that has yet to be justified.)

We should now consider metaphorical uses of 'edax'; it will be remembered that all pre-Augustan uses of the word are literal. We find that, in metaphorical uses, the word catches on in Augustan poetry (and later literature) to a remarkable degree. Vergil and Horace both use it of the physically devouring effect of non-animate physical entities. Vergil has 'ignis edax' at 2.758 (his only example of the epithet):

> ilicet ignis edax summa ad fastigia uento
> uoluitur ...

Straightway the greedy fire rolls before the wind to the rooftops...

and this then begets a host of children (Ov. *Fast.* 4.785, *Met.* 9.202, 14.541,[44] etc., *TLL* V.2.62.18 ff., 31 ff.: legitimizing effect, cf. I.4 *init.*). Horace has 'imber edax' at *Carm.* 3.30.3, 'aere perennius / regalique situ pyramidum altius, / quod non imber edax ... possit diruere'. Ovid then comes up with 'uirus edax' at *Fast.* 5.403; and one or two further ways were excogitated in which 'edax' might qualify a non-animate physical entity.

Still more metaphorical are uses of 'edax' of non-physical entities in Horace and Ovid: Hor. *Carm.* 2.11.18 'dissipat

follows: 'quae piscis edax auido male deuoret ore, / abdere suspensis aera recurua cibis.'

[44] Cf. too Ov. *Met.* 15.354, 'edax' of 'Natura' lacking 'nutrimen' in a context of fire.

Euhius / curas edaces', Ov. *Am.* 1.15.1 and *Rem.* 389 'Livor', *Met.* 15.234 'tempus edax rerum tuque inuidiosa uetustas', *Pont.* 4.10.7 'tempus', and *Met.* 15.872 'opus ... quod ... nec ignis ... poterit ... nec edax abolere uetustas'; and these beget children (*TLL* V.2.62.40 ff., 45 ff., 49).

It is interesting, by the by, that, although Ovid's uses of 'edax' at *Am.* 1.15.1, *Rem.* 389 and *Met.* 15.872 are most directly to be compared with Hor. *Carm.* 2.11.18 (in that they are metaphorical uses with a non-physical entity), Ovid clearly thinks of and draws from in these passages (and perhaps *Met.* 15.234) Hor. *Carm.* 3.30 as well (note the similar topic). On top of this he seems to think too of *Aen.* 2.758 in the context of *Am.* 1.15.41 ('cum me supremus ad*ederit ignis*', and in the context of *Met.* 15.872 '*ignis*' quoted above). So, attracted to a novel use of 'edax', he is put in mind of other such novel uses. The ways in which 'edax' had been put to service by his predecessors were striking and novel enough for him to associate and contaminate them.

The assumption I am making, referred to above, is that Vergil is the first to extend the use of 'edax' in a metaphorical way, that it is in fact he who starts 'edax' off on its profitable career in literature. I am assuming in particular that Vergil does not follow Horace; rather, Horace in the Odes takes a cue from the *Aeneid* before its publication, or hears about Vergil's use in conversation with the great man. Such influence on Horace by Vergil is what I take to be happening on other occasions (cf. 'uxorius' above); and I do not think that this is simply the biased view of a Vergil idolator. But let me do something to justify the assumption here.

'Ignis edax' reflects a tactic of Vergil's that we can observe elsewhere, and the phrase is striking but self-explanatory. It vividly recasts a metaphor well paralleled in other, less striking language: note e.g. ἐσθίω, 'eat', in Hom. *Il.* 23.182 τοὺς ἅμα σοὶ πάντας πῦρ ἐσθίει· Ἕκτορα δ' οὔ τι / δώσω Πριαμίδην πυρὶ δαπτέμεν, ἀλλὰ κύνεσσιν, '[Achilles addresses the dead Patroclus] them the fire eats at the same time as you; but Hector I shall not give to the fire to devour, but to the dogs', *Aen.* 5.683 'lentusque carinas / est uapor', and (of metaphorical fire) Catull. 35.15 'misellae / ignes interiorem edunt medullam', *Aen.* 4.66.[45] So:

---

[45] The image can be reversed: see Hesiod *Erga* 363 with M. L. West ad loc.

Vergil revivifies the metaphor of fire 'eating' by applying to 'ignis' this eye-catching colloquial word for 'greedy' (whose root is 'edo', eat). He *exploits* a word from the living tongue to jerk some life into an old metaphor.[46] His tactic in 'ignis edax' is identifiable and explicable. (We might add that Aeneas is marginally characterized by the popular diction.)[47]

Horace's 'imber edax', where 'edax' is similarly transferred to a non-animate noun, is not similarly explicable. It is indeed worth asking exactly how well the metaphor serves in Horace's context. If not well, why does he use it?

Horace's context (in celebration of the immortal achievement that is *Carm.* I—III) is as follows (3.30.1 ff.):

> exegi monumentum aere perennius
> regalique situ pyramidum altius,
> quod non imber edax ...
> possit diruere ...

I have built a monument more lasting than bronze, higher than the royal site of the pyramids, that greedy rain [etc.] cannot demolish ...

This proclamation requires us to think of the effect of rain on stone (the pyramids) and on memorials of bronze ('aes'),[48] where, so Horace implies, it *can* be destructive, compared with its impact on his poems. In this connection, in connection with its effect on stone and bronze, he calls rain 'greedy' (root, 'eat'). It seems to me a strange image, slightly off-centre, certainly unparalleled. Water wears away stone in a variety of suggestive and plausible expressions,[49] and *rust* 'eats' metal[50] in a believable image (and, e.g., rivers nibble their banks: Lucr. 5.256, Hor. *Carm.* 1.31.8 with Nisbet & Hubbard). But the idea of rain 'eating', being 'greedy', is not a familiar one. Nor does it seem to me, if I am to be honest, an entirely convincing one; eating is too drastic an image for the action of rain. Nor is the image well

---

[46] We should note that on the second occasion when Homer uses the metaphor in the above quotation he uses 'combination' to re'new' the metaphor. Opposed to devouring dogs, devouring fire must be brought vividly to life.

[47] General Aeneas' high-flying imagery is put on a firm, popular footing. For such characterization of Aeneas see V.2 and 3.

[48] Cf. Woodman in Woodman–West 119 f.

[49] See conveniently K. F. Smith on Tibull. 1.4.18.

[50] Cf. e.g. *Georg.* 1.151; for rust and bronze see Woodman, loc. cit.

integrated into Horace's context: the poem does not develop or even make use of the idea of greedy rain.

Vergil therefore uses the striking word 'edax' to recast a well-paralleled metaphor, Horace uses the striking word to add a novel and slightly extrinsic metaphor. His use is not self-explanatory: we cannot say either that he uses the word because the image works well in his context or that he uses it because it recasts a familiar image. But his use is immediately explained if we suppose that he has been stirred to exploit 'edax' by Vergil's example or tuition. Vergil's 'greedy fire' engendered the more paradoxical 'greedy water'. I wonder what Vergil thought of his progeny.

Aen. 2.758 'ignis edax' precedes and engenders *Carm.* 3.30.3 'imber edax'. *Carm.* 2.11.18 'curas edaces' is also I think its child or grandchild. This is probable in view of the situation with 3.30.3 and seems likely enough on its own account; but anteriority is not here quite so demonstrable. We might however infer that pursuit of novelty (awareness that he was building on Vergil's example) suggested to Horace a different kind of metaphorical transference, a transference to a non-physical subject; and that pursuit of novelty also suggested he concoct another neat little effect to enliven metaphorical 'edax', which in Vergil's first use was quite lively enough on its own: 'dissipat Euhius (i.e. *drinking* dissipates) curas edaces (cares that *eat*)'.

5. degusto

At 2.758 Vergil revivifies the metaphor of fire 'eating' with the idea of fire's *greediness*: specifically with the eye-catching colloquial word 'edax'. Lucretius did something closely similar. He provides the idea of fire *tasting* and draws our attention to this notion with the eye-catching prosaic word 'degusto'. 2.192:

> (sc.) ignes
> et celeri flamma degustant tigna trabesque.

(fires) with swift flame taste beams and rafters.

Bailey ad loc. says, 'the poets usually employ *lambere* in this metaphorical sense' (and gives parallels, one of which is *Aen.* 2.684); see further Munro ad loc. *TLL* cites 'degusto' in 'business' prose (Cato, Varro), Cicero, and other prose, but in verse up to and including that of the Augustan age, it provides only Verg. *Aen.* 12.376, Ov. *Pont* 4.10.18 (and Manil. 3.613), besides Lucr. loc. cit. With Lucr. 2.192 cf. *Ciris* 146 'necdum etiam castos gustauerat ignis honores', where the fact that sacrifices ('honores') are the object of the verb enlivens the image.

In Vergil's text the prosaism will probably have been more eye-catching than in Lucretius': Lucretius' subject matter imposes more prosaisms on him as a matter of course than heroic myth imposes on Vergil. 12.376 runs:

> (sc. lancea) summum degustat uulnere corpus.

The lance grazes the flesh and tastes the surface of the body.

Cf. the allied and grim image at 11.804 '(sc. hasta) uirgineumque alte bibit acta cruorem'; on this occasion Vergil uses a neutral word ('bibo') as the key term. Silius imitates *Aen.* 12.376 at 5.274 'leuiterque e corpore summo / degustat cuspis generosum extrema cruorem.' Homeric images in such contexts which specifically involve taste are different in aspect. Cf. e.g. *Il.* 20.258:

> ἀλλ' ἄγε θᾶσσον
> γευσόμεθ' ἀλλήλων χαλκήρεσιν ἐγχείησιν

Come let us forthwith taste one another with bronze-tipped spears.

Il. 21.60

> ἀλλ' ἄγε δὴ καὶ δουρὸς ἀκωκῆς ἡμετέροιο
> γεύσεται

Come let him taste the point of our spear.

This latter is almost the opposite idea to Vergil's. Closer is *Il.* 11.573–4 = 15.316:

> (δοῦρα) ... πάρος χρόα λευκὸν ἐπαυρεῖν,
> ἐν γαίῃ ἵσταντο, λιλαιόμενα χροὸς ἆσαι.

Spears ... before they had enjoyment of the white flesh, stood fixed in the earth, desiring to sate themselves with flesh.

Cf. too *Il.* 21.70 and 168 (ἄω again).

6. porto

It is an over-simplification to call 'porto' 'colloquial' in contrast to 'fero', without further ado.[51] One should be cautious about simply comparing occurrences of 'fero' and 'porto' as if they were denotative synonyms, differing only in tone and connotations. There is a difference in denotation between the two words. A large proportion of the semantic range of 'porto' is occupied with the narrow and literal sense 'carry'; 'fero' is a most flexible, even vague word, its semantic range extensive; it has some similarity to the English word 'bear'.

First I cite some simple numerical statistics, beginning with those provided by the *TLL* survey. I shall, since *TLL* does, indicate the comparative position of 'fero'. But I stress that straight numerical comparisons of 'porto' and 'fero' have limited value in the light of the much greater semantic range of 'fero'. Perhaps the most useful lesson is just to observe who does and who does not make significant use of 'porto'.

TLL s.v. 'porto': 'legitur ... per totam latinitatem, sed apud plerosque multo saepius occurrit *fero*; in oratione soluta *porto* admodum raro inuenitur apud scriptores elegantiores, e.g. Cic. (*oratt.* 13, *phil.* 4, *epist.* 6 ... sed *fero* plus milies), Caes. (6/124), Tac. (6/186), Plin. Epist. (1/74), saepius apud Sall. (13/23), Liv. (65/ca. 850), Curt. (12/70); e poetis haud raro adhibent dactylici, e.g. Verg. (19), Hor. *sat.* et *epist.* (11, bis tantum in *carm.*), Sil. (57), Stat. (36), excepto Lucano (2).' Here are some further indications of frequence ('porto'/'fero'): Plaut. 6/saepissime, Ter. 9/saepissime, Enn. *Ann.* 1/6, *Scen.* 0/5, Catull. 5 (4 in 64, 1 in 66: an interesting grouping)/45, Lucr. 8/saepissime, Hor. 13 (as above)/saepissime, Prop. 9/saepissime, Tibull. 8/s., Verg. 20 (*Aen.* 19, *Georg.* 1)[52] /s., Ov. 31 (plus *Hal.* 1, *Ep. Sapph.* 1)/s., Val. 7/s., Varro *Rust.* 4/30, Vitruv. 3/15.

[51] For a confident statement that 'porto' is colloquial see Löfstedt, *Syntactica*, ii. 338, and *Peregrinatio Aetheriae*, 270–1, both useful discussions in spite of their confidence. Axelson, 30 f. is more cautious, and provides valuable figures. Note too these prudent and informative comments of Ernout (Review 61): 'Trop souvent on a qualifié de vulgaires des mots de sens concret que la langue tend à substituer à des termes plus abstraits, et par là même moins expressifs. C'est le cas notamment pour *portare* qui va remplaçant *ferre*, que condamnent, outre sa double valeur abstraite et concrète, les anomalies de sa conjugaison ... La multiplicité des emplois de *ferre* ... et de ses composés rendait inévitable le recours à un mot nouveau de sens plus précis, et mieux délimité, *porto*, qui se disait uniquement du port et du transport—par mer—des choses matérielles ...'. Palmer, 168, rather unhelpfully says that 'we may assign ["porto"] to the *genus demissum*'.

[52] But 'asportare' (which would require a change of word-order in the line) is a variant at *Aen.* 2.778.

We see that 'porto' clearly had currency in the living tongue (note Plaut., Ter., Horace's distribution). We may assume that it was the regular spoken word for literal 'carry'; this is confirmed by the persistence of the word in this sense into the Romance languages.[53] Further interpretation of the statistics is difficult—we do not have the clear patterns and divisions (e.g. prose / verse) that we might expect. Tentatively, I try. We see that there is a strong objection to the word in some but by no means all poetry (note perhaps especially Lucan). But prose too exhibits qualms, sometimes in unexpected places. For example, Caesar fights shy of it; that is more unexpected than that the fastidious younger Pliny should shun it. The everyday and casual tones that we may assume in it rendered it not to the liking of some prose, and even some 'business' prose, as well as some poetry. On the other hand some poets as well as prose writers desired or tolerated the casual tones of a word that also directly referred to the real and necessary action of carrying. Vergil was conspicuous among them. We may assume that with Ovid, Statius, and Silius the 'legitimizing effect' (I.4 *init.*) is to an extent operative.

Before I attend to Vergil, I cite a couple more details of evidence indicative of the lower and casual status of 'porto' (= 'carry') compared with 'fero' *sim.* in the same semantic field.[54] First, note the different ways in which the refined Caesar and the baser author of the *Bell. Afr.* refer to similar actions of carrying. The *Bell. Afr.* uses 'comporto', e.g. 69.2 'sarcinas in aceruum comportare', where Caesar himself would use 'confero', e.g. *Gall.* 1.24.3 'sarcinas in unum locum conferri ... iussi', 7.18.4. Cf. too *Bell. Afr.* 21.2 'in plostris [a vulgar form] deportare', also 75.3 'portare', and Caes. *Civ.* 1.54.3 'has (sc. naues) perfectas carris iunctis deuehit'. Note too Cicero in a literary speech, *Verr.* 5.27 'lectica octaphoro ferebatur', and Cicero in a letter, *Qu. fr.* 2.9.2 'hominem portarem ... octaphoro Asiciano'.

Most of Vergil's uses of 'porto' are I think to be explained thus: they are part of his campaign to keep the narrative in touch with the realities of everyday life.[55] But sometimes there is a

---

[53] See ch. I p. 12.
[54] Cf. Löfstedt, *Peregrinatio Aetheriae*, 270. Löfstedt cites other material.
[55] Cf. his policy in his account of the war, ch. V.

more particular exploitation.[56] Juno is worth referring to, a goddess who manipulates stylistic register to good purpose.[57] In her first speech in the poem she is made to say the following (1.67–8):

> gens inimica mihi Tyrrhenum nauigat aequor
> Ilium in Italiam portans uictosque Penates.

A people that is my enemy sails over the Tuscan sea, carrying Ilium and its conquered Penates to Italy.

She talks of the Trojans 'carrying' Ilium and the conquered Penates to Italy. This is dismissive, sarcastic, and contemptuous. The sense which the verb naturally signifies (*literal* carrying) represents what the Trojans are doing in its more literal and inglorious aspect. It almost conjures up a picture of the Trojans putting their city and gods into a removal van; to translate 'carting' would be to exaggerate the effect, but would show the direction in which Juno is heading. The casual, everyday tone that 'porto' possessed contributes to Juno's effect, belittling and mocking the Trojan enterprise.

Juno's contemptuous phrasing is echoed by the enraged Dido at 4.598, 'quem secum patrios aiunt portare Penates'. Contrast the more circumspect way in which Aeneas himself refers to the same event: 1.378 f., 'raptos qui ex hoste penates / classe *ueho* mecum' and 3.149 f., 'quos mecum a Troia mediisque ex ignibus urbis / ex*tuleram*'. Note too the mode of expression of the narrator at 1.6 'in*ferret*que deos Latio' and 12.285 f. 'fugit ipse Latinus / pulsatos re*ferens* infecto foedere diuos', and of the narrator (or the Italian embassy) at 8.11 ('in*ferre*'). With Juno— Dido's phrasing on the one hand and that of Aeneas and the rest on the other, it is most interesting to compare the different choices of Caesar and the *Bell. Afr.*, and the different choices of Cicero in *Verr.* and Cicero in *Qu. fr.*, quoted above.

Appendix: 'uxor' and 'coniunx' (fem.) in Propertius and Tibullus

Propertius was taken by Catullus' vision of the beloved as wife,

---

[56] Besides those I discuss, note 5.840.
[57] Cf. II.7.

that romantic adaptation of a real institution,[58] and was more inclined to use the ordinary word 'uxor' than 'coniunx' in this connection. We may infer that he did not want to obscure the reality of what he was romantically adapting (but Catullus himself, we remember, had made nothing of the *word* 'uxor', above p. 44). 'Uxor' is used directly in reference to the beloved Cynthia at 2.6.41 and 42; and it is used of mythical paradigms for Cynthia, thus underlining the relevance of these paradigms to her and Propertius' situation, at 2.28.22 (Andromeda) and 2.32.57 (Pasiphae). In addition to these Propertius uses 'uxor' in the following places. At 2.21.4 he points out to Cynthia (I presume it to be her) that her new lover has a wife. Plain words suit the situation, and the tone of the whole poem is direct, even blunt: note e.g. that in the Odysseus paradigm the hero is referred to as the 'Dulichius iuuenis' (13).[59] At 3.13.18 the Eastern wives who commit suttee are termed 'uxores'. Since their function is to serve as paradigms for contemporary Augustan Rome, the choice seems right. At 3.12.37 the use is subtle. Penelope is described thus: 'casta domi persederat uxor'. She is cited in the poem as a mythical comparison for Postumus' wife Galla ('Postumus alter erit miranda coniuge Ulixes' (23)). But Propertius' eventual conclusion (in 37 f.) is that Galla will *excel* Penelope in 'fides'. Carefully therefore he refers to Penelope on her own as an ordinary 'uxor', and employs the grander word 'coniunx' for direct association with Galla: in 23 quoted above, and 16.

As well as at 3.12.16 and 23 Propertius uses the more resonant, less everyday word 'coniunx' (fem.) in the following places. At 2.6.23 he refers thus to a paradigm (Alcestis) who is adduced as *unlike*, better than, Cynthia: she needs therefore a different and grander word than one employed for Cynthia. At 1.19.7 he uses 'coniunx' of Laodamia. In this poem the question whether the mythical paradigm (Protesilaus and Laodamia) has any relevance to Propertius and Cynthia is really the subject of the poem;[60] Propertius' belief in such relevance is always precarious and in fact collapses at the end: Laodamia and Protesilaus *are* of

---

[58] Lyne, *The Latin Love Poets*, 79–80 and above .

[59] This seems to me to cut the hero down to reality, in spite of Camps ad loc. and Rothstein on 1.20.23.

[60] Lyne, *The Latin Love Poets*, 100–2, 140–5.

a different order from mere ordinary reality. The use of 'coniunx' may therefore be compared (ultimately) with that at 2.6.23. 'Coniunx' is used of Briseis at 2.8.29 in a paradigm which is certainly intended to suit the situation of Propertius and Cynthia; but this is one of Propertius' most carefully wrought, dignified, special (indeed tragic) compositions, and a desire for high diction for its own sake is readily comprehensible. 'Coniunx' also of Juno at 2.28.33 (not a paradigm), and of Tullus' putative future wife at 3.22.42.

I think it is evident that Propertius did perceive and exploit different tone in the two words. In sum, he reserved 'coniunx' for grander contexts than the everyday, but does regard 'uxor' as the more fitting to be used in connection with Cynthia. This latter fact is perhaps not something we should have predicted.

Tibullus too was taken by the Catullan vision of the beloved as wife,[61] but he preferred not to be so specific as to use either 'uxor' or 'coniunx' in that connection. Wives of course figure in his world and are designated: he prefers to denote them with 'uxor', but it is not clear to me that he makes much active use of the tone-difference between that word and 'coniunx'. 'Uxor' of the rival's wife at 1.9.54, of a rustic wife at 1.10.42 and 52; Cornutus will pray for 'uxoris fidos ... amores' at 2.2.11. 'Coniunx' of the wife of Titius, the intended recipient of the erotic teaching of 1.4, at 1.4. 74; and 'coniunx' occurs in a question addressed to the husband of Delia at 1.6.33.

[61] Lyne, *The Latin Love Poets*, 79–80.

IV

Narrative through Imagery

Some of Vergil's characteristic techniques are extreme, and elicit violent metaphors from me. Others are discreet and guileful. Among these is his use of the traditional epic simile. This I shall look at in the present chapter, from one particular point of view. I shall also show, in this and subsequent chapters, how his technique with simile intersects most interestingly with other techniques that I analyse. First, some background is necessary. Since Homer's practice conditions later epic and most if not all of Vergil's methods with simile derive from him, it will be illuminating to approach Vergil through his most important predecessor.[1]

1. The function of epic simile: definition

What is the function of a Homeric simile?[2] The answer is not yet self-evident. First, it is well to clear away misconceptions.

One ancient view of the Homeric simile had great currency in the nineteenth century, and is still very much alive today: I mean the view that a simile typically has a single point of contact or correspondence with the narrative and a single illustrative function in relation to it,[3] but is then developed irrelevantly, self-

---

[1] Vergil's methods derive from Homer via of course Apollonius and others. On Catullus, one of the others, see section 3 *Addendum*. For my present purposes Homer sufficiently illustrates the background to Vergil's practices with similes, and for the sake of brevity and clarity I concentrate in this respect on him. But it should be mentioned that precedents for the techniques of Vergil that I discuss could be cited in, say, Apollonius as well as Homer (and Catullus). For example, at 1.774 ff Apollonius *adds* to the narrative via the 'narrative' of imagery (cf. Section 3), in that the simile foreshadows the erotic impact of Jason on the women of Lemnos; in the same simile he makes use of *irrational* correspondence (Section 4), in that the 'youth' as well as the 'star' bears upon Jason; at 3.971 ὁμαδέω, a verb predominantly used of people, looks to me like a *trespass* of narrative into simile (Section 5).

[2] There is a survey of views in Bassett, 133 f.

[3] In other parlances, it has a single *Vergleichungspunkt*, a 'tertium comparationis'.

indulgently, beyond this point of contact and observable illustrative function. This view is reflected in, for example, the ΣT on *Iliad* 4.482 ff. (the simile for the death of Simoesius): '"like a poplar": thus far things which belong to the comparison. What follows Homer says superfluously, indulging prettily in it and pursuing a pleasurable effect';[4] and in 1973 we find M. D. Reeve appealing to 'a conclusion that few people would wish to dispute: Homer elaborates his similes without regard to the narrative.'[5] I should have supposed that dissenters from such a view were now a majority, but it is difficult to count heads. The correct way of refuting it does *not*, however, lie in the following approach: to suppose and to argue, pressing ingenuity beyond its limits, that *all* details in a simile correspond to and illustrate something present in the narrative. With Homer, the implausibilities that such an approach can produce shows its fallibility;[6] with Vergil (and Apollonius) one can have greater success,[7] but (I would argue) one is missing the main point. There are many details in Homeric, and indeed Vergilian similes, which lack corresponding

[4] ΣT *Il.*4.482 πέσεν αἴγειρος ὥς: μέχρι τούτου τὰ τῆς ὁμοιώσεως. τὰ δὲ λοιπὰ ἐκ περιουσίας ἐναβρυνόμενός φησι καὶ διώκων ἡδονήν. Note however ΣT on 4.484, 'he compares the man who was born by a river to a waterside tree', παρυδατίῳ δὲ φυτῷ εἴκασε τὸν παρὰ ποταμὸν γεγενημένον.

[5] M. D. Reeve, *CQ* NS 23 (1973), 193. See Richardson, 277 for further examples of the view in the Homeric scholia, Clausing, 18, 22 f., 62–4, 67 f., 71, 76, 86–8, Moulton, 12. West began his first article on similes thus: 'Similes in the *Aeneid*, like Homeric similes, have commonly been thought of as similes *à queue longue*, as similes which have *one* point of comparison with the narrative and a large ornamental development.' Contrast e.g. Pöschl 86 f.

[6] e.g. the following efforts are well-meaning, but unhelpful: ΣbT on *Iliad* 6.507, 'the bond (δεσμός) of Alexander is Helen'; ΣbT on 6.509 ἀμφὶ δὲ χαῖται, the horse's mane, 'Paris too has beautiful hair'; ΣT on 6.510, where the horse 'trusts in its splendour', 'this is said suitably of [Paris] the dandy (καλλωπιστής)'. Cf. too the reasons of the ΣT at 15.263–4 for (and against) athetizing 15.265–8 on the grounds that they belong properly at 6.508–11 and not in 15: ἀπὸ δὲ τοῦ εἰωθώς ἀθετητέον: οἰκειότερον γὰρ ἐπὶ Ἀλεξάνδρου κεῖνται (sc. at 6.508–11): οὐ γὰρ ἁρμόσειαν <ἄν?> Ἕκτορι νῦν: τινὲς δὲ ὡς καλὸς καὶ Ἕκτωρ (quoting 22.370–1)· εἰ δὲ τέτρωται, ἀλλ' ὑπὸ δύο θεῶν ἐπαίρεται. ἔστι δὲ ἐπηρμένος καὶ ἐπαγαλλόμενος ταῖς τύχαις. Likewise ΣbT on 20.490–2 is for my taste unhelpfully obsessive in its pursuit of correspondence.

[7] Vergil in particular is clever enough often to provide such correspondences while meantime doing something more important with the simile. To demonstrate such correspondences between simile and narrative in Vergil is the purpose of West's two articles. Apollonius organizes detailed correspondences in e.g. the similes at 3.1380 ff.; but it would do him an injustice to say that we have exhausted the similes when we have observed all these. West does an injustice to Vergil by not touching on the main function of his similes.

items actually in the narrative and are otiose to any strictly illustrative function: we cannot always say that *this* detail in the simile corresponds to and illustrates *that* detail in the narrative. And the pursuit of correspondence in this way is—at best—a diversion on the route that leads to a full understanding of Homeric as well as Vergilian simile.

Two other misapprehensions may be mentioned, one well-intentioned but in fact insulting to the poet, the other superficially attractive and therefore dangerous. Many scholars argue that the (or a) function of similes, in particular those that adduce pastoral or agricultural scenes during the battle narrative, is to provide 'relief' or 'respite' from that narrative.[8] This is, when one thinks abouts it, another but politer way of saying that similes are developed irrelevantly beyond an initial point of contact. But it is surely insulting to the poet to imply that he constructed a narrative so boring that it required interludes to relieve it; and the suggestion is unlikely in itself. It is certainly hard to imagine that the poet himself thought that that was what he was doing. I am particularly moved to refer to this misapprehension because (as I shall show in VI.3) the type of simile that most often gives rise to it in fact contributes a richly important contextual effect.

Superficially attractive but often radically wrong is the view that Homer uses the familiar to illustrate the unfamiliar (with one or more points of contact, depending on simile and interpreter). I should grant that sometimes this view may be at least compatible with the facts. But I would maintain that on very important occasions it demonstrably is not; and it is never the essential explanation of the function of a simile.

Again the view has ancient authority. Cf. e.g. ΣA on *Iliad* 16.364 which says (in passing) ὁ γὰρ Ὅμηρος ἀπὸ τῶν γινωσκομένων πᾶσι ποιεῖται τὰς ὁμοιώσεις, 'Homer makes his comparisons from what is known to all'.[9] Modern proponents of the view are evident.[10] Now it makes sense for an *orator* to draw his

---

[8] Bowra, 123, Stanford, 128, Moulton, 18 n. 1; the otherwise admirable Porter (11 f.) has surprising confidence in the view's validity.

[9] Cf. further Richardson, 280.

[10] Cf. Fränkel, 98, 'Die wohl am häufigsten vertretene Meinung ist die, das Gl. solle veranschaulichen, d.h. durch die Nebenstellung von etwas Bekanntem ein Unbekanntes, durch ein Sichtbares ein Unsichtbares deutlich machen.'

comparisons from the familiar (and orators' practice may have influenced critics' memories of Homer). An orator often finds himself addressing audiences on subjects with which they are relatively unfamiliar and in regard to which he must induce in them a certain point of view; and to draw illustrations from what they do know is in these circumstances an obvious policy. Quintilian enjoins such a policy, on orators (8.3.73): 'debet enim, quod inlustrandae alterius rei gratia adsumitur, ipsum esse clarius eo quod inluminat', 'what is adduced to illustrate something else must itself be clearer than that which it illuminates'. If however we look at the practice of the *poet* Homer, we find that the policy is one which he in fact often demonstrably does not follow. He compares heroes to lions, heroes to gods; and however unfamiliar heroes may have been to Homer and his audience, lions will I imagine have been no more familiar[11] and gods decidedly less so. Very often in fact it seems that Homer and other good epic poets 'illustrate' the familiar with the unfamiliar—as Quintilian acutely observed. The above quotation continues: 'quare poetis quidem permittamus sane eiusmodi exempla ... [and he quotes *Aen.* 4.143 f., Aeneas' Apollo simile] ... non idem oratorem decebit, ut occultis aperta demonstret', 'and so let us grant to poets examples like *Aen.* 4.143 f. (Aeneas' Apollo simile), but it will be quite unsuitable for an orator to do the same, namely, to illustrate the plain by the obscure.' There is sense in what Quintilian says, but we must resolve the paradox that it contains. How can the obscure *illustrate* the plain? It begins to look as if 'illustration' is not what similes in some important respects are doing.[12]

Many ancient scholia in fact exhibit a much profounder understanding of the function of Homeric similes than those referred to above; and modern appreciation should have been revolutionized by Fränkel and others.[13] The upshot of such

---

[11] Cf. Fränkel, 62 n. 3, 98. On the unfamiliarity of many Homeric similes in general, Fränkel, 98, and 15 with n. 2 has excellent comments.

[12] Cf. Fränkel's opinion on the view that 'Veranschaulichung' is the key to the purpose of similes, 15 with n. 2, 98.

[13] See the ΣbT on *Iliad* 4.130 (quoted Richardson 279), bT on 18.318 and 23.222, Richardson, 280 (with many more references). Richardson, 280, concludes: 'These and many other examples show [the scholiasts'] sensibility to the less obvious implications and wider resonance of the similes.' For good modern

more constructive approaches to the Homeric simile is (so I would put it) that we should reckon simile as *adding* to the narrative as well as, perhaps rather than, illustrating things that are, in another form, already there. I shall now attempt a description of the function of simile in my own words, one that applies to Vergil, Apollonius and others, as well as Homer.

First we should grant that similes do usually have a clear point of contact with the narrative and a simple illustrative function in respect of it. Indeed, point of contact and illustrative function are often advertised by verbal repetition. Note e.g. how Homer rounds off his comparison of Hector to a galloping horse at *Iliad* 15.268 f., ῥίμφα ἑ γοῦνα φέρει ... ὣς Ἕκτωρ λαιψηρὰ πόδας καὶ γούνατ' ἐνώμα ..., 'lightly its [the horse's] *knee* bears it ... even so Hector nimbly plied his feet and *knees*': Homer advertises that the simile illustrates Hector's nimbleness of knee. Or note the famous simile in which Apollo's action in destroying the Achaean wall is compared to a child's knocking over a sandcastle (*Il.* 15.361 ff.): ἔρειπε δὲ τεῖχος Ἀχαιῶν ῥεῖα μάλ', ὡς ὅτε ... ἂψ αὖτις συνέχευε ποσὶν ... ὥς ῥα σύ, ἤϊε Φοῖβε ... σύγχεας ..., 'Apollo dashed down the wall of the Achaeans full easily, just as when ... back again the child *obliterates* [the sandcastle] with his feet ... so, O Phoebus, did you *obliterate* ...'. A point of contact is evident in the action of obliteration, and the advertised illustrative function seems to be in respect of the facility of it. (I should say that I return to both these similes.)

In Vergil's similes too there is usually a clear point of contact and illustrative function; and Vergil advertises similarly, though not in explicit terms quite so frequently as Homer. I provide one example (to which I shall also return), Amata's top simile at 7.377 ff.:

> sine more furit lymphata per urbem.
> ceu quondam torto uolitans sub uerbere turbo
> ...
>   ille *actus* habena
> curuatis fertur spatiis ...
>   non cursu segnior illo
> per medias urbes *agitur* ...

In frenzied abandon Amata rages through the city. Just as at times a top

discussion see of course Fränkel, noting in particular his summarizing remarks, 98 f., 104–7; Bassett, e.g. 147; and the very useful book of Moulton.

spins under a whirled whip ... *driven* by the whip it is borne on in great circles .... With no slacker course is Amata *driven* through the midst of the city ...

The advertisement 'actus ... agitur' is reinforced by other verbs suggestive of motion before and within the simile, and we get the point: the whirling top illustrates the whirling motion of the maddened Amata.

There is thus in most similes a visible point of contact with the narrative and an illustrative function tied to it which is often advertised; in many similes further points of contact and illustrative functions can be discerned. But this sort of function is not I maintain the important or main function of a developed simile in the hands of a master. The main function of a simile is not to illustrate something already mentioned in the narrative, but to *add* things which are not mentioned, in a different medium: imagery. The poet is switching modes, switching from direct narrative to 'narrative' in the suggestive medium of imagery; and he capitalizes upon the fact that he is now operating in a suggestive, not an explicit medium. An advertised illustrative function and concomitant point of contact with the narrative may often be seen as a means to an end, as little more than a formal device to effect the switch from direct narrative to 'narrative' in imagery.

That similes are essentially *narrative* I shall show in stages. The first stage is to show that on some occasions a narrative function is more or less irrefutable: I mean when similes demonstrably *substitute* for direct narrative.

2. Substitution

The example I wish to cite from Homer, *Iliad* 15.263 ff. (touched on above)[14] needs a little context. It involves a large episode: the wounding of Hector at the Achaean ditch, his withdrawal, recovery and return, over books 14 and 15.

At 14.402–39 the following events happen. Hector is wounded by a stone-throw from Ajax in the battle at the ditch. He is rescued by comrades and withdrawn by horse and chariot 'towards the

---

[14] On this simile cf. Fränkel, 77 n. 2. For other examples of 'substitution' in Homer see Fränkel, 81, also 73 f.

city', and is then laid down 'by the ford of Xanthus', i.e. some distance from the ditch; here he passes out. The narrative next returns to him at 15.239, where Apollo, who has been dispatched by Zeus to rouse him, arrives and finds him 'seated; and no longer was he lying, and he had gathered to him fresh spirit, θυμός' (240); we note that the resumption, after an interval of over 320 lines, is well dove-tailed. Apollo encourages him, and *inter alia* bids him 'urge his horsemen to drive their horses against the ships'. Then Apollo 'breathes might' into Hector (262), who in 269–70 is described as 'nimbly plying his feet and knees, and urging on his horsemen'. By 279 the Achaeans (at the ditch) see him 'approaching the ranks of men, and they feared', and from then on Hector is back in the fight. I have now accounted for all the lines which are devoted by Homer to the wounding, recovery and return episode except those that immediately follow and those mentioned below in n. 17.

In lines 263–9 of Book 15 there is a simile,[15] which I quote:

> ὡς δ' ὅτε τις στατὸς ἵππος, ἀκοστήσας ἐπὶ φάτνῃ,
> δεσμὸν ἀπορρήξας θείῃ πεδίοιο κροαίνων,
> εἰωθὼς λούεσθαι ἐϋρρεῖος ποταμοῖο,
> κυδιόων· ὑψοῦ δὲ κάρη ἔχει, ἀμφὶ δὲ χαῖται
> ὤμοις ἀΐσσονται· ὁ δ' ἀγλαΐηφι πεποιθώς,
> ῥίμφα ἑ γοῦνα φέρει μετά τ' ἤθεα καὶ νομὸν ἵππων·
> ὡς Ἕκτωρ λαιψηρὰ πόδας καὶ γούνατ' ἐνώμα ...

Even as when a stalled horse that has fed his fill at the manger breaks his bond and runs pounding over the plain, accustomed as he is to bathe in the fair-flowing river, and he exults; on high does he hold his head, and his mane darts about his shoulders, and as he trusts in his splendour his knees bear him to the haunts and pasture of horses: so Hector nimbly plied his feet and knees ...

The advertised illustrative function of this simile I remarked on above (section 1). This scarcely justifies its length and detail, much of which is otiose to such a function. Nor will we find a satisfactory role for the detail by ingeniously pursuing further

---

[15] 15.263–8 = 6.506–11. It seems to me, unlike many, equally appropriate in both places. ΣA on 6.506–11 thinks that its original location is 15.263, a heterodox view I think. For the opposite view see ΣT on 15.263–4, quoted above n. 6.

correspondences and further illustrative functions.[16] In fact the simile has a much more important contribution to make than illustration.

A question arises about the narrative hereabouts. The account of Hector's movements across books 14 and 15, which I summarized above, appears to be dove-tailed and punctilious. Except in one respect: how and when did Hector get *back* to the ditch and the fighting, whence he was removed and taken by chariot to Xanthus? No return journey, no trip back from Xanthus to ditch is actually narrated, as my summary and discussion has now more or less revealed[17] (we only hear of Hector 'plying his feet and knees'). There is an apparent *gap* in the narrative. The answer to this is not that Homer has ceased to be punctilious, but that he has chosen to avoid monotony and to narrate the return journey *in imagery*. The journey of the horse from manger to pasture within the simile is Homer's 'narrative' of Hector's journey from Xanthus to ditch: it *substitutes* for it. Hector's return journey is something that the simile *adds*; it bridges the gap in the explicit narrative. And the advertised illustrative function is little more than a formal means to introduce it. And how well the simile performs its narrative function! The splendid, exulting horse, free from bonds and racing from manger to pasture, aptly conveys the recovered and glorious Hector in motion from Xanthus to ditch. This is 'narrative through imagery'. The poet has simply switched modes, for a purpose: here, to avoid monotony, two descriptions of the same journey. Ruinous to see relevance only in the one advertised illustrative function—and the way to find relevance for the rest of the simile is not to pursue exact correspondences and illustrative functions for the horse's mane, and so on. The imagery adds rather than illustrates.

I should mention that another simile at 15.271–6[18] and its resumption add further narrative of the events during Hector's

---

[16] Cf. the views of those scholars (τινές) referred to by ΣT on 15.263–4 (quoted above n. 6.) who think the simile belongs properly in Book 15.

[17] The only lines that I have not now accounted for in 15.240–80, i.e. in the narrative that picks Hector up at Xanthus and sees his re-entry into battle at the ditch, are 271–8. These are occupied by another simile, together with a two line narrative resumption. I refer to these lines below; they do not affect my argument at this point.

[18] Cf. preceding note.

absence and return, but to keep my account as clear and brief as possible I leave this for the consideration of the reader.

Vergil substitutes similes for narrative, on occasion nearly as visibly as the above example of Homer's. I pick up the text of the *Aeneid* at 11.718 ff. Camilla pursues the deceitful Ligurian, and kills him:

> pernicibus ignea plantis
> transit equum cursu frenisque aduersa prehensis
> congreditur poenasque inimico ex sanguine sumit ...

Fiery-swift she outruns his horse on fleet foot, and, seizing the reins, closes with him face to face and exacts punishment from his hated blood ...

That is the end of the narrative proper of the episode. A question arises. How does Camilla kill him? What does she do to him? In a sense the vague but ominous 'poenasque inimico ex sanguine sumit' bridges any gap we may feel. In another sense it does not. What does she actually do to him? Vergil does not narrate this. Contrast the situation at 12.949 ff. where he or rather Aeneas uses the phrase 'poenam scelerato ex sanguine sumit' and Vergil then proceeds to specify.

After 'poenasque inimico ...' at 11.720, Vergil attaches a simile. It has a clear illustrative function: to show the ease with which Camilla caught the Ligurian (721 ff.):

> quam facile accipiter saxo sacer ales ab alto
> consequitur pennis sublimem in nube columbam
> comprensamque tenet ...

as easily as a sacred falcon from lofty rock overtakes on wing a dove in a cloud on high, then holds her in its clutches ...

The simile's illustrative function is in fact more or less advertised in two respects, overtaking and grasping ('*transit* equum cursu' and '*consequitur*', 'frenisque ... *prehensis*' and '*comprensam*'). But it serves another and more important purpose.

It continues:

> pedibusque euiscerat uncis;
> tum cruor et uulsae labuntur ab aethere plumae.

and with hooked claws tears out her innards; blood and sundered feathers drop from the sky.

The description of the hawk's bloody destruction of the dove, otiose to the illustrative function advertised, covers the gap we sensed. It 'narrates' in imagery how Camilla killed the Ligurian, it substitutes for it. The poet has switched modes, from the explicit to the suggestive one. He is enabled thereby to convey to us that Camilla mangled her enemy brutally, without committing himself to yet another description of human killing; it might be, too, that he wished to tell us that Camilla killed brutally without providing details that could excessively have alienated us from her. At any rate (whatever his motive) we see that he has opted here for the suggestive but inexplicit medium of 'narrative through imagery'. Ruinous (once more) to see relevance only in the advertised illustrative function; and mistaken to seek further illustrative functions and exact correspondences for the dove's feathers and so on.

At *Aen.* 10.369 ff. Pallas rallies the fleeing Arcadians, urging them to fight ('quo fugitis, socii …?' etc.). He himself then in exemplary fashion embarks on a successful *aristeia* (379–404). But what about the Arcadians in general? What do they do in response to his incitement? The narrative tells us the following at 410 f., and this is all it tells us:

> socium uirtus coit omnis in unum
> teque iuuat, Palla.

Your comrades' valour all gathers to one point and aids you, Pallas.

This conveys the idea that the Arcadians[19] eventually regroup around Pallas, and provides some cover for the gap we may feel, more perhaps than 'poenas … sumit' provides in the previous example. Still, one might legitimately expect more detail: how did the Arcadians immediately respond to Pallas' exhortations?

From 405 to 409 there is a simile which illustrates, apparently, the 'gathering of the Arcadians' valour' referred to in 410 f.: 'non aliter' in line 410 seems to point to, if not to advertise, such an illustrative function, '*non aliter* socium uirtus coit omnis in unum …'.; cf. too 'una', 'unum', 407, 410. The simile runs as follows:

> ac uelut optato uentis aestate coortis
> dispersa immittit siluis incendia pastor,

---

[19] We can interpret the phrase 'socium uirtus' along the lines of βίη Διομήδεος (*Il.* 5.781), etc. as = 'valorous comrades'.

> correptis subito mediis extenditur una
> horrida per latos acies Volcania campos,
> ille sedens uictor flammas despectat ouantis ...

And just as in summer, when, in answer to his prayers, winds have arisen, a shepherd launches scattered fires on the woods; suddenly the mid-spaces catch, and Vulcan's bristling battleline spreads unbroken over the broad fields; he from his seat looks down victoriously over the triumphant flames ...

'Fire', we take it, illustrates 'valour', the Arcadians and their 'uirtus', i.e. the valorous Arcadians; and we may infer that the incendiary 'pastor' corresponds to Pallas inspiriting his Arcadian comrades. The simile has, however, an emphasis which is not so much otiose to the supposed illustrative function as conflicts with it. The fire in the simile spreads over a broad area ('extenditur per latos ... campos'), the Arcadians' valour (= the Arcadians) is said by the narrative to *come together*'. An anomaly, to be explained. The answer is that the simile is not in this respect illustrating, it is adding. It is covering the gap that some of us feel: substituting. It 'narrates' (in the spreading line of fire) an aggressive and successful advance by the general body of the Arcadians over a wide front (the result of Pallas' exhortations), an advance that presumably preceded their coalescence;[20] it narrates in the suggestive though less apparent medium of imagery. Once more illustration and correspondence are shown to be insufficient guide to a simile's function.

We should note that the simile's narrative function has here been drawn to our attention: by a special effect, by what Michael Silk might term the 'intrusion' of 'tenor' language into the 'vehicle'. The effect is what I call *trespass*. Here narrative language has trespassed into the simile (we have therefore the reverse phenomenon to the one I pointed to in III.1 ('conlabor')).[21] The spreading fire of the simile is described in terms that would infinitely more naturally suit an advancing line of troops: in particular 'acies', also 'horrida' and 'ouantes', are natural to troops; and 'uictor' and (probably) 'immittit' suit the troops'

---

[20] Some might wish to see 'correptis ... mediis' as illustrating this coalescence. I think rather that it 'narrates' how the inspirited Arcadians form a continuous battleline (they would have to fight to do so) *before* advancing and *then* regrouping around Pallas.

[21] Cf Silk 138 ff. I deal with the topic of trespass fully in section 5.

general (Pallas) more naturally than they suit the incendiary shepherd.[22] So, the Arcadian 'acies' which, together with its actions, we have to supply in the narrative from the substituting simile is actually explicit, with some of its actions, in the diction of the simile. Trespass thus assists simile in its narrative, substitutive function; or it is perhaps truer to say that it helps us to perceive that the simile is continuing the narration and substituting for a piece of explicit narrative that is not there. So, by skilful relocation, 'combination', of what in fact is ordinary diction ('acies' and so on), Vergil reinforces an effect (simile as narrative). The master of imagery is still the master of words. (I take up these points again at the end of this chapter.)

In book 2 Laocoon is destroyed by prodigious serpents. The simile that is attached to his death also substitutes, but less expectedly. The climactic lines are (2.220–4):

> ille simul manibus tendit diuellere nodos
> perfusus sanie uittas atroque ueneno,
> clamores simul horrendos ad sidera tollit:
> qualis mugitus, fugit cum saucius aram
> taurus et incertam excussit ceruice securim.

He strains to tear apart their [the serpents'] coils with his hands, his priestly fillets bespattered with gore and poison; at the same time he raises horrendous cries to the stars: like the bellowings of a bull when it has fled the altar wounded, and has shaken off an ill-aimed axe from its neck.

Here we have once more a declared point of contact, a more or less advertised illustrative function: 'clamores / mugitus'. The bull's bellowing illustrates Laocoon's cries. But much in the simile is arguably irrelevant to any such illustrative function,[23] and in fact does something much more important. To appreciate this we must recapitulate.

---

[22] According to *TLL* 'acies' as a self-sufficient metaphor of fire *sim.* is rare and post-Vergilian: I.400.46 ff. (incidentally 'acies' at *Aetna* 409, cited by *TLL*, is not accepted by Goodyear); the military sense of 'acies' is of course its main and very common one, *saepissime* in 'business' military prose. In Vergil's simile we may infer that it sticks out like a sore thumb. 'Horridus' strongly coheres with this military implication (*Georg.* 2.282 f., *Aen.* 6.86, etc.); on 'immitto' see *OLD* s.v. 2a; 'uictor' and 'ouantes' speak for themselves.

[23] For bellowing-bull similes in Homer that will have been in Vergil's mind, see *Il.* 17.520–2, 20.403–5, 21.237. The *escaping* bull, Vergil's most significant motif, appears in none of these. It is most easy to parallel in descriptions of real sacrifices: see n. 27.

Laocoon's first appearance in the poem sees his challenge to the introduction of the Horse into Troy (2.40–56). There then follows the episode of Sinon, which strengthens the Trojans in their intention to introduce it, and their belief that Laocoon was wrong and indeed impious to oppose it (2.57–198). At 2.199 we are returned to Laocoon, and what then happens clinches the fatal decision.

We find Laocoon sacrificing a bull at an altar—he is a priest, in Vergil's version, of Neptune. 2.201–2:

> Laocoon ... sacerdos
> sollemnis taurum ingentem mactabat ad aras.

Laoocon ... the priest was sacrificing a huge bull at the ceremonial altar.

Then come the serpents. First, they attack and devour Laocoon's children (213–15); then they attack Laocoon (216–20; 220 is quoted above). We wait for the narrative of his death. It does not come: there is a gap. However, the simile (quoted above) does not 'narrate' his actual death either. But it does shift the narrative on, substituting *something else* for the expected narrative of his death. One of the things that the image of the bull adds to the narrative—the bull ineptly struck and fleeing—is that Laocoon does indeed free himself, for a moment, from the coils: in 220 'he strives to tear them apart'; the bull shaking off the axe and fleeing images some momentary success. 'Narrative through imagery' here shifts the action on, but sustains suspense in respect of the action we are in fact waiting for. Does Laocoon escape? Theoretically this is left open. But much in fact suggests to us that Laocoon's death is only seconds away.[24] The priest who defied the introduction of the Horse will be dead in moments, apparently by divine will (226; see below), and his countrymen will in consequence be quite persuaded of his error.

'Narrative through imagery' here advances the action, but sustains suspense by substituting unexpectedly. Its natural powers of suggestiveness are, too, in this instance, put to extraordinary and mysterious effect; more is implied than that Laocoon momentarily frees himself. More is achieved than the mere

---

[24] Ineptly struck sacrificial animals are sometimes, though not always, explicitly killed in the immediate aftermath: cf. Tac. *Hist.* 3.56.1 'profugus altaribus taurus ... longe, nec ut feriri hostias mos est, confossus'.

avoidance of monotony. I make just a couple of summary points. Laocoon the priest sacrificing a bull 'taurum ad aras' becomes himself in the imagery-narrative the victim, the 'taurus' at the 'aram':[25] the imagery implies that Laocoon, in a desperately ironic twist, becomes a sacrificial victim to a god. The idea of humans as sacrificial victims is a dark one which Vergil makes considerable play with in the *Aeneid*, which the Greek tragedians had also exploited to great effect, and which is as old as Homer.[26] Here the suggestion is disturbing but enigmatic. The death of Laocoon convinces his countrymen of his wrongness in regard to the Horse; we have to ponder the implications of his *sacrifice*. We may say with confidence that it seems to be Minerva who wishes him to be thus a victim (cf. 226 with Austin); but further than this it is hard to proceed with certainty, and I leave it to others. Except that this must be said: Laocoon's 'sacrifice' is desperately ill-omened, 'dirum'. When a victim is uncleanly dispatched, the prospects are dire.[27] Clearly, imminent prospects for the Trojans are bad. But is that the direction, or the only direction, of the 'omen'?

We have seen that, by substituting 'narrative through imagery', the poet can achieve a more suggestive if less patent narrative. In Laocoon's simile Vergil capitalizes upon suggestiveness to create mystery and darkness. On other occasions he substitutes such 'narrative' for its powers of *discretion*. Suggestion is discreeter than statement, less vulnerably committed; imagery, guilefully communicating through suggestion, may verge on the clandestine. That suits Vergil. He evolves for substitution the important role of communicating sensitive material.

Part of Vergil's guile on these occasions is to make the gap

[25] Cf. Austin on 2.223–4 ('he is now himself the victim'). Servius on 223 is on the way to seeing the point: 'facta autem comparatio est propter sacerdotis personam.'

[26] Vergil uses the motif with a great variety of explicitness and effects. Cf. e.g. his uses of 'immolo' (notably in 12.949) and 'macto'; note the implications of Priam's death 'altaria ad ipsa' (2.550, cf. Heinze 44), and then Pyrrhus' 'patriasque ... ad aras' (3.332), poetic justice at least; and note Messapus' 'haec melior magnis data uictima diuis' at 12.296; at Aesch. *Agam.* 1056 f., 1118, 1277 there are more or less obvious innuendos of, or allusions to, human sacrifice; cf. Eur. *Orestes* 191, 562; O. Taplin, *Greek Tragedy in Action* (London, 1978), 60, 76, 139; Hor. *Carm.* 2.3.24, with Nisbet & Hubbard ad loc.

[27] Cf. Liv. 21.63.13, Tac. *Hist.* 3.56.1 above n. 24 ('dirum omen'), Suet. *Galba* 18.1, Austin on *Aen.* 2.223–4.

being bridged by the substitution traceable but not over-evident. I adduce two examples. First, 4.69 ff.[28]

There is, I would argue, a gap in the narrative in book 4. For a legitimate question is: what part did Aeneas play in the growth of the love-affair between himself and Dido? We know the part played by Dido. She took Aeneas round town, showed him the sights, demonstrated her emotional confusion in faltering speech, besought him at dinner to retell his story, hung on his every word (4.74–9), etc.: she showed that she was interested in this stranger above and beyond the call of hospitality. In other words, she made up to him. But what part did Aeneas play meantime? There is silence in the explicit narrative. It seems to represent him as a passive partner, contributing nothing until the indirect but unmistakable implications of the cave episode (165–8). Is this plausible? Can he have done *nothing*? Can Vergil mean to imply this? It takes two to tango. Are we not to sense a *gap* in the narrative, which, following the precedent of other occasions, we should expect to be filled by 'narrative through imagery'?

The famous simile at 4.69 ff. runs as follows. A '(love-) wound' lives beneath Dido's breast, and she roams through the city ...

> qualis coniecta cerua sagitta,
> quam procul incautam nemora inter Cresia fixit
> pastor agens telis liquitque uolatile ferrum
> nescius: illa fuga siluas saltusque peragrat
> Dictaeos; haeret lateri letalis harundo.

like a hind shot by an arrow, an unwary hind which a shepherd hunting with darts has pierced from afar amid the Cretan woods, leaving in her the winged iron, not knowing that he has: she in flight ranges through the Dictaean woods and passes; the deadly arrow clings to her flank.

As usual the simile has an illustrative function, more or less advertised: Dido's mad motion through the city ('totaque uagatur / urbe furens', 68 f.) is pictured in the tormented motion of the hind ('peragrat'). There is too a second point of contact perceptible between simile and narrative, drawing attention to, apparently, another illustrative function: Dido's 'wound' of love ('uulnus', 67) is imaged in the wound of the hind (this time a

---

[28] Cf. too *Further Voices*, 194–6.

metaphor in the narrative rather than something literal is picked up and 'illustrated' by the simile).[29] This latter parallel may immediately seem so expressive to us that the word 'illustrative' seems inadequate. However that may be, there is something yet more important to notice, and that is the significance of the 'pastor' and the hunt. We remember our question: what part did Aeneas play in the growth of the love-affair? 'Narrative through imagery', substituting for an explicit account, here tells us; as I shall explain.

All agree that the 'cerua' in the simile parallels Dido in the narrative, and the wound of the 'cerua' parallels Dido's 'wound' in love, also in the narrative; in the latter case simile corresponds to narrative *metaphor*. These are patent correspondences. Now, if I was a certain type of ancient Homeric scholiast[30] or a certain type of modern Vergilian commentator,[31] the type that is committed to correspondences, I would expect that the hunt which occupies a large part of the simile and causes the hind's wound would *also* have a correspondent in the narrative. And it easily might have. For if the hind's wound corresponds to a metaphorical wound, a love-'wound' (Dido's love-wound), then the natural correspondent for the hunt would have been a metaphorical hunt, some 'hunt' of love. And this in fact is a frequent image. Writers on love commonly image a lover who is trying to win the favour of a beloved as *hunting* him or her: it is, we could say, a vigorous image for courtship.[32] So the hunt in the simile could well have paralleled something in the narrative: the courting of Dido by a man, a man's purposeful making up to her, his 'hunting' of her, the 'hunt' that led or contributed to her 'wound'. But there is no such scene in the narrative. A critic committed to correspondence like our aforementioned Homeric scholiasts would be driven to find some other ingenious but wrong-headed parallel. But we know the answer. The imagery of

---

[29] Or as Michael Silk would say (235 f.), metaphor is 'ground term' to simile. (We could also simply talk of 'vehicle' language in the 'tenor'. My favoured designation is a third: I would prefer to talk of simile language trespassing into the narrative. I discuss this phenomenon fully, and refer to this simile again, in section 5 below.)

[30] Those exemplified in n. 6, p. 64 above.

[31] Cf. West's two articles.

[32] Cf. Xenophon *Mem.* 1.2.24, Callimachus *Epigram* 1 GP = 31 Pf., summarized at Hor. *Serm.* 1.2.105 f.; Plaut. *Epid.* 215 f., Ov. *Am.* 2.9.9, *Ars* 1.89, etc., Lyne, *Further Voices*, 195 n. 64.

hunt in the simile guilefully *substitutes* for the scene in question. Aeneas made up to Dido, courted her, 'hunted' her: the imagery discreetly 'narrates' to us this sensitive material. The identification of Aeneas as the 'pastor' is made unavoidable by the fact that Vergil figures him in this role on two other most prominent occasions.[33] (The final point I would stress is that 'nescius' syntactically and logically relates only to 'liquit', not to 'agens'. The shepherd purposefully hunts the hind, is ignorant only that one of his shots has hit. This has obvious but crucial implications for Aeneas' role. For fuller discussion of this point see *Further Voices*, 196.)

We may repeat the lesson already learnt, for in the example just discussed we have striking confirmation of it. It is ruinous to accept that material otiose to illustrative functions, advertised or discernible, is in truth otiose; and the way to find relevance for it is not to pursue further (illusory) illustrative functions and correspondences, but to accept that it *adds*.

There is a gap in the narrative in books 7–12. What are Lavinia's feelings and preferences as war develops over who is to marry her? The explicit narrative tells most readers nothing. In fact, for the acute reader, there is a sign. But there is nothing definite, and what hint there is certainly needs to be confirmed. So let us say: there is a gap in the narrative in respect of Lavinia's feelings about a possible mate.

One way round this would be to say that she has none, either positive or negative. Another would be to say that the articulation of any such feelings would be inappropriate to Vergil's Roman epic. The first resort is hardly plausible. After all, one of the contenders for her hand has been openly and assiduously wooing her (7.55); she must have formed some opinion. Nor is it likely—other things being equal—that she should possess feelings, but that Vergil should deem it socially or generically inappropriate to reveal them, either in her own mouth or in the storyline. Lavinia's Homeric ancestress sets the pace in such matters: Homer's Helen had views on the men that impinged on her, and she uttered them.[34] Perhaps we should seek Lavinia's role model solely in Roman 'uirgines'. But they, while tradition-

---

[33]   2.304–8, 12.587–9 2; cf. Anderson 'Pastor Aeneas', esp. 1–10, Lyne, *Further Voices*, 195.

[34]   Cf. e.g. Helen's views on Paris at *Iliad* 6.349–53.

ally chaste or negative in their inclinations, do tend, if they feature in say history or epic, to reveal these inclinations or to have them revealed:[35] their authors see to it, for the sake of readers of that history or epic.

I say 'other things being equal'. Perhaps they are not. Perhaps some abnormal consideration is silencing Lavinia and inhibiting Vergil. Perhaps Lavinia's inclinations are not so negative or chaste. That would explain Lavinia's own silence. It would also explain why Vergil, committed for the sake of his readers to disclosing something on the topic, might not narrate the news in a way manifest to all. We might expect that, in the circumstances I deduce, he would imply such sensitive material discreetly. And this in fact is what he has done: he has 'narrated' some sensitive news about Lavinia's erotic feelings in the guileful and substitute medium of imagery.

At 12.54 ff.[36] Turnus' departure to fight Aeneas is imminent. Amata pleads with him not to go, passionately and in tears—so passionately that she betrays other emotions besides the kind regards of a possible future mother-in-law; there is much of a Phaedra in her. Lavinia is present, and her immediate and consequent reaction to this is to join her mother in weeping—and to blush. Her tears at this point are part of that hint of her feelings which I mentioned above. They involuntarily reveal a partiality which (I think we are to infer) she does her best at other times to conceal. They reveal her passionate sympathy with her mother's passionate concern for Turnus. Her blush is the other part of the hint. Like the closely analogous blush of the girl in Catullus 65, it reveals her embarrassment, even shame, that she has thus (in weeping) opened a window on to her tender feelings for the young Italian prince.

Vergil then provides imagery and a pair of famous similes to illustrate her blush (12.65–9):

---

[35] Cf. Lucretia at Liv. 1.58.7–10. Note too the fairly loaded and revealing dream-narration of Ilia in Ennius *Ann.* 36–50 Sk. Heroines whose ancestry is in Alexandrian literature and / or Euripidean tragedy are of course so keen to declare their feelings themselves that they can hardly be kept quiet: Catullus' Ariadne, Vergil's Dido.

[36] I discuss these lines fully at *Further Voices*, 114–22, from another point of view. Any opinions that seem summarily stated in the present account are so because they are fully explained in *FV*.

> lacrimis ...
> flagrantis perfusa genas, cui plurimus ignem
> subiecit rubor et calefacta per ora cucurrit.
> Indum sanguineo ueluti uiolauerit ostro
> si quis ebur, aut mixta rubent ubi lilia multa
> alba rosa, talis uirgo dabat ora colores.

... her burning cheeks drenched with tears; a great blush kindled fire in her and ran through her heated face. As when someone stains [more exactly, 'defiles'[37]] Indian ivory with blood-red dye, or when white lilies blush mingled with many a rose: such colours did the maiden's face display.

One of the similes has an explicit point of contact and (we might say) an advertised illustrative function: Lavinia's blush, 'rubor', is pictured in the blushing effect, 'rubent', of roses among lilies.[38] But much in both similes is clearly otiose to any simple illustrative function. What does it do? We are now alerted to Vergil's practice; we allow the imagery to *narrate* to us—the metaphor implied in 'ignem' (and 'flagrantis', 'calefacta': Lavinia is 'on fire') as well as the images in the similes. We find then that a gap which we sensed (what did Lavinia feel?), a gap which Lavinia's involuntary tears and blush did something to make up for, is now completely bridged. The stained ivory simile alludes to a famous simile applied to the wounded Menelaus at *Iliad* 4.141 ff.:

> ὡς δ' ὅτε τίς τ' ἐλέφαντα γυνὴ φοίνικι μιήνῃ
> Μηονὶς ἠὲ Κάειρα ...

As when a woman stains[39] ivory with scarlet, some woman of Maeonia or Caria ...

By allusion therefore Lavinia is cast as someone *wounded*. The metaphor implies she is *on fire*. 'Wound' and 'fire': these were the salient, recurrent and vivid images for Dido's passionate love in Book 4. But they are also Lavinia's images. 'Narrative through imagery' therefore tells us what we may have suspected from Lavinia's actions in weeping and blushing: that she is in love, in love with the hero now departing to his death, Turnus. Sensitive material! Lavinia loves Aeneas' enemy. It is conveyed to us by

---

[37] On the choice of 'uiolauerit' see VI.1.
[38] On 'rubor' ... 'rubent' see too below section 5.
[39] On the choice of μιαίνω see below section 5.

simile in its substitutive function, a device here put to rich and guileful service.[40]

3. Addition in the absence of gaps

The phenomenon of substitution shows us similes *demonstrably* 'narrating'. Gaps more or less patent exist in the explicit narrative and we can see that 'narrative through imagery' bridges them; and the extended imagery in similes, which, if the similes are allowed only an illustrative function, is largely otiose, is revealed to be serving a necessary purpose: as 'narrative'. We should now ask: what of the extended and 'otiose' imagery in similes where there is no patent gap in the narrative? Might it not follow that it too is narrating, but, in the absence of any clear gap, narrating in a way which we cannot so irrefutably demonstrate? I think it follows, and it can be shown to be happening in practice. To sum up therefore: when similes substitute, their 'narrative' adds material which fills a traceable gap in the story; other extended similes add 'narrative' to a story which is apparently, but only apparently, complete without it.[41]

I showed above how substitution by similes can in Vergil's hands verge on a clandestine mode of communication, especially where the gap is a guarded one; it should follow that 'narrative through imagery' where there is no gap at all to put us on the alert is even more covert potentially. This can be so: see e.g. VI.4a, VII.3. But for now I give some quick and plainer examples of addition in the absence of gaps; with Homer in particular I shall choose familiar similes since my purpose is to illustrate an epic narrative method rather than to illuminate byways.

First I return to Apollo's sandcastle simile at 15.361–5, referred to above. It runs:

[40] I have only really picked at the surface of the stained ivory simile; and I have said more or less nothing about the lilies and roses. There is more discussion in *Further Voices*, loc. cit.

[41] There is, it must be said, no exact frontier between 'substitution' and 'addition in the absence ...'; the two categories, separated in my discussion for the sake of ordered exposition, actually shade into one another. It is to be noticed for example that in none of the cited Vergilian examples of 'substitution' is there quite the yawningly visible gap that there is in the case of Hector's return to the ditch in *Iliad* 15. They are already on the road to 'addition in the absence of gaps'.

ἔρειπε δὲ τεῖχος Ἀχαιῶν
ῥεῖα μάλ', ὡς ὅτε τις ψάμαθον πάϊς ἄγχι θαλάσσης,
ὅς τ' ἐπεὶ οὖν ποιήσῃ ἀθύρματα νηπιέῃσιν,
ἂψ αὖτις συνέχευε ποσὶν καὶ χερσὶν ἀθύρων.
ὥς ῥα σύ ... Φοῖβε ...
σύγχεας

Very easily did Apollo dash down the wall of the Achaeans, as when some boy by the seaside makes a plaything out of sand in his childish fashion, and then in his game obliterates it again with his hands and feet; so did you, Apollo, ... obliterate ...

We will take the simile, certainly in the first place, to be illustrating the *ease* with which Apollo destroys the Achaean wall; an advertisement to this effect seems to be indicated in ῥεῖα μάλ', ὡς etc. (see further below). But much of the detail is clearly otiose to such a function, e.g. the elaboration of the fact that the child is engaged on a *game*. It is not otiose however if we allow the simile a 'narrative', *adding* function. It adds to the narrative the thought that Apollo's action is for him not only as easy as a game, it has the *significance* of a game. We could say, it *is* a game. To cause men trouble is for him a matter of no consequence, and it is *fun*. Apollo like other gods finds sport in upsetting the endeavours of men, and in causing them suffering. Such are the thoughts that are added.[42] We are not far from 'As flies to wanton boys ...', and we are on the edge of the great Iliadic theme of divine *Unernst* in interaction with the dreadful *Ernst* of the life of mankind.[43]

In this instance Homer does something to make the narrative function of his simile clearer for us. He only feints in the direction of advertising an illustrative function in respect of facility (leading into the simile with ῥεῖα μάλ' does indeed make us *think* that that is the illustrative function); in the event the explicit point of contact is shown to be between συνέχευε ('obliterates') in the simile and σύγχεας ('you obliterated') *and the narrative which follows*.[44] And what follows is this: πολὺν

[42] Cf. Fränkel, 90, Moulton, 71 f.

[43] Cf. K. Reinhardt, *Das Parisurteil* (Frankfurt, 1938), esp. 12–14, *Die Ilias und ihr Dichter* (Göttingen, 1961), 446 ff.

[44] When the narrative in the *Iliad* syntactically prepares for and leads into a simile (X happened, even as Y ...) as opposed to occasions when the simile starts a syntactical unit, and is connected to the narrative only in its conclusion (Even as Y, so X), the element immediately preceding the simile usually forms the basis of the

κάματον καὶ ὀϊζὺν / σύγχεας Ἀργείων, 'and so did you, Apollo, obliterate much toil and misery of the Achaeans'. In the final count therefore the simile is presented as an illumination of Apollo's action *as it affects the wall which cost the Achaeans labour and misery*. Directed to think of men's labour and *misery* going to nothing because of Apollo's action, we should find it easier to pick up the contrasting message that the simile is adding, the message that Apollo's action for himself is not just easy but *pleasurable*. More than usually Homer helps us to see past a simple illustrative function to an important and profound 'narrative', adding function.

At *Iliad* 4.274 ff. (a simile to which I shall have occasion to return) a mass of foot-soldiers, metaphorically called a 'cloud', advancing under the leadership of the Aiantes, is compared in a simile to a storm cloud:

> ἅμα δὲ νέφος εἵπετο πεζῶν.
> ὡς δ' ὅτ' ἀπὸ σκοπιῆς εἶδεν νέφος αἰπόλος ἀνὴρ
> ἐρχόμενον κατὰ πόντον ὑπὸ Ζεφύροιο ἰωῆς·
> τῷ δέ τ' ἄνευθεν ἐόντι μελάντερον ἠΰτε πίσσα
> φαίνετ' ἰὸν κατὰ πόντον, ἄγει δέ τε λαίλαπα πολλήν·
> ῥίγησέν τε ἰδὼν ὑπό τε σπέος ἤλασε μῆλα·
> τοῖαι ἅμ' Αἰάντεσσι διοτρεφέων αἰζηῶν
> δήϊον ἐς πόλεμον πυκιναὶ κίνυντο φάλαγγες ...

And a cloud of footsoldiers followed with them: just as when from some vantage-point a goatherd sees a cloud moving over the sea before the blast of the West Wind; and to him being afar off it seems blacker than pitch, as it passes over the sea; and it drives a mighty storm; and he shudders at the sight of it and drives his flocks into a cave; such were the packed phalanxes of warriors fostered by Zeus as they moved up to destructive war with the Aiantes.

Here we have a point of contact between narrative and simile like that in *Aen.* 4.69 ff. above: narrative metaphorical νέφος is picked up by the νέφος of the simile. To this I will return. We may infer an illustrative function: the storm-cloud illustrates the

point of contact and signals the illustrative function: cf. *Iliad* 2.144 ff., 3.2 ff, 22.25 ff. We would therefore initially assume ῥεῖα μάλ' to be signalling the illustrative function at 15.361 ff. But in fact Homer switches in this instance from the former type of simile to the latter.

dark masses of the advancing ranks of troops.[45] But a very great deal of the detail in the simile is clearly otiose to such an illustrative function: in particular, the goatherd, his thoughts and actions. What the simile does is *add* to the narrative the idea of the destructive potential of the Achaeans (*storm*cloud), the apprehensiveness of a waiting Trojan commander, probably Hector (goatherd), and his anxiety and precautions, or desire to take precautions, in respect of his men (flocks). And so on: interpretation of the narrative function of this simile could be much extended.[46] But to sum up up one important contribution made by it, we should say that it adds to the narrative another *point of view*, a point of view (Trojan) different from the dominant one at this stage (Achaean).[47] We might not all agree on the details of an extended interpretation, for it is in the nature of 'narrative through imagery' to suggest thoughts and possibilities, not to deliver facts. But that the simile is 'narrating' should be beyond dispute.

A quick example from the *Aeneid*. At 8.588–91 the Trojans and Arcadians are leaving Pallanteum for war; Pallas is compared to the morning star:

> it ... chlamyde et pictis conspectus in armis,
> qualis ubi Oceani perfusus Lucifer unda,
> quem Venus ante alios astrorum diligit ignis,
> extulit os sacrum caelo tenebrasque resoluit.

Then comes Pallas, conspicuous in his cloak and emblazoned arms: even as the Morning Star, whom Venus loves above all other stellar fires, when, drenched from the wave of Ocean, he lifts his sacred face up in the sky and melts the darkness.

---

[45] See Fränkel, 22.

[46] See the excellent discussion of Fränkel, 22 f.

[47] Adding a point of view different from what is perhaps the expected one is what *Iliad* 8.555–61 is doing: this is the simile that provoked the comment of M. D. Reeve quoted above p. 64. On 8.555 ff. see Fränkel, 34. On the general question of 'point of view' in narrative see Booth, e.g. Ch. 1 on 'showing and telling', and pp. 278 ff. on 'point of view' and Henry James; the concept has been refined (as 'focalization') by Genette 185 ff. and Rimmon-Kenan 71–85. On 'point of view' and the *Aeneid*, see Conte *Rhetoric* 152 ff. = *Il genere* 66 ff. (in Conte's hands, however, 'point of view' signifies something larger and more complex than normally); and for a another recent treatment of the *Aeneid* and 'point of view' see Bonfanti. Since Homer's narrative is normally and with much justification seen as 'objective' and univocal (cf. Lyne, *Further Voices*, 218 ff. with bibliography, Conte *Rhetoric* 152 = *Virgilio: Il genere* 66) intrusions of unexpected 'points of view' should be carefully noted.

No illustrative function is advertised, but given that the narrative of Pallas is very visual and that stars, in particular the morning star, are proverbially beautiful,[48] we may take it to consist in the illumination of the young Arcadian's beauty. But the simile then adds, 'narrates', other implications—besides the news that Pallas has incurred the fondness of the troubling Venus.[49]

To compare someone to the morning star was in Vergil's ambience an ambiguous thing to do.[50] The identity of morning *and evening* star was by this time, especially after the neoteric poets, almost a cliché.[51] The morning star on the one hand may connote youth and life (cf. 'Plato' below and Vergil's 'tenebras-que resoluit'), but evening and the evening star connote death. Cf. Soph. *O.T.* 177, where the dead are said to wing their way 'to the shore of the evening god', ἀκτὰν πρὸς ἑσπέρου θεοῦ. And 'Plato' *Epigram* II (Page, *Further Greek Epigrams*, pp. 161–2) epigrammatically exploits both the death connotations of the evening star and the identity of the evening and morning star (as well as the beauty connotations of both):

> ἀστὴρ πρὶν μὲν ἔλαμπες ἐνὶ ζωοῖσιν ἑῷος,
> νῦν δὲ θανὼν λάμπεις ἕσπερος ἐν φθιμένοις.

Formerly you used to shine as the morning star among the living; but now, dead, you shine as the evening star among those who are passed away.

Elliptically, Vergil does something very similar. His comparison of Pallas to the (dual-identity) morning star *entails* in his literary ambience an allusion to the evening star. The simile adverts to Pallas' youth and life *and* adds discreet foreshadowing of Pallas' death. Not dissimilarly to Vergil, but without the ellipse and

---

[48] Cf. Fränkel, 47 f.; Page on 'Plato' below; *RE* VIII 1252; Hor. *Carm.* 3.9.21.

[49] Pöschl, 171 f. does not find the affection of Venus troubling, but he glances usefully at this detail in the simile.

[50] I shall argue that the morning star comparison casts shadows on this scene, intimating the imminent death of Pallas, because the morning star entails the evening star. Senfter, 171 f. argues that the morning star in its own right signals Pallas' untimely death because, owing to its intense but brief period of shining, it was associated with the dead on tombs.

[51] Cf. Cinna fr. 6 f.M, Catull. 62.35, Hor. *Carm.* 2.9.10–12 and the most interesting observations of Nisbet and Hubbard, *Horace*, ii. 144 f. Belief in the identity of morning and evening stars is of course much older than the neoterics: see Page, op. cit. 161.

double allusion, Homer compares Achilles' spearpoint to the evening star at *Il*. 22.317 f. (illustrative function: 'brightness') and adds thereby a foreshadowing of Hector's death;[52] on this simile see further section 4.

Addendum: Addition & substitution, G. Williams & Catullus

Where I talk of similes being otiose as regards an illustrative function, G. Williams would speak of 'over-adequacy' (e.g. *Figures*, 52). Where I talk of imagery as 'narrative', he might talk of the replacement of 'primary statement' by simile (e.g. *Figures*, 48). And what he shows in ch. III of *Figures* is in effect that Catullus richly develops the techniques of, as I would say, substituting 'narrative through imagery' for narrative, and adding to narrative by the same means (but Williams does not distinguish between what I call adding and substituting): in poems 11, 64, 65, and 68. In 68 the Laodamia simile is a spectacular example of addition. This vast 'comparison' exploits the suggestive media of myth and imagery to 'narrate' to us, in a way that explicit narrative never could have, Catullus' idealization of Lesbia, pathetic devotion to her, wish-fulfilling fantasies about her, simultaneous sense of doom, and so on, all of which occurred in the seconds that elapsed between the sound of her foot on the threshold and her entry into the 'domus';[53] and on top of this the simile 'narrates' Catullus' feelings of loss, abandonment, and despair in the face of his brother's death.[54] Williams' chapter is in many respects a useful one, and shows, in effect, the neoteric Catullus adopting a technique from the epic tradition and developing and exaggerating it to a point of unparalleled ingenuity and ostentation—in the neoteric spirit. But Williams does not mention the epic tradition of 'narrative through imagery' at all, implying rather that Catullus' technique sprang fully armed from the head of Catullus; and that, to put it mildly, is misleading. Nor does Williams mention Vergil in this context: he shows the influence of Catullus' practice on Propertius and others, but does not suggest that Vergil might

---

[52] Slightly differently Moulton, *Hermes* 102 (1974), 393–4: 'the evening star represents the end of Hector's day of glory ... At the same time, κάλλιστος (318) focuses attention on Achilles and his supreme heroism.'

[53] See Lyne, *The Latin Love Poets*, 52 ff., Macleod, *Collected Essays*, 160–5.

[54] Cf. Williams, *Figures*, 59, Macleod, *Collected Essays*, 161 f.

have picked up a hint or two. In fact it is surely likely that Catullus as well as Homer (and Apollonius, etc.) influenced Vergil in this matter, though Vergil returns to Homeric discretion in his handling of the contours and relative proportions of simile.

4. Adding and 'irrational correspondence'

'Narrative through imagery' as I have described it to date is made slightly more intriguing by what some would call 'irrational' correspondences. I do not like the term, but it is not wholly out of place.[55]

To approach this topic, I attempt some summary. We have agreed that the main function of a simile is to add to the narrative, not to illustrate what is already there. It follows that we cannot expect correspondence between all details in the simile and details present in the narrative: it is the function of many details in the simile precisely to be new additions. Usually, in fact, the situation may be described as follows (I restate my position in a slightly different way). The poet gives us one correspondence (one point of contact), e.g. the obliteration of the sandcastle / the obliteration of the wall, in *Il.* 15.361 ff. (above); and he leaves us to *construct* other 'correspondences', i.e. he leaves us to insert into the narrative details to which details in the simile may correspond, e.g. child's game / Apollo's *game*—and to infer thereby the important added 'narrative'. Sometimes (I might add) we do not have actually to construct correspondences, merely to recognize a correspondent present but unobvious in the narrative—and proceed to infer the added 'narrative'. So, in sum, we can say: the poet usually provides a patent correspondence for one detail in the simile; we, on top of this, must construct or find the correspondences for other details. This is our basic situation. Possibilities are opened up by irrationality, as I shall now show.

(1) When we are finding or constructing correspondences for details not provided with obvious correspondences by the poet, we should not necessarily be committed to the mutual, rational

---

[55] Cf. West (1969), 42 f. and Hardie, 145. Hardie talks expressively of a 'knight's move connection' in *Aen.* 9.710 ff., mentioned below.

consistency of these correspondences. *Iliad* 15.362 ff., Apollo's sandcastle simile (already quoted and partly interpreted above, IV. 3), is an example. The whole context runs thus (from 355):

προπάροιθε δὲ Φοῖβος Ἀπόλλων
ῥεῖ' ὄχθας καπέτοιο βαθείης *ποσσὶν ἐρείπων*
ἐς μέσσον κατέβαλλε, γεφύρωσεν δὲ κέλευθον
μακρὴν ἠδ' εὐρεῖαν, ὅσον τ' ἐπὶ δουρὸς ἐρωὴ
γίγνεται, ὁππότ' ἀνὴρ σθένεος πειρώμενος ᾖσι.
τῇ ῥ' οἵ γε προχέοντο φαλαγγηδόν, πρὸ δ' Ἀπόλλων
αἰγίδ' ἔχων ἐρίτιμον· *ἔρειπε δὲ τεῖχος* Ἀχαιῶν
ῥεῖα μάλ', ὡς ὅτε τις ψάμαθον πάϊς ἄγχι θαλάσσης,
ὅς τ' ἐπεὶ οὖν ποιήσῃ ἀθύρματα νηπιέῃσιν,
ἂψ αὖτις *συνέχευε ποσὶν καὶ χερσὶν* ἀθύρων.
ὥς ῥα σύ ... Φοῖβε ...
σύγχεας

And before them Phoebus Apollo *easily dashed down* with his *feet* the banks of the deep ditch, and cast them down into the middle of it, and made a bridge, a path broad and long, even as far as the throw of a spear when a man hurls it making trial of his strength. By that route they poured forward in phalanxes, and before them went Apollo bearing the highly-prized aegis. And very *easily* did Apollo *dash down* the wall of the Achaeans, as when some boy by the seaside makes a plaything out of sand in his childish fashion, and then in his game obliterates it again with his hands and *feet*; so did you, Apollo, ... obliterate ...

The poet draws attention to a correspondence between the child's obliteration of the sandcastle and Apollo's obliteration of the wall; we constructed another correspondence between the child's and Apollo's *game* in so doing, and inferred the added 'narrative' (IV.3). But what correspondence do we construct, or find, for the child's *building* of the sandcastle? We can neither construct nor find any, if we expect rational consistency between correspondences: for according to such consistency, if the child obliterating the sandcastle equals Apollo obliterating the wall, then the child building the sandcastle would equal Apollo building the wall; and Apollo did not build the wall. But why should we expect rational consistency between correspondences? The function of a simile is to add, to narrate through imagery; and there is no requirement of imagery to work in the rational manner of explicit narrative. And if we abandon expectations of

such rational consistency, we can find a very important correspondent for the child's building of the sandcastle: Apollo's
building *of the bridge*. Apollo, as the full context shows, first
built a bridge to assist the Trojans across the ditch, then
knocked down the Achaean wall, also to assist them. It is to
this (the bridge-building) that the child's building in the simile
refers ('irrationally'). The text in fact helps us to see that the
simile's range of reference extends back to the building of the
bridge. The destruction of the ditch's banks, part and parcel of
the process of building, is verbally linked (in italicized words)
to the destruction of the wall, which is explicitly referred to by
the simile, and indeed it is verbally linked (πο(σ)σίν) to the
simile itself; or to put it another way, when the words ῥεῖ' ...
ποσσὶν ἐρείπων which initiate the bridge-building description
are picked up by the simile and its explicit point of reference in
the narrative, we may infer that the simile's sphere of influence
extends back to them. We may therefore pick up the correspondence: child's building of the sandcastle = Apollo's building of
the bridge; and we may then infer the same sort of further
narrative significance that we inferred in respect of the two
obliterations. This, the building of the bridge, a desperately
earnest matter for both Greeks and Trojans, is also mere sport
for Apollo—like the building of the sandcastle for the child.
This is what the simile 'narrates' to us, *if* we are fully alive to
simile's narrative function and to the 'irrationality' allowed by
'narrative through imagery'.

Quite similar is Bitias' simile at *Aen.* 9.710 ff.[56] Bitias falls like
a pier which engineers drop into the sea:

> talis in Euboico Baiarum litore quondam
> saxea pila cadit, magnis quam molibus ante
> constructam ponto iaciunt ...
> ...
> miscent se maria et nigrae attolluntur harenae,
> tum sonitu Prochyta alta tremit durumque cubile
> Inarime Iouis imperiis imposta Typhoeo.

So on the Euboean shore of Baiae sometimes falls a stony pier, which,
prefabricated from mighty blocks, they cast into the ocean ... The seas
are in turmoil, and the black sands are churned up. Then at the din

---

[56] Briefly discussed in III.1

trembles lofty Prochyta, and Inarime, a rugged resting place laid over Typhoeus on Jupiter's orders.

In rationally consistent terms Typhoeus, imprisoned under the island of Inarime, can be given no correspondent in the narrative, and certainly not Bitias, to whom the 'pila' (as the poet makes clear) corresponds. But, as has been seen by Hardie,[57] the Giant Typhoeus may not *rationally* correspond to Bitias, but Bitias is indeed in a sense his correspondent, the 'irrational' recipient of his 'narrative' significance. Typhoeus adds the mythical associations of a Giant and Gigantomachy to huge Bitias and his episode.

(2) An additional possibility for 'narrative through imagery' is opened up in the following manner. I repeat the basic situation, summarized above: the poet provides a correspondence for one detail in the simile; we, on top of this, must find or construct correspondences for other details. The additional possibility is this: sometimes we find that the poet provides the correspondence for one detail, as usual; but then we, on top of this, may construct *an additional correspondence for this same detail*. This may seem an irrational thing to do, but there is in fact no reason to limit an image to one function; and some passages of text impose the procedure on us.

For example, *Iliad* 22.317 ff, discussed briefly above:

> οἷος δ' ἀστὴρ εἶσι μετ' ἀστράσι νυκτὸς ἀμολγῷ
> ἕσπερος, ὃς κάλλιστος ἐν οὐρανῷ ἵσταται ἀστήρ,
> ὣς αἰχμῆς ἀπέλαμπ' εὐήκεος, ἣν ἄρ' Ἀχιλλεὺς
> πάλλεν δεξιτερῇ φρονέων κακὸν Ἕκτορι δίῳ ...

Even as a star goes among stars in the dead of night, the evening star, which is the fairest of stars that has its place in heaven, so there went forth a gleam from the well-pointed spear which Achilles brandished in his right hand, intending evil for godlike Hector ...

Here Homer provides a correspondence, bright star / bright spear (suggesting an illustrative function: the star pictures the way the spear gleams, 'even *so* there went forth a gleam ...'). But in its narrative function, so we deduce (cf. IV.3), the star (the *evening* star) adds thoughts of Hector's death, it images the dead *Hector*. This is a correspondence (star / Hector) which we must

[57] Hardie, 144 f.

find *in addition to* the one explicitly provided by the poet—and
one that according to the explicit terms of the simile ('even
so from the *spear* there went forth a gleam') might seem
'irrational'. We are, incidentally, helped to find this additional
correspondence (star / Hector) by the fact that an ominous
remark on Hector lies immediately adjacent to the simile
(φρονέων κακὸν ...).

5. Trespass

In III.1 I showed examples of simile language that had trespassed
into the narrative ('conlabor', 9.708, 4.664; cf. 'uulnus' at 4.67,
above pp. 77 f. and n. 29.); in section 2 of this chapter I pointed
to an example of the reverse, narrative language trespassed into
the simile ('acies', etc., 10.405–9). Michael Silk has admirably
attended to this sort of effect, particularly that of narrative
language in simile, but with special reference to early Greek
poetry (but not Homer).[58] Vergil is adept at contriving and
capitalizing upon both effects, and therefore I must devote some
attention to the topic: particularly so, since he often combines
the technique with others analysed in this book in a mutually
enhancing way. 'Trespass' is the term I prefer to use, as it seems
the simplest and the most graphic.

First, it is worth hazarding a general comment. The first effect,
simile trespass into narrative, is almost bound to produce a
metaphor in the narrative, and the metaphor may well be of a
not too startling sort: a word or idea natural to simile has a good
chance of translating into a not unnatural metaphor. The second
effect, narrative trespass into simile, is more likely to be assertive.
What is native to the narrative is I think less likely to make
familiar metaphor within the world of the simile, and may not
make what can simply be called metaphor at all; so that it will
stand out. Cf. and contrast the effect of 'acies' trespassed from
narrative to simile at 10.408, and 'uulnus' trespassed from simile
to narrative at 4.67: the former is a startling metaphor, the latter
(which I look at again below) quite a familiar one. I would not
however like to insist on this general position; we must assess

[58] For narrative language trespassed into simile ('tenor language intruded into
vehicle') see Silk, 138–42, for simile language in narrative ('metaphor as ground term
to simile'), 235 f. The quoted phrases echo the way Silk describes the effects.

individual instances as they come. Certainly Vergil can contrive simile trespasses into narrative that are arresting: 'conlabor' in III.1 is a case in point.

Next we should recognize that both effects are as old as Homer, and were observed and described by Porphyry. I select some examples.[59]

We should recall *Iliad* 4.141–6, Menelaus' wound:

ὡς δ' ὅτε τίς τ' ἐλέφαντα γυνὴ φοίνικι μιήνῃ
Μηονὶς ἠὲ Κάειρα ...
...
τοῖοί τοι, Μενέλαε, μιάνθην αἵματι μηροὶ ...

Even as when some woman stains [more literally, '*defiles*'] ivory with scarlet, some woman of Maeonia or Caria ... even so, Menelaus, were your thighs *defiled* with blood ...

The repetition of μιαίνω we might initially suppose to be advertising an illustrative function; more usefully, it advertises trespass. μιαίνω, 'defile' rather than 'stain', is appropriate to the description of blood disfiguring flesh, but is unnatural of the action of dye on ivory.[60] Language appropriate to the narrative has trespassed into the simile. And what is produced is remarkable. Within the simile μιαίνω can hardly, it seems to me, be called metaphor and certainly not familiar metaphor. Rather it strikes one—within the simile—as a catachresis, or strange hyperbole. But the ultimate explanation is: trespass. This, I say, is a remarkable and eye-catching example. But, as I shall show, it is limited in its function (below p. 98).

At *Od.* 19.204 ff. Penelope weeps:

τῆς δ' ἄρ' ἀκουούσης ῥέε δάκρυα, τήκετο δὲ χρώς.
ὡς δὲ χιὼν κατατήκετ' ἐν ἀκροπόλοισιν ὄρεσσιν,
ἥν τ' Εὖρος κατέτηξεν, ἐπὴν Ζέφυρος καταχεύῃ·
τηκομένης δ' ἄρα τῆς ποταμοὶ πλήθουσι ῥέοντες·
ὣς τῆς τήκετο καλὰ παρήϊα δάκρυ χεούσης.

---

[59] Porph. *Quaest. Hom.* 1.6 (Sodano) τάς τε γὰρ οἰκείως τιθεμένας φωνὰς ἐπὶ τῶν πραγμάτων πολλάκις εἰς τὰς παραβολὰς μετατίθησι καὶ τὰς ἐπὶ τῶν παραβολῶν εἰς τὰ πράγματα: οἷον ... and he cites excellent examples, esp. *Iliad* 2.87 ff., 4.422 ff. (both narrative to simile), and 18.219 ff. (simile to narrative). Another formulation at 1.17 *init.* with more examples, including 4.273 ff. Cf. Richardson 280–1. It will be noticed that my first example was not spotted by Porph. (and is owed to D. P. Fowler: see next note).

[60] See Fowler, 190. Fowler made this point and drew the correct inference from it.

As she listened her tears flowed, and her flesh *melted*: just as the snow *melts* on high mountains, which the East wind *melts* when the West wind has strewn it; and as it *melts* the rivers flow full; so her beautiful cheeks *melted* as she poured forth her tears.

Again we might have wanted to see in the repetition of τήκω, -ομαι the advertisement for an illustrative function; more truthfully, it spotlights a trespass, this time of simile into narrative. τήκω, -ομαι is used naturally of the melting of snow (cf. Hdt. 2.22, LSJ s.v. II). But, whereas it might have been transferred without violence to, say, flesh actually wasting away (LSJ I 2), τήκομαι makes a most unusual and thought-provoking metaphor (?) applied to the 'melting' of Penelope's cheeks in tears.[61] If I was pressed to label the effect of τήκομαι in 204 and 208 without reference to the phenomenon of trespass, I might call it catachresis again, or relate it to hypallage: τήκομαι, which would have made more sense with the tears on Penelope's cheeks, is transferred to the cheeks. But I prefer to talk of trespass: from snow to cheeks, simile to narrative. And here we have a result as attention-seeking as the narrative–simile example just cited.

At *Iliad* 4.274 ff. we have a less strident example:[62] this is the simile for the Aiantes' phalanxes, discussed above (IV.3). One can say, as I did above, that a metaphor (νέφος) in the narrative is picked up by the νέφος of the simile, and an illustrative function for the latter can be inferred:

ἅμα δὲ νέφος εἵπετο πεζῶν.
ὡς δ' ὅτ' ἀπὸ σκοπιῆς εἶδεν νέφος αἰπόλος ἀνὴρ ...

And a cloud of footsoldiers followed with them: just as when from some vantage-point a goatherd sees a cloud ...

And one can then proceed to identify the simile's narrative 'adding' function which is much more important than the illustrative one. Or we can now put it in a different but equally valid way. We note the verbal repetition of νέφος. This signals a trespass. νέφος, literal and natural within the simile, has trespassed into the narrative where it makes metaphor. The metaphor is paralleled, it is true (*Iliad* 16.66, 23.133), but such a use is

---

[61] Porph. 1.17 τῷ δὲ τήκεσθαι κυρίως ἐπὶ τῆς χιόνος χρησάμενος ἐνδιατρίβειν ὡς ἐναργεῖ πολλάκις οὐκ ὤκνησε καὶ τῷ αὐτῷ χρήσασθαι ἐπὶ τῆς διὰ λύπην τοῖς δακρύοις διαρρεομένης.

[62] Porph. 1.17.

less familiar than the literal use within the simile, so that we gain at least some impression of trespass.[63] Having seen and explained the simile in this different way, we may then, as before, proceed to the main job, the identification of its narrative function. And here is a thought, which may suggest that explanation in terms of trespass is a useful one. Does the demonstrated ability of simile language to trespass into narrative and to appear as narrative help us to see simile's narrative function? Is the narrative appearance of νέφος in 274 a pointer to the fact that νέφος in 275 also narrates? Is trespass designed to break down barriers, to bind narrative and 'narrative through imagery' together? Narrative trespass into simile might have even more impact in this direction: cf. μιαίνω above and examples below. This line of thinking will be resumed.

There is an example of simile trespass into narrative at Verg. *Aen.* 10.802 ff. which is interesting to compare:

> furit Aeneas tectusque tenet se.
> ac uelut effusa si quando grandine nimbi
> praecipitant, omnis campis diffugit arator
> omnis et agricola, et tuta latet arce uiator
> aut amnis ripis aut alti fornice saxi,
> dum pluit in terris, ut possint sole reducto
> exercere diem: sic obrutus undique telis
> Aeneas nubem belli, dum detonet omnis,
> sustinet ...

Aeneas rages, and keeps himself under cover. Just as when storm-clouds pour down with showers of hail, every ploughman, every farmer flees from the fields, and the traveller lurks in a safe stronghold, under river bank or in vault of high rock, while the rain falls on the earth, that so they may pursue the day's task when the sun returns: even so, overwhelmed by weapons from all sides, Aeneas withstands the cloud of war waiting for it to spend its thunder ...

Embattled Aeneas covers up, protecting himself against the onset of the enemy, as ploughman, farmer and traveller protect themselves against a storm. We could see the metaphorical cloud, 'nubes', of war, violence *sim.* which Aeneas withstands in the sentence following the simile as, in a sense, that which is picked up by the storm-clouds simile: compare how we could see

---

[63] I think Silk would call this 'neutral-based interaction': Silk, 85 ff.

Homer's metaphorical νέφος as picked up by the νέφος simile (though Vergil locates his metaphor as a resumption of, not as an introduction to, the simile). But we could also say, with equal validity, that the idea of storm-cloud, which is literal and natural within the simile, has trespassed into the narrative; it is less natural in the narrative, and this gives us our impression of trespass. Vergil's metaphorical 'nubes' is in fact a much less familiar use than Homer's metaphorical νέφος at *Iliad* 4.274. It lacks exact parallel in Latin before Vergil, and is not used again by Vergil himself; it derives primarily not from *Iliad* 4.274, but from another Homeric use of νέφος.[64] We have therefore a slightly greater impression of trespass with 'nubes' than with Homer's νέφος at 4.274. The binding together of narrative and 'narrative through imagery' is thus more ostentatious. Note however that in this instance Vergil does not furnish a strictly *verbal* trespass: the *idea* of 'nimbi' etc. trespasses and appears as 'nubes'. The trespass is therefore in this respect less advertised. But then note that 'detonet', and 'obrutus' also, cohere with the 'nubes' metaphor, reinforcing the trespass and strengthening the bonding of the two media.

There is a very similar situation at *Aen.* 4.67 ff. (discussed above, IV.2). Metaphorical 'uulnus' is picked up and illustrated in the hind simile; or, we could say, the idea (not the word) of the hind's wound trespasses into the narrative to appear as 'uulnus'. At 12.66 ff. (IV.2), Lavinia's blush simile, we have the reverse situation: narrative 'rubor' (this time it is the word) trespasses to appear as metaphorical 'rubent' in the simile. The degree to which this would have been felt as trespass depends on how actively and assertively metaphorical, thus how unnatural, 'rubeo' of roses and lilies appeared.

I now cite an interesting but unobserved example of trespass at *Aen.* 7.582 ff.:

> ... Martemque fatigant.
> ilicet infandum cuncti contra omina bellum,
> contra fata deum peruerso numine poscunt.
> ...

---

[64] Cf. *Iliad* 17.243 πολέμοιο νέφος περὶ πάντα καλύπτει, where νέφος may be in apposition to Ἕκτωρ if one accepts the integrity of line 244 and, accepting it, construes it thus. Cf. and contrast the νέφος metaphor at 4.274.

> ille uelut pelago rupes immota resistit,
> ut pelagi rupes magno ueniente fragore,
> quae sese multis circum latrantibus undis
> mole tenet ...

... they importune for the God of battle. All, against the omens, against the will of the gods, overturning divine sanction, straightway demand war. He [Latinus] like a rock unmoved by the ocean resists, like a rock which, as a great uproar of ocean comes upon it, stands steadfast in its bulk amid many baying waves ...

Crowds of Latins clamour for war, their pressure on Latinus compared to the ocean beating against a rock. Why are the waves in the ocean described as 'baying', literally 'barking' ('latro')?[65] The word is literally suited to dogs, and 'barking' is not a natural metaphor of waves, in spite of the implications of *OLD*.[66] But 'latro' *is* established as a metaphor of the bawling clamour, the 'baying', of unruly speakers (*OLD* 3b and 4); and this provides us with our answer. 'Latro' has, we can say, trespassed from the narrative, from the clamorous and importunate Latins ('fatigant', 'poscunt') whom it might naturally suit (the Latins we infer are 'baying') to the waves which image them in the simile; and applied to the waves it makes a very novel metaphor. Essentially therefore we have a narrative trespass to simile. But this is an striking and sophisticated example. I shall make some observations in respect of it, and then broaden out to some conclusions about trespass in general.

(1) In 7.582 ff. we have what we might call a degree of removal

---

[65] There is nothing to parallel this in traceable Homeric sources, *Il.* 15.618–21, 17.747–51.

[66] *OLD* isolates a subsection (s.v. 1d) '(of waves) to roar'. The subsection contains our line of Vergil, Sil. 3.471, and 5.397; Stat. *Ach* 1.450 f. might have been added. But the subsection is misleading. Vergil's use of 'latro' is not a self-contained metaphor but a special effect *dependent on its own particular context* (narrative trespass into simile), as analysed above. What happens then is that his example *legitimizes* (cf. I.4 *init.* a self-contained metaphorical use (waves 'bark') for Flavian poets who (I would bet) did not realize that he was contriving a special effect dependent upon a particular context. *TLL* VII.2.1014.1 ff. parallels the use at Acc. *trag.* 569 Ribbeck 'curuo litore latratu (latrans, *Scaliger*) unda sub undis labunda sonit', and in late Latin as well as in the above Flavians. All post-Vergilian examples I would bet derive from Vergil; for Accius' use I imagine there was some particular contextual motivation on a par with Vergil's.

Fordyce's comment 'the waves are like a pack of barking hounds' shows that he has not seen what is going on; likewise R. D. Williams' 'Virgil may be thinking of Scylla's sea-dogs'.

which we have not yet seen. In 10.802 ff. (simile trespass to narrative), the trespassed term 'nubes' (etc.) did not repeat a word, only an idea, contained in its source. This was one stage removed from the plainest examples of trespass (e.g. νέφος in *Iliad* 4.274 f.), where the *word* trespasses. Nevertheless the idea (cloud) was paramount in the source, and words closely adjacent to 'nubes' appeared there. In 7.582 ff. no words *closely* adjacent to 'latro' appear in the source (here the narrative), nor is the idea of the Latins 'baying' paramount there: it can be inferred from the narrative context rather than plainly descried therein. This is a further stage removed from the plainest form of trespass.

(2) 7.582 ff. is the first instance of narrative trespass which we have noticed where a narrative *metaphor*, or rather a potential narrative metaphor (baying speakers), trespasses to become another metaphor (baying waves) in the simile.

(3) A simile trespass into narrative binds narrative and 'narrative through imagery' together, and helps us to perceive simile's narrative function (see above). Narrative trespasses into simile help us more directly: a narrative term explicit in the diction of a simile is a very pressing invitation to regard simile as narrative. The more startling the impact of such a trespass, the more 'narrative' it strikes one as being, the more pressing the invitation is: e.g. Vergil's battleline of fire at 10.408 and Homer's defiled ivory at *Iliad* 4.141. Diction on these occasions almost advertises that the similes provide narrative, of Menelaus' defiled thighs and an advancing Arcadian battleline. Vergil's baying waves at 7.588 are perhaps similarly an advertisement, though more is left to our powers of inference.

(4) Narrative trespasses into simile help us to perceive simile's narrative function. And they can do more. Homer's μιαίνω at *Iliad* 4.141 and Vergil's 'rubeo' at 12.68 do no more than help us to see that their similes narrate; they themselves echo something already in the narrative, and additional 'narrative' must be sought elsewhere in the similes. But Vergil's 'acies' at 10.408 and 'latro' at 7.588 help us to see that their similes narrate *and themselves constitute a substantial part of the 'narrative' which they are helping us to see*. 'Acies' and other trespassed terms in 10.405 ff. add the advancing Arcadian battleline to the narrative ('bridging a visible gap', 'substituting'). 'Latro' at 7.588 adds the notion of the baying Latins to the narrative ('adding in the

absence of a visible gap'). The way I put it above was to say that
the idea of the baying Latins can be inferred in the narrative. But
it is not actually there. It is, we can now more exactly say, added
to the narrative by the simile, by in fact 'latro' the trespassed
term.

(5) These effects should be regarded as further evidence of
Vergil's skill in combination ('iunctura'). Consider 'latro', and
how we are steered to an effect which we ought not to miss. In its
combination, it its trespassed position applied to waves, it makes
a novel metaphor. The novelty of the combination should make
us ask: Whence and why? That should make us think of trespass;
for narrative trespasses to simile produce such strange metaphors (catachresis etc.) within the simile. What, we then ask,
does this narrative term in the simile (if such it be) correspond to
in the narrative? What has it trespassed from? Answer: it
corresponds to an idea that we might infer in the narrative but in
fact substantially have to *add* to it from the simile, from 'latro'
itself: the idea of the baying Italians. 'Latro' in fact (we could
say) is the trespassed residue of an element of narrative.

Much therefore is being done in context by one neutral word
('latro'); and by Vergil's combination.

It is worth stressing that all the above effects of trespass and the
effects that trespass produces are ultimately created by no more
histrionic device than the relocation, combination, of ordinary
words. Guileful combination of words that fall into the categories of ordinary diction (μιαίνω, τήκω, νέφος, 'nubes', 'uulnus',
'latro', 'acies') produces these indisputably poetic results.

In later chapters I shall return to examples of trespass in which
other Vergilian techniques are brought in to assist or enhance it
(V.2, VI.1).

V

Exploitation: II

1. The war

Vergil's narrative involves much military action. It was desirable that this should strike his readers as real and immediate. In particular, the second half of the poem sees a war that illustrates many of the agonies and dilemmas of the civil wars of recent Roman history, and Vergil could not want these to be distanced, much less glamorized. To keep reality present in his war narrative, Vergil exploits some of the language characteristic of military prose, the language used for example by Caesar to report the reality and facts of war at the front. Such diction had become prosaic *because* of its assertive association with a topic deemed properly to be prose's: everyday, mundane warfare (cf. Ch. I, pp. 10 f.). For the same reason it could be of service to Vergil. I shall give some illustration of his tactics in this respect, especially in subsections i. and iv.

Prosaisms with other qualities, words prosaic because of associations other than those of everyday war, can also serve to keep a narrative of war real and immediate. These too Vergil exploits, as I shall show in subsections ii, iii, and v.

But of course Vergil's exploitation of all such ordinary language had to be very prudent; and, as I shall also show, it is. Had it not been, the military portions of his poem might simply have become approximations to—say—Caesar. In an epic poem there must be heroism and 'otherness' as well as facts and immediacy. Besides, there are heroes in wars, even in civil wars, and there is heroism. Death may be moving, if not glorious, as well as the final bathos. Poetry's more expressive diction has a major role to play (cf. Ch I, pp. 15 f. on the value of poetic diction).

i. The weapons

Vergil's diction in the simple matter of weapons shows thought and discrimination.[1] As a rule he excludes from the battle scenes[2] terminology that smacks strongly of the contemporary Roman army (prosaisms). Trojans and Italians (and Greeks) fight predominantly with neutral diction, i.e. with terms that might be used of contemporary military equipment, but which were equally at home in poetry: e.g. 'hasta', 'iaculum', 'galea'; or with poetic diction: 'ensis', 'clipeus', 'hastile'. Their heroic pretensions are thus given ample scope; whereas constant use of 'pilum', 'gladius' or 'scutum', prosaisms which emphatically denote the equipment of contemporary military issue, could have limited their heroism to the scale of an everyday legionary. (Notes on all these words which justify the labels just given, together with some comments on their use outside Vergil, are given at the end of this subsection. Vergilian figures that follow in this subsection refer to the *Aeneid*.)

Vergil avoids constant use of prose terminology. But a total ban might have removed his action from all contact with everyday reality. We find no total ban. We find measured and sometimes very acute exploitation of prose terminology. Although 'pilum' is confined to one use in the eccentric Catalogue (7.664),[3] 'gladius' is exposed five times (all in the narrative of the Italian war):[4] this, in spite of the vastly higher number of the corresponding poetic diction word 'ensis' (63), is a relatively large figure, as statistics for other poets show (see end of subsection). Likewise thirteen examples of 'scutum' (eleven in the second half of the poem)[5] is a relatively high occurrence; Vergil uses the poetic diction 'clipeus, -um' fifty times. Not even Lucan, whose Roman *Bellum Civile* clearly has a special interest in the effects of ordinary diction, feels much moved by this particular act of legitimation ('scutum').[6] So Vergil has a relatively high number of very real swords and shields, 'gladii' and 'scuta'.

---

[1] Cf. Heinze, 201–5, Couissin, 'Virgile et l'Italie primitive', esp. 557–69 and 575–6.

[2] Diction in the Catalogue is a special case: all sorts of oddities occur. Cf. Heinze, 201 f., Couissin, op. cit., esp. 559.

[3] On the oddities of diction in the Catalogue see preceding note.

[4] 9.769, 10.313 and 513 (all of Aeneas' sword), 12.278, and 12.789 (of Turnus' sword).

[5] In the body of the narrative at 8.93, 539, 562, 9.229, 666, 10.506, 12.130 and 563. Also at 1.101, designed to be a pair with 8.539; two in the Catalogue at 7.722 and 796; one at 3.237, and one on the Shield at 8.662.

[6] Contrast his attitude to 'pilum' and 'gladius': see the notes at the end of this subsection.

Most poets preferred to signify their swords and shields more or less exclusively by the words 'ensis' and 'clipeus', for these are the weapons of a fabled world, a world other than our own.[7] That is why Vergil generally prefers them too. 'Gladii' and 'scuta' belong emphatically to our world and the reality of Roman warfare. That is why Vergil sometimes prefers them. He must occasionally anchor his heroic narrative in mundane reality.

One of Vergil's uses of 'scutum'[8] deserves special attention. It exploits the value of 'scutum' to particular effect. The elaborate, emotional and *heroic* treatment of the dead Pallas which occurs in Book 11 is discussed in VII.1. When Pallas falls in Book 10 different effects are pursued. Here is one of them.

Pallas is borne from the field of battle thus, 10.505–6:

> at socii multo gemitu lacrimisque
> impositum scuto referunt Pallanta frequentes.

With tears and many a groan his thronging comrades bear Pallas back, placed on his shield.

Pallas borne dead off the field is actually borne off on a 'scutum', the word that refers to the armament of regular army issue. Vergil may not have limited Pallas' heroism in life to the scale of an ordinary Roman legionary, and may in Book 11 inflate his posthumous image way above such a mark. But here he reduces the sombre fact of his death to precisely that scale. In death, at this point, Pallas is an ordinary soldier. The new Patroclus becomes a body on that most ordinary and Roman of objects, the 'scutum'. The mighty are in truth fallen: in a scene which we can incidentally sharply visualize, since we know exactly what a 'scutum' looks like.

It might well be objected: Pallas could hardly be carted off on a 'clipeus'—it is too small (see below). I retort: Vergil had three choices. Either he avoids the scene altogether; or he circumvents the difficulty by using a periphrasis; or he does what he does. The decision to use 'scutum' is a free one, and it is the one he makes. I can in fact prove my point that Vergil might have used a

---

[7] Cf. my remarks in ch. I, pp. 15 f.
[8] On the others see Lyne, 'Diction and Poetry', 84.

periphrasis, for that is what he does in the case of Lausus, at 10.841:

> at Lausum socii exanimem super arma ferebat
> flentes ...

But his weeping comrades bore him off dead on his armour ...

He designs essentially the same pathetic scene for Lausus, the hero borne off on his shield. But the full bathos, the complete *peripeteia* of a hero reduced to being a body in such humbly familiar Roman circumstances, he reserves for Pallas.

Further notes on the diction of weapons:
ensis, gladius
See Axelson 51. There is a useful table at the beginning of the *TLL* 'ensis' article, comparing its occurrence with that of 'gladius'. (But note the emended Vergilian figures given above.) 'Gladius' is prosaic. It denoted the sword of regular army issue, as its uses in 'business' military prose (e.g. Caes.) show us; because of this limited denotative value, it was avoided by the poets. Here are a few indicative figures (see further *TLL*, Axelson). Caesar in *Gall.* and *Civ.*: 'gladius' 20 / 'ensis' 0. Cicero prose: 'gladius' 89 / 'ensis' 0.[9] Cic. *poet.* 'gladius' 0 / 'ensis' 3. Horace: 'gladius' 1 (in the Satires) / 'ensis' 8. Propertius 'gladius' 0[10] / 'ensis' 5. Tibull. 'gladius' 0 / 'ensis' 2. Ovid in *Met.* 'gladius' 13 / 'ensis' 41: the *Met.* is comparatively hospitable to prosaic and colloquial diction, in spite of its apparent genre (see e.g. its attitude to 'puella', Axelson, 58, Watson, 433 f.), but in respect of swords it is only cautiously hospitable.

It is quickly clear from the *TLL* table that 'ensis' becomes poetical (and cf. above). But either this status is not yet established in Ennius' time, or Ennius in this respect pursues realism, for he has three examples of 'gladius' (all in the *Annales*), none of 'ensis'. Soon thereafter, however, 'ensis' is the regular word for the poets. Some apparent exceptions prove the rule. For example, Cato has one example of 'ensis' in the *Origines*. But he is pursuing a special effect; he needs to evoke a *heroic* sword: *Orig.* 71 Peter 'in arbore ensem uiderint quem

---

[9] Unchecked *TLL* figures.
[10] Wrongly transmitted at 4.3.34.

Orestes ... reliquisse dicitur.' The poet Lucan uses 'gladius'
nearly as often as 'ensis' (45/54); but, writing an epic about a
Roman civil war, it would suit him to keep the ugly reality of
swords relatively prominent;[11] cf. his policy with 'pilum', though
not with 'scutum' (both below).

Quint. *Inst.* 10.1.11 perhaps suggests a certain deafness to
connotations though not to denotation: 'sunt autem alia huius
naturae, ut idem pluribus uocibus declarent, ita ut nihil significa-
tionis quo potius utaris intersit, ut ensis et gladius.'

clipeus (-um), scutum

Strictly or originally these two words referred to different types
of shield, 'scutum' to a long oval shield, 'clipeus' to a smaller,
round one: see Couissin, *Les armes*, 70–9, 240 ff. The 'scutum'
was, the 'clipeus' was not, adopted as the regular weapon of the
Roman army of historical times: cf. Livy 1.43.4 'secunda classis
... instituta, et ex iis ... uiginti conscriptae centuriae; arma
imperata scutum pro clipeo ...', 8.8.3 'clipeis antea Romani usi
sunt; dein, postquam stipendiarii facti sunt, scuta pro clipeis
fecere'. Denoting this everyday object, the word 'scutum' came
to be prosaic. 'Clipeus', little used in the real Roman world,
became largely poetic diction, connoting the shield of heroes and
poetry. Of course 'clipeus' could still be used technically to
denote the actual small round shield as used in archaic days, or
by foreigners, or in some other such special, real circumstances
(cf. Livy above). Then it is not poetic diction. But usually it is.
Certainly it is poetic diction, designed to connote the shield of
heroes, in the hands of the poets to whom I now refer.

Here are some figures for 'clipeus (-um)' / 'scutum' in some
poets, and some prose writers: Enn. 4/2, trag. frag. (Ribbeck)
3/0, com. frag. 3/1, Lucr. 0/0, Catull. 0/0, Hor. 1[12]/0, Prop. 0/0,
Tibull. 0/1,[13] Verg. 50/13 (in both cases all *Aen.*), Ov. 29/10, Luc.
4/1,[14] Stat. 58/2, Sil. 60/2; Caesar *Gall.* and *Civ.* 0/12, Livy 13/69.
TLL s.v. 'clipeus' gives more figures for 'clipeus' at the beginning
of the article.

---

[11] Axelson 51 refers to the high occurrence of 'gladius' as 'eine bei seiner sonstigen
Eleganz etwas überraschende Anomalie.' We can see that it is not in fact surprising.
[12] *Carm.* 1.28.11.
[13] 1.10.65: realism is desirable in context.
[14] 9.471, an echo of *Aen.* 1.101 / 8.538.

The 'business' military prose writer Caesar gives us an obviously eloquent figure; and the striking lack of enthusiasm for 'scutum' among the post-Vergilian epicists, in spite of Vergil's potentially 'legitimizing' example, is perhaps an equally interesting indication of the status of the word, and of 'clipeus'. The reasons why Livy uses 'clipeus' when he does are obvious when the contexts are examined: he is technically denoting a special kind of shield (this possibility was mentioned above). A breakdown of Ovid's figures for 'scutum' makes nicely significant reading: *Am.* 1, *Her.* 1, *Fast.* 5, *Trist.* 1, *Pont.* 2, *Met.* 0. He keeps it out of the *Met.*, his world of Fancy ('clipeus', *Met.* 21), but he can use it quite substantially in his calendar of Rome (cf. the breakdown of his 'pilum' figures, below). Vergil's tolerance of 'scutum' is shown to be relatively high.

pilum

'Pilum' refers to the regular javelin of the Roman army, and is on that account (like 'scutum') prosaic. Poets tend to use it only in technically or ostentatiously Roman contexts. Propertius, for example, has four examples, and they all bear this statement out: 3.3.7,[15] 4.1.91, 4.12, 6.22.

Here are some more figures for 'pilum': Caesar *Gall.* and *Civ.* 18 (and 'pila muralia' at *Gall.* 5.40.4 and 7.82.2),[16] Enn. 1, trag. frag. 0, Lucr. 0, Catull. 0, Hor. 1 (*Serm.*), Tibull. 0, *Corp Tib.* 1 (= 3.7.90, the *Panegyricus Messallae*), Verg. 1 (and *Georg.* 1), Ov. 4, Luc. 20,[17] Sil. 10, Stat. 7, Val. 1.

Vergil's single use in the *Aeneid* (in the Catalogue, 7.664) is a telling statistic, considering his subject-matter. Lucan's subject-

---

[15] 'Horatia pila'. Propertius refers to an event supposedly sung by Ennius and commemorated by a monument with this name. He means 'pila' to be n. plur., as his syntax shows. Dionysius of Halicarnassus 3.22.9 refers in the same connection to a Ὁρατία πίλα, i.e. a fem. 'pila' or column. Livy 1.26.10 calls the monument 'Horatia pila' in a sentence which strictly speaking leaves the 'pila' ambiguous (fem. or n. plur.?), but on balance I think it is more likely that he meant it to be n. plur.: '*spolia* Curiatiorum fixa eo loco qui nunc *pila* Horatia appellatur ostentans ...'. (Dionysius knows of these spoils, and tells us that they used to be placed on the pillar. Probably there existed a site plus pillar, on which once upon a time there had been spoils, and both interpretations of the name 'Horatia pila' coexisted.)

[16] Also the phrase 'primi pili centurio' at *Gall.* 3.5.2, *Civ.* 1.13.4, 1.46.5, and 'primum pilum ducere' at *Civ.* 3.91.1. There seems some doubt in these cases whether the word is the familar 'pilum' or a different word 'pilus'.

[17] And 'pilum' / 'pilus' at 1.356: cf. n. 16.

matter is not only war, but Roman civil war, and his large use reflects his desire to make the poem immediate; cf. the situation with 'gladius', though not with 'scutum'. On occasions Lucan exploits the essential and contemporary Romanness of 'pilum' very blatantly.[18] However, Silius and Statius are also showing more tolerance, though not Valerius; Valerius' one use (6.403) occurs in a simile with Roman legionaries as subject matter. Of Ovid's four uses, one occurs in the *Am.*, three in the *Fast.*, a *Roman* poem: cf. the breakdown of his 'scutum' figures.

hastile

'Hastile' occurs at Enn. *Ann.* 392Sk., then in Vergil, in Ovid, and frequently subsequently; but it remains almost exclusively a poetical word, especially when used of the whole spear. (Caes. *Gall.* and *Civ.* 0.)

ii. *Killing*

Killing is one of the two most popular activities in war. Diction to express it is instructive, for the poets are generally choosy.

Of the words for 'kill', 'neco' is prosaic and a rather special case.[19] 'Interficio' seems the most normal and everyday: it is, for example, the word vastly preferred in the 'business' military prose of Caesar, who according to one count has 210 examples of 'interficio'. The same count gives him 24 examples of 'oc-

---

[18] e.g. he uses it programmatically in the exordium, 1.6 f. 'infestisque obuia signis / signa, pares aquilas et pila minantia pilis'. At 7.517–19 'pilum' is again used to betoken of itself *Roman* weapons: 'sceleris sed crimine nullo / externum maculant chalybem: stetit omne coactum / circa pila nefas'.

[19] See J. N. Adams, 'Two Latin Words for Kill', *Glotta* 51 (1973), 280 ff. In early Latin it was a legalism with the sense both of 'execute' and 'murder'. Its function then widened. By the end of the republic it is disproportionately common in application to murder without the use of a weapon, and above all to that by means of poison. But, stresses Adams, its uses are not limited to killing without a weapon (as Festus, Wölfflin, Axelson, and others maintained; see too Skutsch on Enn. *Ann.* 573 for a refinement of this view). Its legal base probably accounts for its prosaic status. As Bömer in a useful note on *Met.* 9.679 remarks, poetry tends to talk of killing in a heroic sphere which attracts a different moral evaluation from killing in our own context. 'Neco' is bound, as the word for 'execute' and 'murder', to carry with it our contemporary moral evaluation and is therefore undesirable to poets. Bömer provides some statistics, including the information that Ovid eccentrically and interestingly has sixteen examples of 'neco'. Vergil has the one mentioned below: the monstrosity of Mezentius' action is suddenly described from today's perspective—an interesting effect.

cido'.[20] 'Occido' is (as its derivation might suggest) a more colourful, 'butchering' word. It is the word hugely favoured by the more histrionic prose of orators and rhetoricians. Some figures:[21] Seneca *rhet.* has 'occido' 320 times, 'interficio' only 5 times; Quintilian in the declamations is very similar in his preference. Cicero shows the same tendency, but more moderately: his speeches contain 160 examples of 'occido', 121 of 'interficio'; conversely, the less coloured style of his philosophical works offers 27 'interficio' against 10 of 'occido'. The orators therefore incline to 'occido'. In the spoken tongue, too, this colourful word was popular. This is indicated by the partiality of Petronius ('occido' 16;[22] 'interficio' only once, in the parodic epic, at 123.228); and we can infer its spoken role from the persistence of the word in Italian ('uccidere').[23]

Striking is the objection of poetry to all three words, 'interficio', 'occido' and 'neco'. Axelson gives excellent and eloquent figures.[24] 'Interficio' we might think of as metrically uncongenial; no such feeling can be entertained in regard to 'occido', or 'neco'. I pick out just one indicative statistic from Axelson. In all the pages of Ovid there is no example of 'interficio' and only one (*Fast.* 2.693) of 'occido'. The poets, Ovid and Vergil among them, opt generally for words or phrases with more colour than 'interficio' and colour different from that contained by the somewhat lurid 'occido' of popular and rhetorical parlance: 'sterno', 'perimo', etc.[25]

Like most poets Vergil avoids all use of 'interficio'. He stands out from most however in that he admits 'occido' three times:[26] at 10.312, 11.193, and 11.811. (And he uses 'neco' once at

---

[20] Löfstedt, *Syntactica*, ii. 344 f.; cf. Sallust: 'interficio' 21, 'occido' 16.

[21] From Löfstedt, loc. cit.

[22] In addition, Buecheler restores an example in 74.

[23] Cf. Palmer, 168–9, Löfstedt, *Syntactica*, ii. 342 f.

[24] Axelson, 65 f.

[25] Axelson, 67.

[26] The three examples in the *Aeneid* are the only three in all Vergil. Figures for use of 'occido' by other poets (from Axelson, 66): Lucr. 1, Catull. 0, Horace *Carm.* 0, Tibull. 0, Prop. 0, Luc. 0, Val. 0, Sil. 1. Only Seneca matches Vergil with four in his tragedies. It is unsurprising that these rhetorical tragedies should tolerate the rhetorical word. It is perhaps surprising that Vergil's example did not give more legitimation to 'occido' in the eyes of Lucan and the Flavians. Instinctive feeling against it must have been strong.

8.488.)[27] He will not completely remove his narrative from the familiar butchery of ordinary speech and orator's conjuration. Particularly notable is his application of the verb to the butchered Latins in the scene of cremation, at 11.193; note another grim effect alongside, 11.200 'ardentis spectant socios'.[28] Remarkable too is the use of the familiar verb to refer to, more exactly to anticipate, the death of the warrior maiden Camilla in the 'narrative through imagery' at 11.811 'occiso pastore … magnoue iuuenco'.

iii. Dying: obeo, obitus

Dying is the other most popular activity in war. In poetry one tends to die pathetically, emotively, colourfully. The neutral term 'morior' possessed enough of the right qualities to make it acceptable to poets; in addition poetry favoured terms like 'pereo', 'occumbo', 'occido',[29] of which at least the last two may still strike us as resonant and suggestive, if we think of their derivation.

'Obeo', effectively a periphrasis ('mortem' *sim.* may be expressed or not),[30] seems a dull and uncoloured way to express 'die' compared with, say, 'occumbo' and 'occido'. It certainly did not appeal to the Roman poets. Lucretius for his own rather special purposes can use it, and Horace puts it to service three times in the Odes (2.17.3, 20.7, 3.9.24). But the evidence of our literary sources would suggest the label 'prosaic' in the Augustan age (and afterwards); 'obitus' = death seems prosaic in the same way.[31] However, we should note that neither word is popular in all prose. Although *TLL* 'obeo' reports that, with 'mortem', the verb 'spectat ad mortem uiolentam passim' (and reports similarly for 'obeo' absolutely and 'obitus'), Caesar has no 'obeo' in this sense and 'obitus' thus only at *Gall.* 2.29.5; and Livy offers (as far as I can see) only 5.39.13 and 28.22.8 (but 'mortem obeo' is frequent e.g. in Cicero). It looks as if 'obeo', 'obitus' may be

---

[27] Mezentius' monstrous executions: 'sanie taboque fluentis / complexu in misero longa sic morte necabat'; cf. above, n. 19.

[28] See II.1.

[29] Axelson, 104 f.

[30] Cicero always uses it with an object expressed: cf. *TLL* s.v. 'obeo', Axelson, 105 n. 24.

[31] Axelson, 105, with n. 27. But Axelson misses the evidence of the inscriptions: see below. Statistics too in Austin on 4.694.

not so much uncoloured as possessing the *wrong* colouring—for some prose as well as poetry.

There is a further fact to be mentioned in connection with the two words. 'Obitus' and 'obeo' (in combination with 'mortem' *sim.* or, usually, absolutely) belong to the parlance of tomb-stones.[32] The death of person after person is recorded in this spare manner. Here is how Everyman recorded the death of Everyman, on occasion after occasion. Everyman chose not to differentiate the deaths that he experienced from those experienced by another, and he chose not to emotionalize the event with poetical words. So here is a special nuance possessed by 'obeo' and 'obitus': they reflect the death of everyday, the deaths that are recorded on the tombstones of ordinary people. This everyday colour will have kept them out of poetry. To Caesar the words seemed (I guess) civilian; to Livy, wrongly coloured (and civilian).

Vergil makes a small use of the words. Emotive and colourful deaths crowd the *Aeneid*, in suitable diction. But just occasionally Vergil sounds a less glamorous note. Observe a subsidiary invocation at 12.500–3:

> quis mihi nunc tot acerba deus, quis carmine caedes
> diuersas obitumque ducum, quos aequore toto
> inque uicem nunc Turnus agit, nunc Troius heros,
> expediat?

What god would now unfold to me in song so many bitternesses, what god the diverse slaughters and decease of generals, whom now in turn Turnus, now the Trojan hero hounds over the plain?

'Obitus' is the kind of death a poet does not normally sing, the death of everyday ('caedes', partnering it here, is more dramatic and frequent in poetry). For Vergil death is ordinary as well as heroic: the death of generals may not always be so different from the decease of Everyman, and there is room in his song to make this point.

The everyday tone of 'obitus' is again exploited, very arrestingly, at 4.694:[33]

---

[32] The quickest way to verify this is to consult the index volume of *CIL* VI.

[33] The prosaism is noted, given statistics, and discussed by Austin ad loc. Austin makes much of the plural, to me implausibly ('May the plural here not be "intensive", marking the slow agony of Dido's death, the tortured moments one by one?' He compares uses of θάνατοι. I doubt whether the plural in itself is very significant).

> tum Iuno omnipotens longum miserata dolorem
> difficilisque obitus Irim demisit ...

Then all-powerful Juno, pitying her long agony and the difficulties of
her death (decease?), sent down Iris ...

The massive emotions, the dignity and heroism, that Dido *in
extremis* has displayed, are here, at the last moment, cruelly
reduced. The process of death can be the final bathos, even for a
heroine, and such is the case, from one point of view, with Dido.
Vergil's 'obitus' classes her with unnumbered ordinary people
gone to their everyday deaths. Then, however, Iris' action in
cutting a lock of her hair to dedicate to Dis casts her in the role
of Alcestis.[34] She transcends again. Dido, transcendent and
ordinary: Vergil preserves a balancing act in characterization
which we shall see repeated below (sections 2 and 3).[35]

Vergil's single example of the verb 'obeo' in the sense of 'die' is
a special case, quite different from the above, but very interesting. At 10.641 the 'umbra' concocted by Juno to deceive Turnus
is compared to a ghostly apparition (another sort of 'umbra'):

> morte obita qualis fama est uolitare figuras.

like the shapes which are said to fly about after decease.

The phrase 'morte obita' focuses us on an allusion to Lucretius'
scientific account of ghostly 'simulacra'. Cf. Lucr. 1.131–5:

> uidendum
> ... quae res nobis uigilantibus obuia mentis
> terrificet morbo adfectis somnoque sepultis,
> cernere uti uideamur eos audireque coram,
> morte obita quorum tellus amplectitur ossa.

We must see ... what thing it is that meets us and frightens our minds in
waking life, when we are afflicted with disease or when we are buried in
sleep, so that we seem to see and hear in our presence those whose bones
earth embraces after decease.[36]

Lucretius takes up the topic in 4.33 ff., featuring the verb 'uolito'
(36 and 42).

---

[34] Cf. Eur. *Alc.* 74 ff., Servius on 3.46, Austin on 4.698. Vergil *allusively* (cf. Lyne
Further Voices, ch. III) casts Dido in the role of Alcestis.

[35] Cf. too how 'caedes' balances 'obitus' above.

[36] Lucretius balances the prosaic and the suggestive in line 135 much in the
manner that Vergil was to adopt: cf. above p. 109.

If Vergil's simile projects a belief in ghosts, Vergil is 'recharging his Lucretian model with the mythological content that Lucretius had striven to dissolve'.[37] On the hand if we detect a touch of scepticism in Vergil's 'ut fama est', the allusion to Lucretius the scientist confirms it, with interesting results. The allusion is here ambiguous, the intertextuality enigmatic—but certain.

iv. Combat

Much of Vergil's narrative of fighting is demonstrably imaginative and 'other': poetical in diction, and content. He needs to establish that his warriors are not mere legionaries. Turnus throws, but it must be admitted throws ineffectively, a stone 'which twice six men of today's quality would scarcely shoulder' (12.897 ff.). But if Vergil is to induce us to see in the war a reflection of our own civil war, he must also anchor its combat in our reality. We find touches of diction exploited to do precisely that.

Phrases involving 'confero' were common prosaic methods to signify battle being joined (*TLL* IV.180.5 ff.). Such phrases signified everyday, contemporary battle being joined, and thus were not liked by the poets. Very common in prose was 'signa confero' (IV.180.40 ff.); Vergil exploits this phrase, at 11.517, to anchor his narrative (or rather, direct speech in narrative): 'tu Tyrrhenum equitem conlatis excipe signis'; the use of 'excipio' in this line is also quite prosaic (*TLL* V.2.1255.24 ff.). But we note his caution. This is his only use of 'signa confero'. Other very common prosaic 'confero' phrases (e.g. 'castra c.' IV.180.73 ff., 'pedem c.' IV.180.16 ff.) he does not use at all.

A 'confero' phrase that is prosaic but less frequent (perhaps less assertively everyday), one that for Vergil the heroic poet helpfully stresses single combat, is 'manum, manus confero' (*TLL* IV.180.55 ff., e.g. Cic. *Font.* 12, Liv. 9.5.10). This Vergil uses several times: 9.44 'ergo etsi conferre manum pudor iraque monstrat' (here the hypotaxis, in particular the conjunction 'etsi',[38] reinforces the prose tone of Vergil's utterance), 9.690,

---

[37] Hardie, 91; cf. the description of this common Vergilian procedure as *remythologization* at Hardie, 178.

[38] Axelson, 88; on hypotaxis, prose and poetry see Quinn, 428 ff., Norden, *Aeneis Buch VI*, Anhang II.2, Wilkinson, *GLA*, 189 ff.

10.876, 11.283, 12.345, 480, 678. He echoes Lucretius' variation
on 'confero' phraseology, 'conferre manu certamina pugnae'
(Lucr. 4.843, *Aen*. 10.146 f. 'inter sese ... certamina belli /
contulerant'). He also concocts his own phrase at 10.734 f.
'obuius aduersoque occurrit seque uiro uir / contulit.'[39] In these
examples we may again judge Vergil to be anchoring his combat
narrative, but with even more caution in the exercise of his
policy, discriminating between and adjusting 'confero' phrases.

'Manum, -us, consero' ('join battle'), somewhat like 'm.
confero', is prosaic, but not over-common, and is perhaps not
assertively ordinary (Pl. *Mil*. 3, then Caes. *Civ*. 1.20.3, etc., but
also Ov. *Her*. 12.102, *Fast*. 3.282, and some later poetry; *TLL*
IV.416.21 ff.). Vergil makes this more vivid, particular, and
colourful by writing 'consere *dextram*' at 9.741 (in which he was
followed by Stat. at *Silv*. 1.6.60). Cf. how Ovid adjusts 'manum
confero' to 'dextram confero' at *Fast*. 1.569 (thus too Amm-
ianus, cf. *TLL* IV.180.65 f.). Ovid and Vergil here anxiously
keep their diction in touch with, but just outside, mundane
military parlance. Cf. how Aeneas in book 2 says 'proelia ...
conserimus' at 2.397 f., a phrase which is used by Livy (28.16.5,
42.65.7) and occasionally by later writers, and is allied to other
phrases ('certamen', 'pugnam', etc. 'consero') which are used
in prose, but far from commonly or exclusively so (*TLL*
IV.416.43 ff., 417.10 ff.). Aeneas is given a soldierly, but not too
soldierly phrase. On the topic of Aeneas' diction see sections 2
and 3.

v. The action of weapons

On a couple of occasions Vergil brings heroic conflict abruptly
into our experience. He brings what weapons do abruptly into
our range of perception, by using prosaic words. But this time
they are not *military* prosaic words.

At 11.10 occurs Vergil's single use of the verb 'perfodio', in a
description of the dead Mezentius' armour:

---

[39] Two constituent elements here are (1) 'uiro uir', cf. Hom. *Il*. 13.131 ἀσπὶς ἄρ '
ἀσπίδ' ἔρειδε, κόρυς κόρυν, ἀνέρα δ' ἀνήρ, Furius (*Annales Bellici Gallici* IV) fr.
10M 'pressatur pede pes [cf. Enn. *Ann*. 584 Sk.], mucro mucrone, uiro uir' (*Aen*.
10.361) and (2) the common phrase 'se conferre' (*TLL* IV.182.72 ff.). Combined
they produce a notable new effect, which among other things recalls, but is far
from limited to recalling, military phrases involving 'confero'.

> bis sex thoraca petitum
>
> perfossumque locis

his breastplate attacked and dug through in twice six places.

'Perfodio' is a word avoided by the poets in Vergil's time. It does not occur at all in Enn., Lucr., Catull., Hor., Prop., Tib. or Ovid. Prose uses it for various manual and technological tasks: digging channels through land obstructions and the like: Liv. 4.22.6 'donec perfosso ... monte erecta in arcem uia est', 33.17.6 'freto, quod perfossum manu est', Vitruvius 2.1.5 'itinera perfodientes'. In Plaut. and Ter. we find two examples, consonant with these: Plaut. *Mil.* 142 and *As.* 563 of holes dug through walls (also *Mil. Argumentum* II. 10 similarly). It is because of this kind of unglamorous denotation, the word's attachment to familiar kinds of jobs, that most poets found the word unstimulating and therefore avoided it.

Vergil transfers it to the action of a weapon. There it is effective. The action on which it normally unglamorously focuses (digging) is familiar to us. We may be relatively unfamiliar with the action of a weapon, or disinclined to think about it. The verb, eye-catching in itself (*qua* prosaic in a poem), exploits our familiarity with the one area of life forcibly to illuminate the other. We must appreciate the graphic idea of a weapon digging its way through.

The action described here has important implications; Vergil has an ulterior motive in composing a striking phrase for it. This damage was not done to Mezentius' breastplate during the battle, so far as we can judge (10.783–6, 856 f., 893 ff.). It is presumably due to posthumous mutilation. Aeneas did not therefore comply with Mezentius' request at 10.904 f.[40]

I should add that 'confodio', also used of the action of weapons by Vergil (9.445, Vergil's only example), may not have the same effectiveness as 'perfodio', at least not by Vergil's own time. The verb is fairly prosaic,[41] but its application to weapons is at least as old as Sallust (*Catil.* 28.1, 60.7).

Vergil is the first to transfer 'perfodio' to weapons, according to our evidence. His precedent then legitimizes a use, in the common manner: Luc. 3.660, Stat. *Theb.* 9.767 etc., also Tac. *Ann.* 3.15.

---

[40] This insight is owed to Dr D. P. Fowler. Contrast R. D. Williams on 10.905: 'he fears that his body may be found and maltreated by those he had caused to hate him. Virgil does not tell us whether Mezentius' request was granted.'

[41] Bömer, 5.

A not dissimilar effect is achieved by Vergil with the word 'perforo'. He has two examples in all. At 10.485, Turnus' spear hits Pallas thus:

> loricaeque moras et pectus perforat ingens.

through the delay offered by his breastplate, through his huge chest it bores.

And at 10.589 Lucagus is smitten in the groin:

> tum laeuum perforat inguen

it bores through his left groin.

'Perforo' is a prosaic word, in particular a 'business' prose word, employed in various technical or semi-technical and scientific contexts. It is in some respects a similar sort of word to 'perfodio', but it tends to be used of smaller scale operations and actions ('bore through', 'pierce', rather than 'dig through'). Cf. *Bell. Alex.* 46.5 'multae (sc. quadriremes) ... rostris perforatae merguntur', Liv. 38.7.11 'operculum ... dolii ... pluribus locis perforatum', Colum. *Arb.* 8.3 'antiqua terebra ... urit eam partem quam perforat', etc. It is frequently employed by the medical writer Celsus (13 examples). It is a verb he uses to describe a variety of perforations that occur naturally (e.g. 8.1.11 of the perforations in the middle of spinal vertebrae) or by medical operation (e.g. 7.25.3 of infibulation). I return to Celsus below.

Because of this narrow, precise, and fairly uninteresting denotation, poets found little time for it. There are no examples in Enn., Catull., Prop., Tib., or Hor., one example in Lucr., which is consonant with the prose use (5.1268 'et leuia radere tigna / et terebrare etiam ac pertundere perque forare'), and three in Ovid (stimulated by Vergil, see below). Vergil found a use for it. He uses it of the action of a weapon, not a thing that writers normally do. As with 'perfodio', he exploits our familiarity with one area of life—we know what 'piercing' or 'boring' involves—to enhance our perception of what a spear does to human flesh, which may not be so familiar. Wounds are brought abruptly into our ken. Their effect is conveyed to us with disturbingly unexpected, 'clinical' precision.

There is a difference between the effect of 'perfodio' and the effect of 'perforo' which we should notice. The action of the verb 'dig through' ('perfodio') is familiar to us, but the verb is not familiar to us in its application to weapons; it is illuminating of the action of weapons, but, considering its normal sort of context, it is applied to weapons pretty *metaphorically*. The action of the verb 'pierce through' ('perforo') is familiar to us, but the verb is not familiar in its application to weapons; it is illuminating of the action of weapons, and, I would imagine, though not familiarly applied, is quite literally applied to them: cf. Celsus below. (We might note that the effect of 'perforo' and 'perfodio' is again similar in that both *qua* prosaic in a poem are eye-catching.)

Celsus, as I said above, uses 'perforo' thirteen times, utilizing the word's precise denotation to describe precise actions and conditions. Interestingly, on three occasions he too uses it of a wound, not a thing that writers normally do: 7.4.3A 'nam uenter saepe etiam telo perforatur', 7.16.1 'nonnumquam autem uenter ictu aliquo perforatur ... si tenuius intestinum perforatum est ...' Vergilian influence is hardly likely. Celsus simply observes and describes the action and effect of a wound with the same clinical objectivity which he accords to describing, e.g. a doctor's operations. He is being clinically precise, and this clinical precision has produced the unexpected locution. The effect in context is rather different. Clinical precision of description does not surprise or disturb in a clinical text, it does in a poem. Vergil and Celsus arrive at the same end by different routes, for different reasons, and with different effects.

Note (*a*) the coupling of this prosaic and in context ugly word 'perforo' with the more suggestive 'moras' at 10.485. Vergil likes such combinations of the acutely concrete and the abstract.[42] Another and closely related example may be cited. Columella and Lucr. above show that 'perforo' and 'terebra', 'terebro' are semantic near neighbours. Vergil makes pointed use of 'terebro' too. 'Terebro' is a 'business' prose word for 'bore'.[43] Vergil exploits it for special effects at 2.38 and (especially) 3.635:

---

[42] Cf. 3.366 'denuntiat iras' below p. 126.

[43] Cf. Cato *Rust.* 41.3, Vitruv. 9.8.4, 10.16.5, Colum. 5.9.15, etc. 'Terebro' is not used by Enn., Catull. Prop., Tibull., Hor., Luc., Val., Sil., Stat. There is one example in Lucr., two examples in Ovid. Lucr. 5.1268 quoted above and Ov. *Fast.* 6.697 use the technical word straightforwardly for its technical sense. *Met.* 6.260 puts it to

> et telo lumen terebramus acuto.

and we bore through his eye (but 'lumen', poetical for 'eye', more literally means 'light') with the sharp weapon.

Again we find the telling combination of prosaic concrete and expressive abstract. Vergil's phrase here is a creative distillation of an effect that Homer achieves by means of a quite lengthy simile (*Od.* 9.384 ff., 'even as when a man bores a ship's timber with a drill ... even so we whirled the stake in his eye.')

Note (*b*) that we are accumulating quite a bag of Vergilian special effects in connection with the death of Pallas: 'perforo' at 10.485, 'petit ore cruento' at 10.489, 'impositum scuto' at 10.506; and 11.67 ff. are discussed in VII.1.

Ovid's three uses of 'perforo' are, revealingly, stimulated by Vergil: *Fast.* 5.711, *Met.* 12.377 'uno duo pectora perforat ictu', *Trist.* 3.9.26. There is little sign this time of further legitimizing effect.

2. Aeneas' narrative of the sack

Vergil exploits some of the language of 'business' military prose in the narrative of the sack in book 2. We could say that he does so for the same general reason as moved him in the narrative of war in books 7–12, outlined at the beginning of this chapter. It may also be that he has an eye to the characterization of Aeneas. Aeneas has been shown to think and act on important occasions like a Roman general;[44] perhaps Vergil has a mind to give him a touch of the parlance of a general too. I have mentioned one partial example of this already (Aeneas' use of 'proelia consero', above, V.1.iv), and I cite another forthwith. I shall then show Aeneas using other ordinary diction, besides military diction, which may also have the effect of characterizing him.[45]

Military language occurs at 2.347. The band of desperate Trojans gathers; Aeneas narrates thus:

---

splendidly grim effect, perhaps under Vergilian influence: 'sanguis ... emicat et longe terebrata prosilit aura.' Even in prose, outside the most technical of 'business' prose, the word is rare (no examples in Sall., Caes., Cic., Liv.). Plautus finds it useful for a humorous metaphor (*Bacch.* 1199); also at Fr. 13 and 14.

[44] See Nisbet, '*Aeneas Imperator*'.

[45] Ernout, 'Review' 59 remarks that we might expect to find prosaic turns of phrase in characters' speeches; and he cites a couple of examples.

quos ubi *confertos* ardere in proelia uidi ...

When I saw them in close order burning for battle.

Describing troops in close order, Aeneas calls them 'confertos'. This is a largely prosaic word, a technical term very commonly used by 'business' military prose (Caes.; still technical in Vegetius; Livy, etc.; on the poets see below) to describe troops in massed order. It is a technical term whose normal denotation involved a phenomenon of contemporary military practice. Such military practices were deemed properly the province of prose genres. Hence the word is largely prosaic.

We should, however, note, by the by (but the point will be germane in a moment), that the word offered poets some imaginative possibilities *outside* military contexts, and these possibilities were exploited. Outside a military context, its normal prosaic sense becomes an exploitable connotation; and the use of the word can be almost metaphorical. Cf. e.g. Enn. *Ann.* 378 Sk. 'conferta rate', Lucr. 6.509 'nubes', Verg. *Georg.* 3.369 'confertoque agmine cerui', Luc. 3.575 'conferta cadauera', *TLL* IV. 171.81 ff. In the Lucan passage, for example, 'conferta' denotes the mass of corpses; but it brings to mind (by its connotations) the close order of living troops, producing a grim irony, a kind of ghastly quasi-metaphor.[46] Lucan produces an inventive combination, almost (to put it another way) an oxymoron, 'corpses in close order of battle'; and he will have been alert to the fact that the word would be eye-catching in his context from the beginning *qua* prosaic in a poetical text.

Aeneas' use at 2.347 is not inventive in this way. It is a relatively straightforward use of the prosaic word in its normal sense. This understandably is very rare in the poets, who avoided it in favour of more imaginative modes of conveying massed soldiers (modes suggesting 'otherness'). From *TLL* (IV.172.28 ff.) I can gather no more than the following examples in poetry, besides *Aen.* 2.347, and they are close to it rather than exact parallels: Sil. 4.158 'conferta per arma', 7.390 'densis legio conferta maniplis', 10.75 'membra ... conferta uirum', Stat. *Theb.* 6.261 'conferti ... bellatrix sedere cohors'. (The paucity of

---

[46] Housman ad loc. defends the reading with his customary patience (there is a v.l. 'conserta'), and adduces parallels.

examples in post-Vergilian epic is notable, given Vergil's precedent and his frequent ability to legitimize, I.4 *init.*) Vergil, I surmise, exploits its militarily precise tone to characterize the language of general Aeneas. But, lest he should be too dully characterized, hero Aeneas is promptly provided with more expressive language ('iuuenes, fortissima frustra / pectora ...'): the balancing act.[47]

What Lucan and others do with 'confertus', Vergil does with 'confligo'. 'Confligo' is a largely prosaic word, and its predominant use is to refer (intransitively) to military conflict (= 'clash', 'do battle'): cf. Caes. *Gall.* 5.15.1 'acriter proelio cum equitatu nostro ... conflixerunt' etc. (it is a good 'business' prose word), *TLL* IV.239.1 ff.; Lucr. 3.833 is among the very few poets to use the word thus (and he has another and more imaginative use at 2.86: see below). It will be prosaic *because* its use was largely monopolized by a contemporary military action ('doing battle'). Cf. the situation with 'confertus'. Cicero uses it in a marginally extended way (*Cat.* 2.25, 'causae'), but its sense is, in Vergil's time, very largely the limited military one—which scared off most poets. Not, however, Vergil; or in fact Lucretius.

Here is Vergil's (single) use (2.416 ff.):

> aduersi rupto ceu quondam turbine uenti
> confligunt, Zephyrusque Notusque et laetus Eois
> Eurus equis ...

As when at times a tornado breaks and hostile winds do battle, the Zephyr, the South wind, and Eurus rejoicing in his Orient horses ...

He uses it to denote the collision of winds. But because of its normal use it brings to mind the clash of *troops*. Its effect in this context is therefore metaphorical. Cf. how Lucan had exploited 'confertus'. In fact Lucretius had done something similar with 'confligo' itself, using it of the clash of atoms at 2.86: 'cum cita saepe / obuia conflixere'. I would call this metaphorical, and describe Lucretius' procedure as essentially the same as Vergil's.

Now, military imagery is commonly enough applied to storm winds in Vergil and others, but here there is a particular effect. These storm winds make up a simile for human military conflict: the conflict between the Trojans and the gathering Greeks

---

[47] Cf. pp. 110 and 125–7.

(413–5). 'Confligunt' can therefore be termed an example of trespass (IV.5), narrative language trespassing into the simile, here making within the simile a not unfamiliar metaphor.[48] Or rather, the metaphor itself is essentially familiar (human conflict imaging storms), but this is an arresting instance: for the word 'confligunt' is, *qua* prosaic, intrinsically eye-catching in our text, and it focuses our attention on very everyday, *real* conflict. Vergil effects therefore a striking trespass. And Aeneas is characterized. His high-flying imagery (storm-winds) is put on a solid and soldierly footing by this item of military ideolect.

There is another point to be made. The conflict between the gathering Greeks and Trojans imaged in the simile is not actually described. This is how the simile is introduced (2.413–5):

> tum Danai gemitu atque ereptae uirginis ira
> undique collecti inuadunt, acerrimus Aiax
> et gemini Atridae Dolopumque exercitus omnis:

Then the Greeks, with groaning and anger at the snatching of the girl, gather from all sides and attack, fiercest Ajax, the two sons of Atreus, and the whole host of the Dolopians:

Narrative brings Trojans and Greeks into *imminent* conflict, no more. The *actual* conflict is 'narrated' in the 'battle' of the winds. In other words the simile *substitutes* for an explicit narrative of human conflict in the manner described in the previous chapter (IV.2). 'Confligo' has trespassed from a narrative which we in fact have to supply from the imagery of the simile. It is the trespassed residue of such a narrative.

Compare 'latro' at 7.588 (pp. 96 ff., esp. 98 f.). Like 'latro' 'confligo' signals, *qua* narrative trespass into simile (a narrative term explicit in the diction of the simile), that the simile 'narrates'. And it itself, like 'latro', constitutes a substantial part of that 'narrative'. But the two cases are different as well as similar. Unlike 'latro' (and like, say, 'acies' at 10.408) 'confligo' is a member of a fully substitutive simile. This means that whereas the narrative content of 7.588 was desirable, that of 2.416 ff. is essential. But 'confligo' has a quality different from that of 'latro': it is prosaic. This helps us not to oversee the simile's

---

[48] Cf. Homer's trespassing use of συμβάλλω at *Il.* 4.453, recognized as trespass by Porph. 1.17.

essential material. *Qua* prosaic, 'confligo' catches the eye; it then directs our attention on to its crucial sense (human conflict) without obfuscation or diverting resonances: for that is in the nature of such a denotative prosaism. 'Confligo' is being exploited for much else besides the characterization of Aeneas.

The simple verb 'gemo' is strikingly preferred to the compound 'congemo' in imaginative prose, 'business' prose, and poetry. For example, Cicero use 'congemo' once, at *Mur.* 51 'congemuit senatus frequens', but 'gemo' twenty times (*Or.* 12, *Phil.* 4, *Rhet.* 0, *Epist.* 4). Vergil uses 'congemo' once, at 2.631, but 'gemo' eighteen times (*Ecl.* 1, *Georg.* 4, *Aen.* 13). The question arises: What quality excludes 'congemo' from more common literary use? And what makes Vergil (and Cicero) resort to it on a single occasion?

A tendency towards compound rather than simple verbs is exhibited by both prose and the spoken tongue (and poetry typically exhibits the opposite tendency).[49] Compounds where the preverb simply intensifies (as 'con-' does in most if not all the surviving examples of 'congemo') are more especially the product of the popular language.[50] Cicero's figures for 'congemo' / 'gemo' (among others) confirm that 'congemo' is not prosaic. And a small amount of positive evidence suggests that we are right to call it colloquial. Exceptionally, therefore, Vergil would be resorting to a word of the popular tongue. (Likewise Cicero?—but Cicero may have an additional or other reason in that he wished to say that the senate gave vent to a joint and simultaneous groan: i.e. the 'con-' preverb with him may not be simply intensive.)

Before attending to Vergil I assess the positive evidence for colloquial status in 'congemo'.

The appearances of 'congemo' are according to *TLL* as follows: Cic. *Mur.* 51, Lucr. 3.934 (constructed with a direct object), Verg. *Aen.* 2.631, Petronius 23 (where it was emended by Jahn but retained, I think correctly, by Warmington) and 100, Val. 5.12, Stat. (2), Suet. (1), Apul. (1), and then a few examples in later Latin.

---

[49] See Bömer, 4, also Bömer on Ov. *Met.* 4.233, Palmer, 170, LHS 2.298 ff., R. D. Williams on *Aen.* 5.41, Norden on 6.620.

[50] Cf. Marouzeau, *Traité*, 130 ff.

Valerius and Statius probably use the word simply because Vergil does ('legitimizing effect').[51] The two examples in Petronius ('gemo' 4, of which three are, interestingly, in verse) are the only positive colloquial evidence *prima facie* (besides the inference from the fact that the verb is a 'con-' compound). But Lucretius' use (3.934) is notable, for the context is special. A personified 'Natura' mocks mortals for bucking death ('quid mortem congemis ac fles?'). Now a popular, even vulgar tone in 'congemo' would cohere with the general tone of this speech; in particular it would cohere with the wording of Natura's preceding and first line, which is demonstrably colloquial: 'quid tibi tanto operest, mortalis, quod nimis aegris / luctibus indulges?.'[52] Even more obviously it would cohere with the opening wording of Natura's second speech, 955 ff.: 'aufer abhinc lacrimas, baratre, et compesce querellas.'[53] And this I conclude is why Lucretius exceptionally admitted 'congemo' ('gemo' 2): because it was colloquial and thus cohered with Natura's other diction. *Qua* colloquialism 'congemis' directed Lucretius' readers to a common sort of everyday groaning, not the politer activity of literature. Nature, generally brusque and abrasive in her parlance, is here piqued that men should moan about death, and bluntly says so. (Note, however, that Lucretius slightly mutes the colloquialism by setting it in an artistic transitive construction.)

Vergil and Aeneas also exploit the value of the colloquialism. 2.624 ff.:

> tum uero omne mihi uisum considere in ignis
> Ilium et ex imo uerti Neptunia Troia:
> ac ueluti summis antiquam in montibus ornum
> cum ferro accisam crebrisque bipennibus instant
> eruere agricolae certatim, illa usque minatur
> et tremefacta comam concusso uertice nutat,
> uulneribus donec paulatim euicta supremum
> *congemuit* traxitque iugis auulsa ruinam.
> descendo...

[51] All three Flavian passages carry other clear echoes of Vergilian diction. In particular note that Stat. at *Theb.* 10.791 f. uses 'uicta' in close proximity, cf. Vergil's 'euicta'; at 2.569 'tremefactum' in proximity. (In the latter example the 'con-' prefix is given a particular point, making the example a special case.)

[52] See E. J. Kenney on Lucr. 3.933.

[53] It is by no means certain that Lucretius wrote 'baratre' but, as Kenney *ad loc.* says, 'one thing is clear, that Nature is made to employ a colloquial term of abuse, at home in diatribe-satire but alien to the didactic epos.'

Then indeed all Ilium seemed to me to settle into the fire, and Neptune's Troy to be overturned from its foundations: even as when on mountain tops farmers emulously press to overturn an ancient ash-tree which has been hacked with many a blow of iron and axe; ever it threatens, and it nods with trembling leaves and shaken crest, until gradually vanquished with wounds it *groans* for the last time and torn from the ridge comes crashing down. I descend ...

Aeneas uses 'congemo' to denote the groaning noise emitted by the toppling tree. Within the simile, the use is metaphorical since the verb naturally refers to human groaning. Cf. the use of 'confligo' above, though here the metaphor is plainer; there are other similarities between this and the 'confligo' passage which may be noted (my discussion of the two words and their effects may be compared). Vergil uses a groaning metaphor of the toppling tree; but the tree makes up a simile attached to the fall of Troy. 'Congemuit' can thus be seen as an example of trespass, narrative trespass to simile (IV.5): the fall of Troy encompasses much groaning of men, and this notion has trespassed to appear in the 'groaning' tree. It is a striking trespass. The colloquial 'congemo' is intrinsically eye-catching in a poetical text, and it focuses our attention on a vividly familiar, real groaning, the groaning that you and I do, not the politer article. Vergil therefore effects a striking trespass. And Aeneas is characterized. His high-flying imagery (the toppling tree) is put on a very human footing by this word of familiar parlance.

There is another point to be made. The groaning of humans resulting in the trespassed term 'congemuit' is not actually described, any more than the 'conflict' of Greeks and Trojans was. In the narrative (see lines 624 f., quoted above), only the physical fall of the structure of Troy was referred to; and it was to illustrate this that the simile was ostensibly adduced. The suffering of humans—their groans—which accompanies this structural fall is narrated *by the simile*, by the groaning of the ash-tree. The simile *substitutes* for such a narrative; 'congemuit' is the trespassed residue of such a narrative. The simile substitutes for other manifestations of human suffering, besides groans. 'Vulneribus', 'euicta' and probably other items of diction in the simile are proper to the human condition, and have trespassed like 'congemuit'.

Once more (as for example in the case of 'confligo'), trespass, the presence of narrative terms in the diction of the simile, helps us to see the narrative function of a simile; and once more the trespassed terminology itself constitutes a large part of that narrative. And 'congemuit' is special. *Qua* colloquial, it directs our attention to a very particular but relevant kind of groaning, the groaning of ordinary people, *our* groaning. Ordinary people suffer even in the sack of heroic cities. So the diction—obliquely—tells us. 'Congemuit' is exploited for much else besides the characterization of Aeneas.

In these last two examples we see Vergil brilliantly enhancing one characteristic technique with another, his practice of constructing 'trespass' with his exploitation of ordinary diction.

3. Aeneas' parlance, continued

I now give some more examples of lower range diction exploited by Vergil to characterize Aeneas in book 2. Our hero's epic narrative is given a welcome grounding in the speech of Roman men.

At 2.469 ff. Pyrrhus is pictured at the threshold of Priam's palace. Aeneas the narrator rises to a splendid, epic snake simile (2.471–5). Then, says Aeneas (476), along with Pyrrhus was Periphas and Automedon, Achilles' charioteer:

> una ingens Periphas et equorum agitator Achillis,
> armiger Automedon ...

Along with him was huge Periphas, and Achilles' charioteer, armour-bearing Automedon ...

For 'charioteer' Aeneas says, not 'auriga' the normal literary word,[54] but 'agitator (equorum)'. 'Agitator' is the regular and common colloquial word for a charioteer in a circus race.[55] This is shown perhaps most strikingly by epigraphic evidence. 'Agitator' is the standard term on inscriptions for references to charioteers in the games. See Ruggiero s.v. ('E l'auriga proprio dei ludi circensi ... così detto più frequentemente nelle lapide'), with examples and very interesting analysis, and *TLL* I.1329.40 ff;

---

[54] Ennius is so keen to depart from the everyday that he avoids even 'auriga', essaying a metaphorical 'gubernator' at *Ann.* 465 Sk.; this is quoted at Quint. 8.6.9 as a 'tralatio' for 'agitator'.

[55] Cf. Servius *auct.* on 2.476: 'agitator: auriga, secundum usum communem.'

inscriptions often interestingly record the factions to which charioteers belonged, e.g. *CIL* VI.10048.1 '[C. Appu]leius Diocles agitator factionis russatae'. The rare occurrences in literature clearly support such a description of the word, and I will not waste time adducing them: *TLL* I.1329.17 ff. I comment only on those that might appear to contradict it, but in fact rather confirm it.

Cicero at *Lucull.* 2.94 uses the word, but in a simile, and we may infer that the speaker is affecting a colloquial image and tone: '"nihil me laedit," inquit, "ego enim ut agitator callidus prius quam ad finem ueniam equos sustinebo"'.[56] Manilius 5.71 f. alludes thus to the constellation normally known in Latin as 'Auriga' (*TLL* II.1499.82 ff., Hyg. *Astr.* 2.13.1 'Heniochus. hunc nos Aurigam latine dicimus'):

> ille [Heniochus] dabit ... caeloque retentas
> quas prius in terris agitator amauerat artes.

He will provide ... the skills which, as a charioteer, he once loved on earth, and now retains in heaven.

Why does Manilius says 'agitator', and not e.g. 'auriga', given that the scansion could be arranged? Because, I imagine, he wishes to draw a contrast between the erstwhile mortal skills of the eponymous charioteer and their present manifestation in the heavens: what is now so magnificent was once lowly; the comparatively lowly word 'agitator' accentuates a contrast between 'then' and 'now'. Finally, Vergil himself has one other example of the word, at *Georg.* 1.273 'tardi ... agitator aselli'. He chooses the word because, I think, it can yield the general sense 'driver' *sim.* that he needs and at the same time allows him to pun humorously on the sense 'charioteer'.

General Aeneas is thus given a *popular* word at 2.476. We might note, however, that users of 'agitator' did not normally deem it necessary to add 'equorum', as Vergil does at 2.476; and as Ovid does at *Am.* 3.2.7 'o cuicumque faues, felix agitator equorum'. The phrase thus specified probably has a more formal impact than the word on its own. The proper and idiomatic racing enthusiast, the man who uses 'agitator' in a genuinely

---

[56] 'Callidus' I suspect had popular tone. Cf my feelings expressed in connection with 'calleo': ch. I, n. 23.

colloquial way, has no need to specify; a man distanced from the track and its language might think it necessary to make the addition (cf. a cricketer's use of the word 'bowler', where a stranger might while trying to affect the cricketer's ideolect add, in a stilted fashion, 'bowler *of the ball*'). This interpretation is supported by the context of *Am.* 3.2. The speaker makes it clear, in an amusingly ponderous periphrasis, that while trying to participate in the sport for his own present purpose, he is no habitué of the circus (1, 'non ego nobilium sedeo studiosus equorum'). The addition of 'equorum' may thus slightly diminish the colloquial tone at *Aen.* 2.476, counteracting an excessive impression that Aeneas is a man of the track. Note too that before he descends to the language of ordinary men with 'agitator', Aeneas rises to the heights of the snake simile; and after 'agitator' he ascends once more to the dignity of 'una omnis Scyria pubes'. Vergil performs a balancing act with the diction of Aeneas.

To conclude the section, I cite in list form a few further examples of diction which seem to me designed to give hero Aeneas some anchorage in the parlance and reality of everyday men (viz. colloquialisms and prosaisms). I refer only to examples which are unique or almost unique to Aeneas' diction. This list is of course not supposed to be exhaustive; the examples have struck me from time to time rather than resulted from a rigorous search. I cite all occurrences of each word in Vergil. (Similar items of diction could be cited from the direct speech of other characters, e.g. Sinon, Juno.)[57]

aedifico. At 2.16. Prosaic. *TLL*: 'legitur inde ab Enn. per totam latinitatem; poetae uero raro uerbo usi sunt hi: Enn. (semel), Plaut. (8ies), Verg. (semel), Hor. (quater), Ov. (semel) ...'. Horace uses it thrice in *Serm.* (and all in the same satire, 2.3), and once in *Epist.*, i.e. the prosaic / colloquial genres. Lucr. 0, Prop. 0, Tib. 0. The 'business' prose writer Caesar uses it five times in *Gall.* and *Civ.*, Sall. 2, Liv. 35.

trucido. At 2.494, also 12.577 (narrative). Prosaic. Austin on 2.494: 'It suggests business-like, matter of fact butchery'. Axel-

---

[57] On Juno's diction see II.7 and Lyne, *Further Voices*, 52–3.

son, 66 f. illustrates the avoidance of the word by poets. Livy uses it 43 times, but Caesar in *Gall.* and *Civ.* not at all, and Sall. only once. Sallust's example (*Cat.* 58.21) is instructive: 'sicut pecora trucidemini'; cf. Liv. 5.44.7 'uelut pecudes trucidandos'. The word was more coloured than Austin implies (too coloured for Caesar?), but coloured in the wrong way for poetry.

attrecto. At 2.719. Prosaic. *TLL* provides perspicuous evidence of its prosaic status. 'Attrecto' was quite frequently used idiomatically of forms of sexual 'handling' (e.g. Plaut. *Poen.* 350, Cic. *Cael.* 20; cf. Adams 186 f.), which might have alienated some poets. For a use close to ours, cf. Liv. 5.22.5 'primo religiose admouentes manus, quod id signum more Etrusco nisi certae gentis sacerdos attrectare non esset solitus.' More congenial to most poets would have been 'tracto', simplex pro composito, more poetarum: cf. 'congemo', 'gemo' above.

incredibilis. At 3.294. Prosaic. *TLL* 'inde a Plauto, Ter., Rhet. Her., Varrone, Cic.; e scriptoribus adamat Cic. (238ies),[58] raro legitur ap. Liv. (7ies), deest e.g. ap. Cels., Petron. e poetis habent Plaut., Ter., singulis locis *Com. Pall.*, Verg., Hor.' Horace's single example occurs at *Carm.* 2.17.21.

denuntio. At 3.366, also *Georg.* 1.453. Prosaic. *TLL* 'praeter Verg. (bis) et singulis locis Lygd., Prop., Ov., ... uocem deuitant poetae; frequentant Cic. (88ies),[59] Liv. (48ies)[60] ...' Note that Vergil conterbalances its tone by putting it in a suggestive combination with 'iras'.

lassus. At 2.739 (P²w, Austin, recte, 'lapsa' M, 'rapta' P¹adr), also 9.436 where it has trespassed from narrative into Euryalus' poppy simile; and *Georg.* 4.449. Colloquial. See Austin on 2.739, a good note; among other illustrative material he cites *CIL* 1.2138.4 'heus tu uiator lasse qui me praetereis'. See too Axelson, 29 f. ('*lassus*, das den Komikern ... geläufig, in der gesamten Prosa des Goldalters aber nur durch bell. Alex. 30.2 zu belegen ist ...').

explico. In the sense of 'expound', 'narrate' at 2.362. Also at

---

[58] 241, according to my count assisted by IBYCUS.
[59] With IBYCUS I count 94.
[60] IBYCUS:47.

Georg. 2.280 and 335 in other senses. Prosaic, especially in the sense of 'expound', 'narrate', as the evidence in *TLL* shows. Catullus uses it twice, but in indicative ways, at 1.6 and 53.3. In the first he refers to the practice of an historian, in the second to that of an orator; and in both cases he may be assumed to be reflecting the diction that an historian / orator might use to describe his own actions. Note how Vergil combines the prosaic word with a phrase that is suggestive and expressive: 'quis funera fando / explicet.' That balancing act again.

VI

Imagery, Extortion, Exploitation

1. Further trespasses

Aen. 8.241–6:

> at specus et Caci detecta apparuit ingens
> regia, et umbrosae penitus patuere cauernae,
> non secus ac si qua penitus ui terra dehiscens
> infernas reseret sedes et regna recludat
> pallida, dis inuisa, superque immane barathrum
> cernatur, trepident immisso lumine Manes.

But the cave of Cacus and his vast palace were uncovered and visible; deep within the shadowy cavern lay open: even as if the earth should by some force gape deep within and unlock the infernal abode, opening up the pallid kingdom hated by the gods, and the Shades should tremble at the incoming light, as the vast abyss was descried above them.[1]

Hercules tears open Cacus' cave. The simile (deriving from *Iliad* 20.61 ff.) has a clear 'narrative' function: the Underworld imagery adds to the story an insinuation which Vergil makes in other ways,[2] namely that Cacus has chthonic, Underworld affinities. A question occurs. Why is Cacus' cave called a royal residence, a palace, a 'regia'? 'Quia ibi tyrannidem agitaret', Tib. Claud. Donatus; 'sicut Cacus putabat', Servius;[3] 'with undertones of despotism, like *arx* and *aula*', Eden, comparing (after Servius), *Aen.* 1.140, Aeolus' 'aula'; 'hendiadys' (with 'specus'), Gransden.

---

[1] 'Superque' is written from the point of view of the 'Manes': see Eden ad loc. In the translation I have reversed the order of the last two clauses to make the English slightly more natural.

[2] Cf. Galinsky 38 ff.

[3] This I think is incorrect, but it is an interesting comment. Servius means, I take it, that in this word Vergil is narrating from the point of view of Cacus: he thinks that 'regia' is an example of what Heinze, 362, would call 'die Empfindung der handelnden Personen' written into the narrative, and Otis, 46–8, would call 'the subjective style'; cf. too Lyne, *Further Voices*, 227 ff. This is wrong, I think (contrast 'superque', n. 1), but it is interesting that he should be aware of the possibility.

None of these is very helpful. Cacus, it should be noted, was no
king and no Aeolus. At his 'aula' Aeolus did rule, over the winds.
No similar role was performed by Cacus. Cacus was a monstrous
terrorist rather than a monarch.

The simile adds the suggestion that Cacus is chthonic, specifically it adds an affinity between Cacus' dwelling and the
Underworld, between Cacus' 'specus' and the 'infernas ... sedes',
the '*regna* ... pallida'. Here is the source of 'regia'. The idea of
'regnum' has *trespassed* from the simile and produced its cognate
'regia' in the narrative. Now we can see the function of 'regia': it
reinforces the suggestion that Cacus' dwelling is hellish; both
'narrative through imagery' and narrative imply the infernal status
of Cacus' dwelling, imply an affinity between it *and the kingdom of
the dead*. What is important about 'regia' is that, because it is
produced by trespass, it suggests *infernal* (royal) abode; its basic
sense of palace, royal abode is comparatively unimportant.

Because it is the result of trespass, 'regia' implies '*infernal*
royal abode'. This is a sense which it cannot naturally or in
isolation have. We might say that the process of trespass *extorts*
this unexpected sense from 'regia'. In this case simile trespass
into narrative has an effect on diction which it does not on, say,
'nubes' at 10.809 or νέφος at *Iliad* 4.274 (IV.5).

'Manes' (246) also trespasses into the narrative. It appears in
'umbrosae'. When we realize that 'umbrosae' is the result of
trespass, we see that unexpected sense is being extorted from it
too. Intrinsically this is quite an inoffensive epithet, a word
which means usually no more than 'shady' or 'shadowy'. Produced by trespass here, it is given the penumbra of the 'Umbrae',
the Shades. Such a sense is more directly and explicitly extorted
by Seneca at *Med.* 741 'opacam Ditis umbrosi domum'.[4]

Aen. 12.65–9:

> cui plurimus ignem
> subiecit rubor et calefacta per ora cucurrit.
> Indum sanguineo ueluti uiolauerit ostro
> si quis ebur, aut mixta rubent ubi lilia multa
> alba rosa ...

---

[4] H. Nettleship in Conington–Nettleship comments: 'With "umbrosae cavernae"
may perhaps be compared Homer's ἠερόεντα Τάρταρον Il. 8.13'. Misplaced I
think, but the instinct is interesting.

A great blush kindled fire in her and ran through her heated face. As when someone stains [more exactly, 'defiles'] Indian ivory with blood-red dye, or when white lilies blush mingled with many a rose ...

I remind us of the conclusions which we have already come to concerning this simile (IV.2). Imagery hereabouts suggests that Lavinia is 'on fire'. The stained ivory simile adds *by allusion* the notion that Lavinia is wounded. Wound and fire: images of Lavinia's love, just as much as they had been images of Dido's love. Narrative insinuation and narrative through imagery tell us that Lavinia is in love with Turnus. Another conclusion was that there is a patent trespass of narrative to simile here in 'rubor' ... 'rubent' (IV.5). This helps us to see a narrative function in the simile in question, as such narrative trespasses always do. But 'rubent' is not a particularly interesting example. It does not itself provide much of the narrative we are invited to see: it has trespassed from something that is still explicit in the narrative.

'Violauerit' here is arresting, likewise 'sanguineus'. 'Violo' is a startling and novel word to use of the action of dye. For a start, it has very strong moral connotations: a fair translation of it is 'pollute' or 'defile'.[5] In addition Vergil and others often use it of physical injury: in four out of its eight other uses in the *Aeneid* (all Vergil's examples of 'uiolo' occur in the *Aeneid*) it makes up a formula 'uiolauit uulnere' *sim.*[6] This latter nuance (a sense of 'wound') is obviously reinforced by 'sanguineus', 'bloody', which is by no means an inevitable epithet of purple.

The novelty of the combination, 'uiolo' and 'sanguineus' with mere dye, might make us ask: Whence and why? And it might make us think of trespass. For the novelty of 'uiolo' / 'sanguineus' seems to be alerting us in the same way as 'latro' did at 7.588 (Ch. IV. p. 99): again we have strange metaphor (perhaps rather, catachresis) within the simile, the sort of phenomenon that narrative trespass to simile produces. So we then ask: what might this novelty of sense correspond to, what might it have

---

[5] Clearly Vergil's 'uiolo' has its origins in Homer's μιαίνω at *Iliad* 4.141, in the source simile for *Aen.* 12.67 ff. As I showed above (IV.2), *Aen.* 12.67 ff. alludes to *Il.* 4.141 ff. I considered the effect of the allusion in general terms, but not in the particular respect of 'uiolo' / μιαίνω. Nor do I do so here. The point I wish to make about 'uiolo' here is more clearly communicated if the question of the intertextuality is left on one side; but a complete interpretation would have to take account of it.

[6] 11.277, 591, 848, 12.797.

trespassed from in the narrative? Or is the simile, as was the case at 7.588, substantially adding the notion to the narrative, the notion of which 'sanguineus' and 'uiolo' are the trespassed residue? Thus at 7.588 'latro' was the trespassed residue of the notion of 'baying Italians', which the simile, in fact largely 'latro' itself, added to the narrative. In combination the words 'uiolo' and 'sanguineus' suggest *wound*. And that is the notion which the simile, *by allusion*, adds to the narrative. So we have our solution. 'Sanguineus' and 'uiolo' are the trespassed residue of a narrative to the effect that Lavinia is wounded, i.e. a narrative of an *image* of Lavinia's love, which is in fact added to the narrative by the *allusive* power of the simile—and by the trespassed terms 'uiolo' and 'sanguineus' themselves.

'Violo', as well as connoting wound, also connotes *moral* defilement. 'Violo' has trespassed from a narrative of Lavinia's wound, i.e. an image of her love. Vergil therefore suggests that Lavinia's love defiled her—a suggestion which he counters with another.[7]

This example of trespass, 'sanguineus' and 'uiolo', is like 'latro', but subtler and at a further remove from perspicuity. We should also note that Vergil is making two words (one neutral, one poetical[8]) work very hard. Or we could say that he is extorting a great deal of sense out of them.

2. ludus

Aeneid 7.377–84:

>   immensam sine more furit lymphata per urbem.
>   ceu quondam torto uolitans sub uerbere turbo,
>   quem pueri magno in gyro uacua atria circum
>   intenti ludo exercent—ille actus habena
>   curuatis fertur spatiis; stupet inscia supra
>   impubesque manus mirata uolubile buxum;
>   dant animos plagae: non cursu segnior illo
>   per medias urbes agitur populosque ferocis.

---

[7] Cf. *Further Voices*, 122.

[8] 'Sanguineus' looks like a poetical word popularized by Vergil himself. Here are some figures: Enn. 0, Lucr. 0, Cic. *poet*. 0, Hor. 1 (*Carm*. 1.27.4), Verg. 13 (*Ecl*. 2, *Georg*. 1, *Aen*. 10), Prop. 0, Tib. 1, Ov. 9, Luc. 7, Val. 9; Caes. *Gall*. and *Civ*. 0, Cic. 1 (*Div*. 2.60), Liv. 2, Sall. 0. On adjectives in -*eus* and their extenstion in the poetical language see Leumann, 148 = Lunelli, 163 f.

In frenzied abandon Amata rages throughout the great city. Just as at times a top spins under a whirled whip; boys intent on the game urge it in a wide circle around an empty court; it, driven by the whip, is borne on in a curving course; the youthful throng bend over the whirling boxwood, puzzled and amazed; their blows give it life: with no slacker course is Amata driven through the midst of the city and its fierce people.

The advertised illustrative function of this simile was mentioned in IV.1. It is in fact a simile which furnishes several patent correspondences: whip / Allecto's snake, top / Amata, boys, youthful throng / Allecto. It is also a simile which far from being limited to illustration makes striking additions to the narrative.[9] I mention just one such addition here. It is stressed that the actors in the simile are children and that they are engaged upon a game: emphases irrelevant to any perceptible illustrative function. We should be reminded of Apollo's sandcastle simile (IV.3): ours is making a similar point. For Allecto, the cruel attack has the mere significance of a game; for her it *is* a game, it is fun. 'As flies to wanton boys.' So the simile 'narrates'. As not infrequently Vergil picks up the Iliadic theme of divine 'Unernst'.

The word 'deludo', 'deceive', 'dupe', was probably colloquial in Vergil's time; contrast the neutral words 'decipio', 'fallo'. This is however one of those occasions where precisely contemporary evidence is deficient.[10] The 'de-' preverb makes the claim *prima facie* not unlikely;[11] and the fact that a majority of pre-Vergilian examples of the word fall in Plautus is also prepossessing. Here is a fuller picture. *TLL* cites eighteen examples in Plautus (and one in the *Argumentum* to *Amph.* [add one in *Arg.* to *Tri.*], 2 in Ter., 2 in Cic. (*S. Rosc.* 26, *Agr.* 2.79), a fr. of Varro in Pliny (in an abnormal sense),[12] Hor. *Serm.* 2.5.56 'recoctus / scriba ex quinqueuiro coruum deludet hiantem' ('a civil servant rehashed from a minor official will cheat a gaping crow'), Prop. 2.15.31 'terra prius falso partu deludet arantes' [add Prop. 2.29b.41, if Housman, *Classical Papers*, i. 316 is right], and three in Ovid (*Am.* 1,

[9] Cf. *Further Voices*, 24 f.
[10] Cf. I, pp. 11 f.
[11] Cf. Marouzeau, *Traité* on compounds with intensifying preverbs; though I suppose our 'de-' is not simply intensifying. Cf. 'congemo', V.2
[12] Varr. ap. Plin. *Nat.* 36.203 'gladiatores, cum deluserunt [= finished their 'ludus'], hac iuuari potione'.

Met. 2 (and 1 in *Hal.*)). These are the only examples which *TLL*
cites up to and during the Augustan age.[13] Plautus shows the
colloquial status of the word in his time. The fact that Horace
uses it once in the Satires (and only in the Satires) is some slight
confirmation of its continuing colloquialism; note too Horace's
demotic, although not pellucid, context. The other rare occurrences are consonant with a basic colloquial status and with the
tone in the word that we shall in consequence infer. It is very
plausible to suppose for example that Cicero's examples are
exploiting such status and tone.

'Deludo' will have been colloquial because, essentially, it
referred to the duping of everyday. It suggested, I think, deceptions that were not very serious in their results or implications;
or, if serious in results or implications, were undertaken with a
degree of unseriousness, even frivolity; the prominence of -*lud*- in
the word will have kept such connotations foremost. Cicero in
his two examples will intend the second of these nuances, and
will be implying *inter al.* that the deceivers were contemptuous of
their victims.

Vergil uses 'deludo' twice, at 6.344 and 10.642. We will assume
that on these occasions he is *exploiting* the word, exploiting the
fact that the word catches the eye (*qua* colloquial) and directs the
attention to the sort of everyday duping just described. Here is
6.344; Aeneas speaks to the dead Palinurus:

> namque mihi, fallax haud ante repertus,
> hoc uno responso animum delusit Apollo,
> qui fore te ponto incolumem finisque canebat
> uenturum Ausonios.

For Apollo, never before discovered to be deceptive, duped me in this
one response: his utterance foretold that you would be safe on the deep
and would come to Ausonian lands.

Aeneas sees that Palinurus is dead: Apollo's prophecy that he
would reach Italy in safety is apparently false. Aeneas recalls that
prophecy in language which respects and suits a divine utterance
(prophetic 'cano', poetic diction 'pontus', the grand periphrasis

---

[13] Then two in Phaedrus, and later examples. I have checked this information. I
have made a couple of necessary additions in [ ], but otherwise the information, and
the negative implications of it, seem correct. Here are some figures confirming those
negative implications: Enn. 0, Lucr. 0, Catull. 0, Tib. 0, Caes. 0, Sall. 0, Liv. 0.

'finis Ausonios'). But he refers to the deception that the prophecy has apparently proved to be with the colloquial 'deludo': 'fallax haud ante repertus Apollo *delusit*'. Note that he rejects the word he might obviously have chosen for 'deceive' ('fefellit': note 'fallax' just previously) for the lower one. It is more bitter in its import. Aeneas implies (cf. Cicero) a trick casually undertaken by Apollo—though frightful in its implications. The contrast in tone between 'delusit' and 'qui fore te ...' is powerful. Grandly uttered promises were just an everyday cheat.

Aeneas implies that Apollo undertook his deception in a frivolous spirit (though the implications were terrible). It was a 'ludus'. Aeneas exploits the word to get at the familiar message. The gods sport with us. 'As flies to wanton boys ...'

Note that Palinurus both corrects Aeneas' facts and restores propriety of diction, 347 f.:

> neque te Phoebi cortina fefellit,
> dux Anchisiade ...

Neither did the tripod of Phoebus deceive you, general, son of Anchises ...

As well as the high style, we observe the prim reinstallation of 'fallo'. But when I read the facts as Palinurus then presents them, I am inclined to think that Aeneas was right.

As a final comment on this passage, we may deduce that Aeneas, by employing a colloquial word, is again characterized by diction: cf. V.2 and 3.

At 10.636 ff. Juno constructs a phantom Aeneas to fool Turnus. Two comparisons are provided for it (641–2):

> morte obita qualis fama est uolitare figuras
> aut quae sopitos deludunt somnia sensus.

Such as are the shapes that men say fly about after death; such as are the dreams which cheat the senses when overcome with sleep.

In the second[14] comparison we hear that the phantom is like the dreams that cheat sleepers. As the *TLL* material shows and as we might infer, 'deludo' is most commonly and naturally used with indisputably animate subjects. In Prop. 2.15.31 cited above the verb reinforces an incipient sense of animation in its subject

---

[14] On the first see V.1.iii.

'terra'. At *Aen.* 10.642 it may do the same for 'somnia'.
Alternatively or in addition, the verb should strike us as an
example of trespass, narrative into simile. 'Deludo' has trespassed from an animate subject in the narrative, with which it
would be natural, to this inanimate one in the simile. It has
trespassed from something we can infer in the narrative, Juno's
deceiving intentions in fashioning the image ('effingit', 640)—just
as 'latro' trespassed from something we could infer (7.588, Ch.
IV. p. 98); and, in the manner of 'latro', it is 'deludo' itself which
in the final count actually adds such a notion to the narrative (in
the immediate context we only learn of the fashioning; 'deludunt'
is a 'trespassed residue').

Vergil thus indirectly attributes the word and action 'deludo' to
Juno. He exploits it, and the technique of trespass, obliquely to
make a point about Juno not so dissimilar from Aeneas' point
about Apollo. Although Juno's action here is apparently serious,
and benevolent in intention (she wishes to deceive Turnus in order
to rescue him), the diction implies that her energies and feelings
are not earnestly engaged. Ultimately the root 'lud-' hovers in the
background, questioning the seriousness of the goddess's under-
taking. One is reminded of Iliadic gods, who are apparently, but
only apparently, serious in their concern for mortals.

3. Contrast similes, and perversion of agriculture imagery

At *Iliad* 22.111 ff. Hector debates with himself the possibility of
an unarmed overture to Achilles. After a few lines he rejects it as
absurd: Achilles will just kill him out of hand. And he draws this
comparison (126 f.):

> οὐ μέν πως νῦν ἔστιν ...
> τῷ ὀαριζέμεναι, ἅ τε παρθένος ἠΐθεός τε,
> παρθένος ἠΐθεός τ' ὀαρίζετον ἀλλήλοιιν.

It is in no wise possible now ... to chat with him as a girl and youth do,
as a couple, a girl and boy chat with one another.

For a change a *negative* comparison is drawn.[15] Hector and
Achilles are *not* like a young flirting[16] couple in respect of the

[15] On negative comparisons cf. *Rhet. Her.* 4.59.
[16] This is the obvious implication of ὀαρίζω here.

way they can converse (advertised illustrative function: ὀαρίζειν, (not) chatting). The negative comparison adds a *contrasting* picture. The contrasted picture provides momentary narrative of a happy, peaceful normal life, denied or imminently to be denied to both Hector and Achilles. Vistas of a lost world are suddenly opened up, as the simile pointedly juxtaposes present cruel reality with a reality which might have been. The picture focuses the bleakness of the explicit narrative, 'narrates' how bleak it is. And so on. Such negative pictures can narrate most expressively. I just scratch the surface, pointing in the direction of what Homer means. (I do not touch, for example, the levels of irony which Hector is directing against himself.)

At *Iliad* 22. 158–61 negative imagery, though this time not a developed simile, is employed to comparable effect. Achilles pursues Hector, and

> πρόσθε μὲν ἐσθλὸς ἔφευγε, δίωκε δέ μιν μέγ' ἀμείνων
> καρπαλίμως, ἐπεὶ οὐχ ἱερήϊον οὐδὲ βοείην
> ἀρνύσθην, ἅ τε ποσσὶν ἀέθλια γίγνεται ἀνδρῶν,
> ἀλλὰ περὶ ψυχῆς θέον Ἕκτορος ἱπποδάμοιο.

In the front fled a good man, but there pursued him a much better, swiftly, for it was not a sacrificial beast or an oxhide that they were striving to win, things such as are men's prizes for swiftness of foot; they were running to win the life of horse-taming Hector.

Here the contrasted picture gives momentary narrative of inoffensive competition, an ordinary might-have-been, highlighting thereby the frightful earnest of the actual pursuit. The touch of narrative pertaining to peaceful racing stresses for us, by the contrast, how destructive and deadly this one is.

Immediately after this explicitly negative image, Homer says this (22.162–6):

> ὡς δ' ὅτ' ἀεθλοφόροι περὶ τέρματα μώνυχες ἵπποι
> ῥίμφα μάλα τρωχῶσι· τὸ δὲ μέγα κεῖται ἄεθλον,
> ἢ τρίπος ἠὲ γυνή, ἀνδρὸς κατατεθνηῶτος·
> ὡς τὼ τρὶς Πριάμοιο πόλιν πέρι δινηθήτην
> καρπαλίμοισι πόδεσσι·

As when single-hooved, prizewinning horses run nimbly round the turning-posts; and a great prize has been set forth, a tripod or a woman, at a man's funeral; even so the twain circled with swift feet thrice around Priam's city.

First imagery presents a race (between men) for prizes as *unlike* the race between Hector and Achilles. Then this simile apparently says almost the opposite: that a race (between horses) for prizes is *like* their race. And the two images are made emphatically similar to one another by the repetition of ἀεθλ-, and by the parallel of a pair of prizes. How do we make sense of this?

The first image *states* the negative, is explicit about the contrast, and shows by the contrast how destructive and deadly this present contest is: it is for no ordinary prize. The simile then repeats the prize motif so exactly that we must *infer* from the preceding negative that this is still a contrasting feature. But while we infer this contrast, we may look to see what the simile adds that does not contrast; for it is after all positively phrased. The simile adds a narrative of an inoffensive contest that is, when we are made to think about it, *like* that of Hector and Achilles in that one contestant (Achilles) pursues another (Hector) in what might be mistaken for an innocuous manner—while being *unlike* it in that what is at stake is no mere tripod. It juxtaposes a normality which might have been (a peaceful contest) with an actuality (a lethal contest) which has clear similarities with it as well as the crucial contrast that we infer. The simile thus makes the pursuit of Hector appear something like a ghastly parody of itself, a nightmare version. But here the nightmare is the reality. The simile 'narrates' to us that nightmare has become real.

We may call such similes, where we *infer* a contrast, contrast similes; there are many of them in Homer.[17] In the example I have just looked at Homer helps us to perceive the effect of contrast by placing an explicit negative in parallel imagery immediately preceding. Usually we must dispense with such overt assistance. In a contrast simile a scene is presented as comparable to the explicit narrative, which *is* comparable in certain ways, but which in vital and most powerful ways in fact *contrasts* with it. A contrast simile, where we must infer the contrast, is more expressive than an overtly negative one (like Hector's 'boy and girl') by virtue of the fact that it suggests we absorb similarities as well as dissimilarities. Usually the scene in the simile is evocative of some peaceful normality, while the

---

[17] The article of Porter is most stimulating on this topic. Cf. too Moulton 31, C. W. Macleod, *Iliad Book XXIV* (Cambridge, 1982), 48 f.

narrative tells of war and killing. Seeing similarity as well as dis-
similarity, sensing likeness (a ghastly likeness) as well as unlike-
ness between the simile scene and our battle narrative, we get the
impression that we are witnessing a nightmarishly parodic version of the peaceful reality, not just, as might be the case with an
explicitly negative simile, a reality cruelly different from the lost
might-have-been.

A very common type of contrast simile in Homer involves
agricultural or pastoral scenes. In these the poet juxtaposes a
might-have-been that is supremely peaceful and productive with
a reality (battle, slaughter) which contrasts by its patent destructiveness, while offering similarities that are in truth ghastly. Such
similes are a most fruitful source of the effect of nightmarish
parody, giving us the sense ('narrating' to us) that peace and
productiveness are being distorted and perverted by the present
events. (What they do not add, I would say, is 'relief' or 'respite'
from the battle narrative:[18] properly read they intensify its
horror.)

Iliad 2.474–7 run as follows:

> τοὺς δ’, ὥς τ’ αἰπόλια πλατέ’ αἰγῶν αἰπόλοι ἄνδρες
> ῥεῖα διακρίνωσιν, ἐπεί κε νομῷ μιγέωσιν,
> ὣς τοὺς ἡγεμόνες διεκόσμεον ἔνθα καὶ ἔνθα
> ὑσμίνηνδ’ ἰέναι ...

Just as goatherds easily separate the broad herds of goats when they are
mixed up on the pasture, so did the Achaean leaders muster the heroes
hither and thither, to proceed to war.

The scene to be imagined in the simile is probably herdsmen
dividing up the goats on the pasture into their distinct groups
—each herdsman musters his own goats—with the intention of
driving them home.[19] There is a patent correspondence between
simile and narrative in the action of mustering. Here is the
simile's 'illustrative function': even as the goatherds mustered
their flocks, so did the Achaean leaders muster their troops. We
may infer a positive 'narrative' contribution in connection with
the correspondences herdsman / leaders, herds / army;[20] but

---

[18] A common view, shared in part even by Porter: see p. 65 n. 8.
[19] Fränkel, 76.
[20] We might infer *protectiveness* in the Achaean leaders. Cf. IV.3 and Fränkel,
22 f. on *Il.* 4.274 ff.

there is a contrast to be seen which is crucial.[21] The narrative of
the simile is peaceful and productive. The Achaean commanders
marshal soldiers for the destructive business of war. The contrast
is at its most acute if we imagine, as I think we are supposed to
imagine, the herdsmen organizing their flocks *to go home* while
the Achaeans marshal their men *to go out* to war, ὑσμίνηνδ'. The
simile therefore adds a scene of peaceful normality, a might-
have-been, which has similarities to the actuality of the battle
narrative but also crucially contrasts with it, which is like it but
then crushingly unlike it. We should get the impression that we
are witnessing a nightmarishly parodic version of a peaceful
might-have-been; the simile 'narrates' that peace and productiveness are being distorted and perverted.

I cite a striking example from the end of *Iliad* book 20, lines
495 ff.:

> ὡς δ' ὅτε τις ζεύξῃ βόας ἄρσενας εὐρυμετώπους
> τριβέμεναι κρῖ λευκὸν ἐϋκτιμένῃ ἐν ἀλωῇ,
> ῥίμφα τε λέπτ' ἐγένοντο βοῶν ὑπὸ πόσσ' ἐριμύκων,
> ὣς ὑπ' Ἀχιλλῆος μεγαθύμου μώνυχες ἵπποι
> στεῖβον ὁμοῦ νέκυάς τε καὶ ἀσπίδας· αἵματι δ' ἄξων
> νέρθεν ἅπας πεπάλακτο καὶ ἄντυγες αἳ περὶ δίφρον,
> ἃς ἄρ' ἀφ' ἱππείων ὁπλέων ῥαθάμιγγες ἔβαλλον
> αἵ τ' ἀπ' ἐπισσώτρων· ὁ δὲ ἵετο κῦδος ἀρέσθαι
> Πηλεΐδης, λύθρῳ δὲ παλάσσετο χεῖρας ἀάπτους.

As when a man yokes broad-browed oxen to tread white barley on a
well-founded threshing floor, and quickly is the grain threshed out
beneath the feet of the loud-bellowing oxen: even so at great-hearted
Achilles' hands did his single-hooved horses trample alike on shields
and corpses; and with blood was all the axle beneath sprinkled, and the
rims about the chariot, which drops smote from the horses' hooves and
from the hoops of the wheels. And the son of Peleus pressed on to win
glory, and with gore were his invincible hands bespattered.

This example should more or less speak for itself. Achilles' action
in trampling the dead is presented by the simile's narrative as a
nightmare parody, a perversion of the supremely peaceful and

---

[21] This is not seen by Fränkel, 76. In consequence he is embarrassed by a detail of
the contrast, by the fact that the goatherds are (so he assumes, rightly I think) going
home: 'der Auszug zur Schlacht kann nicht gut mit der abendlichen Heimkehr
verglichen werden. So bleibt dieser Teil der Gleichnishandlung mit gutem Bedacht im
Dunkel.'

productive action of threshing. The brutal destructiveness is thereby focused.

A final example, *Iliad* 11.67–71:

> οἱ δ᾽, ὥς τ᾽ ἀμητῆρες ἐναντίοι ἀλλήλοισιν
> ὄγμον ἐλαύνωσιν ἀνδρὸς μάκαρος κατ᾽ ἄρουραν
> πυρῶν ἢ κριθῶν· τὰ δὲ δράγματα ταρφέα πίπτει·
> ὣς Τρῶες καὶ Ἀχαιοὶ ἐπ᾽ ἀλλήλοισι θορόντες
> δῆουν ...

As when reapers opposite one another drive a swathe through a field of wheat or barley belonging to a man blessed;[22] and the handfuls fall thick and fast: so the Trojans and Achaeans leapt on one another, slaying ...

There is a ghastly similarity, implied this time rather than stated: Achaeans and Trojans cut down the opposing ranks like harvesters cutting down corn. But the contrast between this productive and peaceful agricultural act and the slaughter of the actuality is glaring. The result is that the might-have-been, told by the simile, adds to the narrative the idea that the narrative reality is nightmare, parody, and perversion.

The effect achieved by the last example, killing as harvest, should be familiar to us; it was disseminated by *metaphor*. Metaphor was able instantaneously to project the message that killing is perversion and parody of what is good and productive by terming it, in a bitter irony, 'harvest', vel sim. Thus we have Ares the harvester at Aesch. *Suppl.* 638:

> τὸν ἀρότοις θερίζοντα βροτοὺς ἐναίμοις.[23]

who harvests mortals in bloody fields.

At Aesch. *Agam.* 536 Paris is said to have 'reaped as harvest the house of his fathers, together with its land', i.e. *caused* it to be reaped as harvest:

> αὐτόχθονον πατρῷον ἔθρισεν δόμον.

---

[22] A hint of Hades? μάκαρ is usually an epithet of the gods. The same hint is present, I think, in Vergil's 'dominus diues' at *Aen.* 12.473. Both I suppose would be examples of 'irrational correspondence' (IV.4).

[23] ἐναίμοις Lachmann, ἐν ἄλλοις MSS.

Horace produces Orcus the harvester at *Epist.* 2.2.178 'si metit Orcus'. And the idea is quite popular.[24]

Vergil's use of actual contrast similes I shall glance at in the next section. By and large he does not choose to imitate Homer's great agricultural or pastoral contrast similes of war. But he does capitalize upon the tradition of such agricultural metaphors, centring on harvest. Relying on the familiarity with such a tradition that could be assumed in his readers, relying too on his own deftness in activating ordinary diction through combination, he seeks such effects sometimes with the slightest of touches. Some spectacular examples of this I examine in VII.1 and 2. I show some more conventional material here.

Juno instructs Allecto to set the war in Italy in motion. She includes these words (7.339):

> sere crimina belli

Sow the accusations that lead to war.

The basic sense of 'sero' is sow *seeds*, etc. It may be thought that the image in metaphorical 'sero' is by Vergil's time pretty inert: cf. Sall. *Hist.* 1.77.7 'tumultum ex tumultu, bellum ex bello serunt', *OLD* s.v. 4. If it is inert, it is in my opinion vivified by the immediate context, by 338 'fecundum concute pectus'; for this, I think, is also agricultural imagery, cohering with 'sere'.[25] But in

---

[24] Cf. simile and metaphor (or simile and simile trespass into narrative) deployed with slightly different impact at Euripides *Hyps.* 60.93 (with Bond ad loc.) ἀναγκαίως δ' ἔχει / βίον θερίζειν ὥσ[τε κάρπιμον στάχυν, translated in Cic. *Tusc.* 3.59 as 'uita omnibus / metenda ut fruges'. Grim refinements and details are introduced into the metaphor at *Iliad* 19.222 f. Apollonius uses the metaphor punningly in connection with the killing of the Earthborn, who are in one sense literally a 'crop' at 3.1382 and elsewhere. Cf. n. 27 below. See further C. O. Brink on Hor. *Epist.* 2.2.178–9.

[25] Fordyce glosses 'concute': 'search', 'ransack', saying the metaphor is from shaking out a garment (the metaphor is common, as Fordyce says, with 'excutio'). He compares Hor. *Serm.* 1.3.34 ff 'te ipsum / concute num qua tibi uitiorum inseuerit olim / Natura'. This passage of Horace is a vital parallel, but its significance is not understood by Fordyce (once again I was helped here by Andrew Crompton). In this passage Horace extensively utilizes agricultural imagery: note, as well as '*inseuerit* Natura' (cf. Juno's 'sere'), how the passage continues: 'aut etiam consuetudo mala; namque / neglectis urenda filix innascitur agris.' 'Concute' presumably coheres with this imagery, and the sense behind it is probably 'rake', 'harrow', *sim.*: Horace is saying 'rake through youself, to find whether there are any *uitia*, moral weeds, *filix*.' I can find no exact parallel for 'concutio' in such an agricultural sense, but other agricultural senses can be shown in other '-cutio' compounds: e.g. 'discutio', 'excutio' = 'thresh' at Varr. *Rust.* 1.52.1, and there are more examples of 'excutio'

any case, a line of linked[26] agricultural imagery develops from 'sere', and must retrospectively confirm the metaphor in it. Linked lines of imagery can work like local 'combinations' to extort, should it be necessary, more or less unobtrusive senses.

Allecto sows 'crimina belli', the seeds of war. A line of agricultural imagery starts. Most conspicuous is this: as a result of Allecto's *sowing*, a *crop* of swords appears, 7.525 f.:

> atraque late
> horrescit strictis seges ensibus.

Far and wide there bristles a dark crop of drawn swords.

This, a change from the idea that *men* form the 'crop' of war (as in *Il.* 11.67–71 above), is essentially as old as Homer.[27] In Vergil's context it makes the familiar ironic point from a different direction. The metaphors of 'sero' and 'seges' tell us that instead of seeds we have 'crimina', and instead of corn we have swords. Different detail, but the same fundamental message: war is the perversion of what might have been, a ghastly parody of what is good, peaceful and productive. The destructiveness of war is again highlighted by a bitter irony. (And, be it noted, if the metaphor in 'sere' was inconspicuous—a possibility

thus used (*TLL* V.2.1309.32 ff.; one can 'excutere spicas' or 'grana e spicis'). I think, given the parallel of Horace, that Allecto is being told to 'rake through' her breast; and Juno's implication is probably that she should find *weeds* to *sow*, a suitable paradox. 'Fecundum' of course coheres well with this imagery. And the imagery vivifies 'sere'.

[26] On linked imagery in Vergil see *Further Voices*, 19 f., 193–200.

[27] The origin of the metaphor of a crop of swords lies I think in Homer, e.g. *Iliad* 13.339 ἔφριξεν δὲ μάχη φθισίμβροτος ἐγχείησι / μακρῇς: *Iliad* 23.599 φρίσσουσιν ἄρουραι (sc. σταχύεσσι) shows the image that must be presumed in ἔφριξεν (see too LSJ s.v. φρίσσω). Apollonius clearly assumes such a metaphor in Homer's ἔφριξεν, for he alludes to it, and in a sense puns on it, when describing the emergence of the Earthborn warriors (a 'real' crop), 3.1355 ff.: φρῖξεν δὲ περὶ στιβαροῖς σακέεσσιν ... Ἄρηος τέμενος φθισιμβρότου. Cf. his punning use of the 'harvest' metaphor, above n. 24. At Enn. *Ann.* 384 Sk. 'horrescit telis exercitus asper utrimque' I imagine that the same metaphor is implied as in Homer ('horresco' = φρίσσω): cf. Verg. *Georg.* 3.198 f., of literal crops, 'tum segetes altae campique ... / ... horrescunt flabris' and 1.314 'spicea iam campis cum messis inhorruit'; cf. too Enn. *Sc.* 143J = 140V, with Jocelyn ad loc. Cf. too Polydorus' description of himself at *Aen.* 3.45 f. 'hic confixum ferrea texit / telorum seges': here Vergil, like Apollonius, refers to a 'real' crop while alluding to the metaphor; even more like Apollonius is *Georg.* 2.142 'nec galeis densisque uirum seges horruit hastis; / sed grauidae fruges.' Purely metaphorical again is *Aen.* 12.663 'strictisque seges mucronibus horret / ferrea.' It takes a context like Vergil's in *Aen.* 7 above fully to exploit the image.

I admitted above—the conspicuous 'seges' must retrospectively illuminate it.)

Vergil expands and continues this pair of images with others, the most interesting of which I shall attend to in VII.1 and 2. For now I would point out that such contrast metaphors, what we may call 'perversion of agriculture' metaphors, have particular point in the second half of the *Aeneid*. For the war breaks out actually among Italian *farmers*. Note e.g. 7.520 f. 'raptis concurr-unt undique telis / indomiti agricolae', and especially 523 ff.:

> non iam certamine agresti
> stipitibus duris agitur sudibusue praeustis,
> sed ferro ancipiti decernunt atraque late
> horrescit strictis seges ensibus ...

No longer is the quarrel a rustic one, conducted with hard sticks or fire-hardened stakes, but with two-edged iron they try the issue, and far and wide there bristles a dark crop of drawn swords.

The agriculture metaphors thus make the general, underlying suggestion that war is a ghastly parody, a nightmare perversion of what is good, even as farmers themselves are actually being twisted by the powers of Fate, Allecto, and Rome into soldiers. The events of the narrative give substance and reality to the message of the imagery, furnishing the most pointed concrete example possible. And of course the events of this 'mythical' narrative were quite close to home: 'squalent abductis arua colonis' (*Georg.* 1.507).[28]

4. Contrast similes in Vergil

I said above that Vergil does not choose substantially to imitate Homer's great agricultural contrast similes. But he does, as I have shown, capitalize upon the tradition of agricultural contrast metaphors. He does too have other sorts of contrast similes. And one agricultural simile demands attention.

(a) 10.803–9

10.803–9 is a simile I have discussed in another context (IV.5). It is necessary to recall it:

[28] Cf. the symbolic statement there, *Georg.* 1.508 'curuae rigidum falces conflantur in ensem', with the imagery of 'seges ensibus' above.

> furit Aeneas tectusque tenet se.
> ac uelut effusa si quando grandine nimbi   (803)
> praecipitant, omnis campis diffugit arator
> omnis et agricola, et tuta latet arce uiator
> aut amnis ripis aut alti fornice saxi,
> dum pluit in terris, ut possint sole reducto
> exercere diem: sic obrutus undique telis
> Aeneas nubem belli, dum detonet omnis,
> sustinet ...

Aeneas rages, and keeps himself under cover. Just as when storm-clouds pour down with showers of hail, every ploughman, every farmer flees from the fields, and the traveller lurks in a safe stronghold, under river bank or in vault of high rock, while the rain falls on the earth, that so they may pursue the day's task when the sun returns: even so, overwhelmed by weapons from all sides, Aeneas withstands the cloud of war, waiting for it to spend its thunder ...

I concentrate now on the figures of the 'arator' and the 'agricola' who, according to the obvious correspondence of the simile, parallel Aeneas.

For Vergil and for readers of the *Aeneid* the 'agricola' and his world have very special significance. The farmer's capacity to connote peace and productiveness is evident and vital in the tradition of agricultural imagery examined in the previous section. But the *Georgics* had signally enhanced that capacity. In the *Georgics* Vergil had, in the war-ravaged context of the end of the republic, presented the farmer as the embodiment, or rather the possible embodiment, of a peaceful, productive, and moral life. In the *Aeneid* he often alludes to the farmer or to aspects of his world precisely because, in the aftermath of the *Georgics*, he may be seen as pre-eminently representing such values.[29] Thus, for example, at 12.450 ff. he makes his readers anxious at Aeneas' imminent destruction of the Italian enemy by figuring them in the deeply positive and sympathetic role of 'agricolae'.[30]

Here we have Aeneas imaged as 'agricola' and 'arator': imaged therefore in roles embodying qualities of peace, productiveness, and morality. The simile adds to the narrative such thoughts, thoughts of Aeneas' peacefulness, morality and so on. This is hard to gainsay. On the other hand, it is hard not to say

---

[29] Cf. Lyne, *Further Voices*, 7 f.
[30] Lyne, loc. cit.

something else. We shall see in the process how elusive and guileful a medium 'narrative through imagery' can be.

Two facts give us pause:

(1) The simile occurs in Book 10 after Aeneas' long sequence of vengeful and merciless killings,[31] and immediately before his final killing, the killing of Lausus (and immediately preceding the simile, in line 802, Aeneas has been described as 'furit').

(2) There is the long tradition of contrast similes and metaphors to reckon with. In these, heroes and their violent actions in battle are compared to productive rural figures and events precisely for the effect of *contrast*, to highlight the *destructiveness* of those heroes and their actions. Remember for example Achilles trampling corpses, imaged as a thresher of corn.

Does not the first of these facts, that the context is a battle and, in particular, that Aeneas has been at his most destructive, suggest that we should interpret the simile according to the direction of fact (2)? This would mean that what the simile 'narrates' to us is that Aeneas is now the *perversion* of this productive and moral figure, a parody, a nightmare version of a peaceful might-have-been. I think in fact that this is an inescapable implication. Of course, very many of the reasons why Aeneas is thus at this time are not his own fault. But I think that the interpretation of the simile as a contrast simile is unavoidable, and the highly disturbing message is there—and true.

Two points remain to be made. First, I said above that the positive interpretation of the simile cannot be gainsaid. That is right. It is in the nature of 'narrative through imagery' to imply not state, and it can imply not only multiple but contrary messages.[32] We can if we like see the simile in its positive interpretation as foreshadowing Aeneas' humane reaction to Lausus' death at 10.821 ff.

Secondly, when we see the simile as a contrast simile, we deduce from 'agricola' and 'arator' that Aeneas is the perversion of the man of peace and morality, and so on: we should reflect on the extraordinary quantity and extraordinary nature of the sense that is being thus *extorted* from these neutral words. Vergil uses the context he has established and our knowledge of literary

[31] On which see *Further Voices*, 110 f., and VII, p. 154.
[32] Cf. my deductions about the roses and lilies simile at 12.68 f. in *Further Voices*, 122.

traditions and procedures to extort sense from the words 'agricola' and 'arator' which we could not expect them to convey; just as he used more local combinations to the same end in the passages analysed in ch. II.

(b) 6.309–12

At 6.309–12 the souls of the dead at the river Acheron are described thus:

> quam multa in siluis autumni frigore primo
> lapsa cadunt folia, aut ad terram gurgite ab alto
> quam multae glomerantur aues, ubi frigidus annus
> trans pontum fugat et terris immittit apricis.

As many as the leaves that fall in the woods at the first chill of autumn, as many as the birds that flock to land from the ocean, when the chill season puts them to flight across the sea, and sends them to sunny lands.

Two similes, in both of which there is a more or less advertised illustrative function: numbers, 'multae'. In neither case is this an important function.[33] The first comparison, that of the dead souls to autumn leaves, I shall attend to in VII.4. It adds to the narrative thoughts of the insubstantial and unimportant nature of the souls, and of the human beings they once were: a sad piece of 'narrative' in context.

The second simile compares the souls to migrating birds. There are two prominent sources.[34] The first is *Iliad* 3.2 ff.

> Τρῶες μὲν κλαγγῇ τ' ἐνοπῇ τ' ἴσαν ὄρνιθες ὥς,
> ἠΰτε περ κλαγγὴ γεράνων πέλει οὐρανόθι πρό,
> αἵ τ' ἐπεὶ οὖν χειμῶνα φύγον καὶ ἀθέσφατον ὄμβρον,
> κλαγγῇ ταί γε πέτονται ἐπ' Ὠκεανοῖο ῥοάων ...

The Trojans advanced with shouts and cries, like birds, like the cry of cranes before the sky, which flee from winter and unutterable rainstorm, and with cries they fly to the streams of Ocean ...

The second is Soph. *O.T.* 174 ff.

---

[33] R. D. Williams on 309 f.: 'The main point of the simile ... is the large number of ghosts; ... a second point of similarity...' and so on. He does not touch on the most important function of either simile.

[34] Norden on *Aen.* 6.308 ff. speculates on a lost single source. On the sources see further Clark 254, Thaniel 241 ff.

ἄλλον δ' ἂν ἄλλῳ προσίδοις ἅπερ εὔπτερον ὄρνιν
κρεῖσσον ἀμαιμακέτου πυρὸς ὄρμενον
ἀκτὰν πρὸς ἑσπέρου θεοῦ

You might see one [dead soul] upon another like a well-winged bird flying swifter than irresistible fire towards the shore of the evening god.

We should note that in the first migration to better climes is more or less explicit, as in Vergil's version. In Sophocles the flight is towards 'the shore of the western god', as suits an image for the dead.[35]

That last thought should draw a point to our attention. Migration to a sunnier clime may suit, at least it is not incompatible with, an image for the living Trojans. But surely it does not suit an image of the dead souls seeking admission to the Underworld. Migration 'to the West' will suit (Sophocles). But migration from cold ('ubi *frigidus* annus') to warmth ('terris apricis') is the reverse of what we expect. Warmth is the condition of life, and cold of death, as the previous Vergilian simile shows: 'autumni *frigore* primo' there evokes chill, finality, death.[36] And whatever else Vergil's Underworld may be, it is not *sunny*, the usual sense of 'apricus'.[37]

What of course we have is a contrast simile. The simile adds a picture of a flight to life and warmth, to highlight the cool passage to the Underworld. The passage to the Underworld is shown by the simile-narrative to be a parody, a perversion of a pleasant might-have-been. And so on. It is clearly richly expressive. Vergil, eschewing large imitation of Homer's agricultural contrast similes, confects another and very pathetic example.

It is a contrast simile in one other respect. The birds are sent across the ocean to *warmth*. That is one contrast with the souls. The fact that the birds are sent across *at all* is another contrast with some souls. Some souls are refused even this privilege. The

---

[35] Cf. IV, p. 86. In Sophocles there is so much 'trespass' that one cannot tell if 'the shore of the evening god' is metaphorical with the souls, or part of the bird simile, or both; I would opt for the last.

[36] 'Frigus' both literally and metaphorically is a very death-signifying word. Cf., for example, the penultimate line of the *Aeneid*; and see *OLD* 'frigus' 4a.

[37] Thaniel, 245: 'the ghosts are aptly likened to the defenseless birds that always fly from the seasonal chill of death but like the transmigrating souls eventually return to the shores of light.' This might be a justifiable interpretation in the long term, but does not explain the simile in its immediate context.

unburied must wait; they wander on the banks of Acheron for a hundred years before they can cross. Line 329:

> centum errant annos uolitantque haec litora circum.

They wander for a hundred years and fly around these shores.

They must wait, says the Sibyl, *flying around*. 'Trespass' points to this further contrast. Flying is not unsuited to souls, but I think it is right to detect a touch of trespass, from simile to narrative, from birds to (unburied) souls. This connects the simile to the particular class of unburied souls, and helps us to pick up the fact that the birds are 'narrating' by contrast not just the general fate of the dead, but the peculiarly ill-starred plight of the unburied.

Two other similes with elements of contrast are 2.355 ff. and 8.408 ff. I discuss these (albeit for another purpose) in *Further Voices*, 212 f. and 42 f.

VII

Incitement

Vergil will catch the eye with, say, a prosaic word and then exploit its particular sense (chs. III and V). He may do this just once ('uxorius', III.2) or several times ('conlabor', III.1). In the latter case each example may produce a self-contained effect. Or Vergil may use one exploitation, by its nature 'eye-catching', to initiate a pair or sequence of related effects. We may regard an example of exploitation as a potential incitement to pursue a sequence, for Vergil likes to integrate effects elaborately into his text. Or we can have another, kindred situation. We may be struck by a word, not necessarily prosaic or colloquial, that in its combination is eye-catching, and infer that some important effect is operative; yet scrutiny of the immediate context may leave us unenlightened as to what that full effect is. We should regard this too as an incitement, an incitement to search further abroad for the full explanation. Nothing in Vergil is without explanation or purpose.

1. harvests

I shall here show not just an example of incitement, but an example of Vergilian allusion, i.e. the purposed recall of another text. I shall also show Vergil exploiting 'perversion of agriculture' imagery (VI.3).

The beginning of book 11 stages scenes of burial and lamentation. In particular, Vergil shows us Aeneas lamenting the dead body of Pallas, and preparing it for its last journey home. This is a very dense passage, laden with the tragedy of the dead young hero. Pallas of course was killed back in book 10, his killing attended by various special effects (p. 116). Here we have a kind of reflective epilogue, with further spectacular effects.

At 11.68–71 Vergil compares the dead body of Pallas to a plucked flower:[1]

> qualem uirgineo demessum pollice florem
> seu mollis uiolae seu languentis hyacinthi,
> cui neque fulgor adhuc nec dum sua forma recessit,
> non iam mater alit tellus uirisque ministrat.

They place the young man aloft on a rustic bier: he was like a flower, harvested by a maiden thumb, of soft violet or drooping hyacinth, whose radiance and beauty have not yet faded, but no longer does its mother earth nurture it and give it strength.

This simile is one of a substantial family. The picture of flowers cut down or in some way destroyed had had two basic uses. It had (1) imaged the loss of female virginity in epithalamial contexts, exploiting what must be universal symbolism ('defloration'). And (2) Homer had employed the comparison in connection with the death of heroes, perhaps transposing established epithalamial imagery:[2] the essential fragility of a heroic but mortal frame was thereby eloquently narrated—and much else too.[3] Cf. Sappho fr. 105c (almost certainly epithalamial),[4] Catull. 11.21–4 (an exploitation and inversion of epithalamial imagery),[5] Homer *Iliad* 8.306 ff. (the death of Gorgythion), 17.53–8 (Euphorbus), Vergil *Aeneid* 9.436–7 (Euryalus, based on Homer's Gorgythion).[6] See further Fowler, 'Virgins', especially 187–91, an excellent discussion. But the most important of such passages for *Aen.* 11.68–71 is an epithalamial example, Catull. 62.39–47. Indeed I would argue that Vergil *alludes* to this passage—unless it is to Catullus' source in Sappho. For practical purposes we will have to work with Catullus.[7]

---

[1] On these lines see Putnam 11 ff. Putnam and I clearly worked on these lines at the same time, and without contact. We come to interestingly different conclusions. As always Putnam's work is rich and stimulating.

[2] This is the plausible assumption of Fowler, 'Virgins', 188.

[3] Cf. Fowler, 'Virgins', 188.

[4] Cf. D. L. Page, *Sappho and Alcaeus* (Oxford, 1955), 121.

[5] Fowler, 'Virgins', 189.

[6] Cf. *Further Voices*, 229. In this part of the simile Vergil draws on Homeric precedent; in the first part, 9.435 f. he draws primarily on Catullus and epithalamial / erotic imagery: *Further Voices* loc. cit.

[7] It might well be that if we possessed Sappho 105c complete, this would be revealed as a close source of Catull. 62.39 ff., and as much of a source and as much of an object of allusion for Vergil as Catullus himself; indeed Sappho might be revealed

Catullus 62.39–47 runs as follows:

> ut flos [qui][8] in saeptis secretus nascitur hortis,
> ignotus pecori, nullo conuolsus aratro,
> quem mulcent aurae, firmat sol, educat imber;
> multi illum pueri, multae optauere puellae:
> idem cum tenui carptus defloruit ungui,
> nulli illum pueri, nullae optauere puellae:
> sic uirgo, dum intacta manet, dum cara suis est;
> cum castum amisit polluto corpore florem,
> nec pueris iucunda manet, nec cara puellis.

As a flower which grows secluded in closed gardens, unknown to the flock, torn up by no plough, which breezes caress, the sun strengthens, the rain brings up; it many boys, many girls desire; the same flower, when it has been culled by a slender finger nail and lost its bloom, no boys, no girls desire. So a girl, while she remains a virgin, is dear to her own; but when she has lost her chaste flower, her body polluted, she is neither pleasing to the boys nor dear to the girls.

Particularly similar between Vergil and Catullus is the motif of Nature's support and nurture of the flower, active in Catullus (41), withdrawn in Vergil (71). And Vergil I think in fact *signals*[9] a connection with this piece of Catullus (or its Sapphic source). He identifies the agent who plucks the flower in his simile as a girl ('uirgineo pollice'). In so doing he picks up and interprets a detail peculiar to Catullus 62 ('tenui ... ungui'): in no other surviving example of this family of similes is the plucking agent similarly identified.[10]

as the primary source and primary object of allusion. Note Vergil's specification of 'hyacinthus' at 11.69 and Sappho's ὑάκινθον in 105c. (Fowler 'Virgins', 189 sees *Aen.* 9.435 'purpureus' as looking directly back to Sappho 105c πόρφυρον ἄνθος.) But in the absence of Sappho we must work with Catullus. The argument is not materially affected. Vergil alludes either to Catullus, or to Catullus' source (Sappho) mirrored by Catullus, or to both (on 'double allusion' in the Latin poets, see J. C. McKeown's edition of *Ovid: Amores*, vol i. 37–45). In these circumstances Catullus is sufficient to show what Vergil is getting at.

[8] 'Qui' is added by Spengel and accepted by Goold, correctly I think. Goold also accepts Spengel's supposition of a lacuna after 41 (to achieve a numerical balance between boys' and girls' stanzas).

[9] For Vergil's practice of signalling allusions see *Further Voices*, index: 'Signals' to other texts.

[10] One can easily imagine this detail starting with Sappho. It is she who might most naturally think of a girl as an agent. Catullus' specification '*tenui* ... ungui' is most naturally, but not inevitably, interpreted as a female finger: cf. Prop. 1.20.39, of Hylas: 'quae modo decerpens tenero pueriliter ungui'.

So, Vergil compares the dead Pallas to a plucked flower, a comparison which is one of a family; and simultaneously he signals a connection with a particular source passage, with Catull. 62.39 ff. Now it is my belief that when Vergil uses Catullus in this way, especially if he signals his use, his use is *allusive*—just as much as when he uses Homer. He is alluding to the source text, expecting us to remember it and its context, expecting us to apply them to the new occasion. Now Catullus' plucked flower imaged a girl who *castum amisit polluto corpore florem*, a deflowered bride. Allusively, therefore—in terms of the Catullan text to which he refers—Vergil casts Pallas *in the role of a deflowered bride*: he uses the Catullan text to cast Pallas in this role, just as, for example, he used Homer's text at the beginning of *Aeneid* 1 to cast Aeneas in the role of Odysseus.[11] Now this may seem a strange idea (Pallas as a deflowered bride); but we shall shortly see that it is confirmed, extended, explained. For the moment, we may simply admit that there is no great surprise in Vergil's depicting a beautiful young hero in ambiguous sexual terms.[12]

I put this conclusion temporarily on one side, and turn to consider 'demessum', the word which Vergil uses for the picking of the flower. It stands out and catches the eye, for two reasons. The first is this: as *TLL* swiftly shows, 'demeto' is prosaic, like so many 'de-' compounds.[13] It is a 'business' and other prose word for 'harvest' (Cato, Caes., Cic., Liv., Colum.). Exact figures and examples from a range of poets will support and amplify the *TLL* evidence: Enn. 0, Cic. *poet.* 0, Lucr. 0, Catull. 1 (64.354, a line I shall have reason to quote below: a literal use, within a simile), Prop. 0, Tib. 0, Hor. 1 (in the Satires, a humorous and coarse metaphor which exploits the prosaism, *Serm.* 1.2.45 f. 'accidit ut cuidam testis caudamque salacem / demeteret ferro'),

---

[11] Cf. Lyne, *Further Voices*, 100 ff.

[12] Note Euryalus' comparison to a 'flos succisus aratro' at 9.435. This imitates Catull. 11.22 ff. In both, the male side is figured in female imagery (the virgin flower, cf. above), as the victim of male imagery (plough: Adams 24, 154). Catullus is fond of sex-role reversals in his imagery. We may note too that 'uirgineo ... pollice' at *Aen.* 11.68 images Pallas' destroyer as a maiden girl. The detail of a female picker probably derives from Sappho (cf. note above), and is in any case to be found in Catullus 62. But Vergil's preservation of it carries with it interesting implications—on top of signalling the Catullan-Sapphic connection—which ought not to be ducked.

[13] Cf. above, p. 120 on compounds ('congemo').

Verg. 1, Ov. 0[14] , Luc. 0, Val. 1 (showing the influence of Vergil),[15] Sil. 3,[16] Stat. 0. (Horace and Vergil seem to generate all the poetical examples referred to which are subsequent to them.) The second reason why 'demessum' catches the eye is this. 'Harvest' ('demeto', 'meto') is not a natural word to use of a *flower*—as the *TLL* articles and (for example) Catull. 62.43 quoted above and Prop. 1.20.39 quoted n. 10 show. One gathers or picks, e.g. 'carpit', a flower, one harvests *crops, vel sim.*[17] The collocation with the specific and minute 'pollice' will have rendered the oddity particularly apparent ('demeto' and 'meto' operate naturally with, say, a 'falx'). So the verb's prosaic register catches the eye; and then we find that its area of sense is not an obvious one (we have a slight and designed catachresis). In fact it *adds* a notion to the one we can infer of picking flowers: harvesting. *Pallas*, who corresponds to the flower, has been *harvested*: so this catachresis implies.

This fits into Vergil's line of 'perversion of agriculture' imagery (VI.3). To demonstrate the destructiveness of war, to suggest that war is a nightmarish parody of a peaceful and productive might-have-been, Vergil uses images of agriculture to depict it: a bitter and expressive irony. Allecto was instructed to 'sow', 'sere', the 'crimina belli' (7.339); the result was a 'bristling crop'

---

[14] Unless it is rightly restored (Heinsius, *recc.*) to *Met.* 5.104, which is transmitted in the *uett.* as 'decutit ense caput'. If it is rightly restored, it looks like a derivation from Hor. *Serm.* 1.2.45 f. above. See further n. 16.

[15] Val. 3.157 'hinc rigido transcurrens demetit ense / Protin'. This uses the word 'demeto', as Vergil does at 11.68, but in a context more like that of Vergil's 'meto' at 10.513 (below). Val. has conflated the two, consciously or unconsciously. He may too have been influenced by Seneca or Ovid. See next n. Colum. 10.304 offers a straight imitation of *Aen.* 11.68.

[16] Sil. 4.213 'demetit auersi Vosegus tum colla', 5.286 'ora citato / ense ferit, tum colla uiri dextramque micantem / demetit', 16.102 'tantum acies hominumque ferox discordia ferro / demetit'. The first two of these seem imitated most directly from Sen. *Ag.* 987 'impium ferro caput / demetere', itself probably deriving from Hor. *Serm.* 1.2.45 f. above (unless from *Met.* 5.104: see n. 14). The third Silian example is perhaps more a product of Vergilian influence, 11.68 and 10.513.

[17] An apparent exception with 'meto' confirms the rule, Ov. *Fast.* 2.706 'Tarquinius ... uirga lilia summa metit'. For Tarquinius is *not* 'picking' the lilies: his action is a drastic and violent one (note 'uirga'), and a symbolic one, intended to tell his son to 'metere' in the sense of 'caedere' (i.e. 'metere' as at *Aen.* 10.513 below) the 'principes' of Gabii; which is what his son does (2.709). Ovid's diction is designed to convey both the drastic and the symbolic aspects of Tarquinius' action. (Mart. 10.93.5 'ut rosa delectat metitur quae pollice primo' is an imitation of *Aen.* 11.69 which misunderstands or obscures Vergil's special effect.)

of swords, 'atraque late / horrescit strictis seges ensibus' (7.525 f.); and so on. Now we have this touch, added by 'demetit': Pallas is part of the 'harvest' of war.[18] 'Demeto' is skilfully exploited.

Clearly this sort of 'perversion of agriculture' imagery is a bitter mode of expression. The perpetrators of such 'harvests' (for example) are not flattered by their imagery. Vergil extends the bitter implications of his imagery to Trojans and Italians alike. In particular he extends it to Aeneas; as I shall show.

We know that 'demessum' fits into a line of imagery ('perversion of agriculture'). But 'demessum' itself is particularly striking, an eye-catching exploitation. We might ask if there are any exact parallels. Is there any other example of 'harvest' itself, 'de(meto)' or cognates, used as part of the 'perversion of agriculture' sequence, and making particular point with our present passage? We may be justified in regarding an exploitation like this as a potential incitement to pursue a sequence; Vergil's practice elsewhere indicates that he is inclined to integrate such effects elaborately into his text.

There is one parallel in the *Aeneid* for 'harvest' itself ('(de) meto', 'messis', 'messor') used as part of the 'perversion of agriculture' imagery, and one only. 'Meto' is thus used, for the first time in such a metaphor in surviving Latin,[19] at 10.513:

> proxima quaeque metit gladio latumque per agmen
> ardens limitem agit ferro ...[20]

All that meets him he harvests with his sword, and, aflame, drives a broad path through the column with iron.

At this point in the narrative, Aeneas has been enraged by the death of—Pallas. In revenge he embarks upon a sequence of merciless and ugly killings, a sequence which is troubling for our estimation of the hero.[21] 10.513 is the beginning of it. Vergil images this beginning as a 'harvest', 'proxima quaeque metit'.

---

[18] For this use of 'harvest' cf. Homer, *Iliad* 11.67–9 and other passages cited in VI.3.

[19] See *TLL* VIII.890.35 ff.

[20] 'limitem agit' may be seen as a less explicit version of Homer's ὄγμον ἐλαύνωσιν at *Iliad* 11.68 (see note 18). (But the most important parallel for *Aen.* 10.513 is Catull. 64.353 ff. cited below.)

[21] Cf. VI.4(a), Lyne, *Further Voices*, 110 f.

Right at the start therefore, by the bitter irony of this imagery, he shows that he regards Aeneas as unflattered by his vengeful actions. He shows Aeneas' actions as fitting into a lamentable, nightmarish pattern, one started by the demon Allecto (7.339 ff.). Allecto sowed the seeds of war; Aeneas reaps a harvest. He plays his part in the 'ghastly parody of what is good, peaceful, and productive'.

But the particular connection which we are incited to see and to reflect upon is between Aeneas and Pallas, between the 'harvest' that is Pallas (his death) and the 'harvest' which Aeneas reaps (revenge), stimulated by the death of Pallas. Pallas' 'demessum' directs us to Aeneas' 'metit' and incites us to reflect upon the nature of the relation between the two. We know the relation to be causal: Pallas' death provokes Aeneas' revenge. The imagery shows it to be troubling. One lamentable action is shown to provoke another lamentable action. We lament the 'harvest' that is Pallas at 11.68, its lamentable nature expressed by the imagery; but lamentable too is the revenge, also expressed as a 'harvest', to which it inspires Pallas' protector and avenger in 10.513 ff. But such is the tragic cycle of war: brutality does breed brutality; harvest inspires harvest. This sort of point is there to be taken, if we are sensitive to 'perversion of agriculture' imagery in general and to the significance of 'demessum' and 'metit' in particular, and to the connection between them. And we must too be ready to respond to incitement.

I add a final point on 'demessum' and 'metit'. Beneath all this there is another text, and a splendid allusion. It is well known that Aeneas is substantially modelled during the killings of 10.513 ff. on the vengeful Achilles of *Iliad* 21;[22] and this allusion has troubling implications for our Augustan hero.[23] It is less well known[24] that a splash of colour has been added to Aeneas' Homeric Achilles model from the bloody Achilles of Catullus 64,[25] Achilles the harvester. Vergil alludes to Catull. 64.353–5 at *Aen.* 10.513. Catull. 64.353–5 run:

---

[22] Cf. e.g. Knauer 301 f., Camps 24 and 142.

[23] Cf. Lyne, *Further Voices*, 110 f.

[24] This point was drawn to my attention by Andrew Crompton.

[25] On the particularly brutal colour that Catullus has given to his Achilles, see J. C. Bramble, *PCPS* NS 16 (1970), 25–6.

> namque uelut densas praecerpens *messor* aristas
> sole sub ardenti flauentia *demetit* arua,
> Troiugenum infesto prosternet corpora ferro.

Just as a *harvester* gathering the dense ears of corn *harvests* the yellow fields beneath the burning sun, so will Achilles with his hostile steel lay low the bodies of those born of Trojan stock.

Vergil's 'metit', the first example in surviving Latin of 'meto' used as a military harvest metaphor (see above), recalls Catullus' 'demeto' used eye-catchingly (it is prosaic) in a military harvest simile.[26] Allusion to the Catullan Achilles further brutalizes Aeneas' model, and the implications for our Augustan hero are the more troubling. We should also notice that at *Aen.* 11.68 too, where Vergil uses the compound 'demeto' with a hint of military harvest metaphor, there is allusion to Catullus 64.353–5, indeed from one point of view more direct allusion than at 10.513: Catull. 64.354 is one of the exceedingly few poetical parallels for the use of the compound at 11.68 (see above). Into the agonized scenes of mourning which characterize the beginning of book 11, scenes which display the humanity of Aeneas, Vergil intrudes a hint of the vengeful Aeneas' brutal model: which might suggest to us a variety of emotions.

We left the dead Pallas above allusively imaged as a deflowered bride. Bride? Deflowered? It may seem a strange suggestion. It is confirmed and clarified a few lines later, at 11.77. Aeneas takes out garments[27] to cover the dead Pallas' head[28] and veils him. The phrase Vergil uses for this veiling is:

> arsurasque comas obnubit amictu

and he veils the hair that was about to burn with a garment.

This involves another eye-catching word, though not one that can simply be called prosaic: 'obnubit'. The verb 'obnubo'

---

[26] The striking quality of Vergil's 'meto' takes us to Catullus' striking 'demeto', in the same context. Then behind both is Hom. *Il.* 11.67 ff.; cf. above n. 18.

[27] On these garments see VIII.3.

[28] Vergil writes 'comas' rather than 'caput' *vel sim.* as at 3.405 and elsewhere. In our context it has the great positive advantage that it admits the grim detail 'arsuras'.

(= 'veil') is rare, solemn and archaic: it is used for example in an ancient legal formula.[29]

Aeneas veils Pallas' head. He does so because it is customary to perform that action for the dead.[30] But Vergil uses this unexpected verb: it is *not* customary for that act. Why has Vergil chosen to exploit this verb? It requires some explanation from us. 'Obnubo' was rare and odd enough to attract the attention of ancient scholars. Some grammarians derived the word 'nuptiae' from 'obnubo': marriage, 'nuptiae' ('nubo') was so named, they said, because the bride's head at a Roman wedding was, as is well known,[31] regularly and ceremonially veiled, i.e. 'obnupta', with the 'flammeum'. Festus (p. 174L = 170M) quotes the earlier antiquarians Aelius Stilo and Cincius: 'nuptias dictas esse ... [sc. aiunt] Aelius et Cincius, quia flammeo caput nubentis obuoluatur, quod antiqui obnubere uocarint.'[32] Whatever may be the truth about the supposed derivation of 'nuptiae' or 'nubo' ('marry') from 'obnubo' ('veil') (and it is not to be dismissed out of hand),[33] it is the reverse connection which would certainly and naturally make itself felt: Vergil's reader, meeting the unfamiliar word 'obnubo', would inevitably think of the familiar 'nubo'. More particularly, when Aeneas veils Pallas in death and Vergil uses for that action the word 'obnubo', the reader must surely be made to think of that other and very familiar veiling, the veiling of a bride. So the whole passage from 11.68 ff. now comes together, a partnership of suggestions. Allusively cast as the deflowered bride in the simile of 68 ff., Pallas finds his hinted bridal veil in 77, in 'obnubit amictu'. Who is the bridegroom? The bridegroom of course is Death.

---

[29] See Cic. *Rab. perd.* 13 'Tarquini ... ista sunt cruciatus carmina quae tu ... libentissime commemoras: "caput obnubito, arbori infelici suspendito", quae uerba, Quirites, iam pridem in hac re publica non solum tenebris uetustatis uerum etiam luce libertatis oppressa sunt'; similarly at Liv. 1.26.6, 11. None of my normal labels fits 'obnubo'. It was an archaism in Vergil's time, but not poetical, as most archaisms discussed in literary contexts are. As an archaism that survives typically in legal language, we might call it a legal archaism. Not unexpectedly Vergil's use encourages its adoption by the Flavian epicists—it *becomes* poetical.

[30] Onians, 133 n. 1, 154.

[31] Onians 153.

[32] Cf. too Servius ([DServius]) on 11.77: ' "obnubit" autem uelauit, translatio a nubibus quibus tegitur caelum: unde et nuptiae dicuntur, quod nubentum capita [obnubantur, id est] uelantur'; Ambrose *Abr.* 1.9.93; Varr. *Ling.* 5.72. It is worth stating that in no example available to us (outside the grammarians) is 'obnubo' itself actually used of *marriage* veiling.

[33] See Ernout-Meillet and Walde-Hofmann s.v. 'nubo'.

To suggest the pathos of his young hero's untimely death, Vergil had many images and ideas available to him. For example, he could have intruded the general idea of Pallas' dying ἄγαμος (unmarried) or 'having death instead of a wedding': these are familiar *topoi* in lamentations for the ἄωροι, the untimely dead. Conte argues indeed that such an idea—that Pallas gets death instead of a wedding—is projected by the depiction on his belt (10.496 ff.: the fate of the sons of Aegyptus, the 'thalami cruenti' of their wedding night).[34] I think this is right. When, however, Vergil comes to the lamentation scene in book 11, Pallas' reflective epilogue, he particularizes, pulling off what I think is a spectacular coup. Sophocles had given concrete and grimly vivid form to the idea of 'death instead of wedding': Antigone lamented that she would be the *bride of Death*. At 11.68 ff. Vergil indulges a pattern of feminine imagery[35] to suggest for his hero the same tragic role. Sophocles' Antigone sees herself as marrying Death (*Ant.* 816):

Ἀχέροντι νυμφεύσω

I shall marrry Acheron.[36]

With his characteristically ambivalent perception, Vergil presents his hero Pallas similarly: as the Vergilian Antigone, married to Death—and by Death deflowered.[37] In the words of the text to

[34] On Pallas' belt and the way it signals Pallas' fate as an ἄγαμος and ἄωρος see Conte, *Il genere* 97 ff. = *Rhetoric* 190 ff. For 'death instead of wedding', *sim.*, in lamentations for the untimely dead in literature and on inscriptions, see Conte *ibid.*; the motif derives its power from the belief that τέλος ὁ γάμος, that the goal of life is marriage, and is used of male and female: cf. e.g. W. Peek, *Griechische Vers-Inschriften I: Grab-Epigramme* (Berlin, 1955), 1584.5–6 (of a boy), ἀντὶ δέ μοι θαλάμοιο καὶ εὐιέρων ὑμεναίων / τύμβος καὶ στήλλη καὶ κόνις ἐχθροτάτη ('Instead of the marriage chamber and holy hymenaeal hymns, there was for me a tomb, a gravestone, and most hateful dust'). Note too the inscription of Phrasikleia, the Merenda *kore*: 'I shall ever be called maiden (*kore*), the gods having allotted me this title instead of marriage': see J. Boardman, *Greek Sculpture: The Archaic Period* (London, 1978), 73 and plate 108a. See too n. 37 below. (Cf. too Lucretius' account of Iphigeneia, 1.87–100, and other conceits connected with weddings and funerals listed by J. C. Bramble at *PCPS* n.s. 16 (1970), 31 n. 2.)

[35] Cf. Fowler, 'Virgins', 187 on Homer, *Iliad* 17.50–60. Fowler assumes that feminine bridal imagery is being exploited for Euphorbus.

[36] Cf. too *Ant.* 654, 891.

[37] 'Marriage to Death' became something of a topos, partnering the more general 'death instead of a wedding' (above, n. 34): cf. Eur. *Or.* 1109, *I.A.* 461 τί παρθένον; Ἅιδης νιν, ὡς ἔοικε, νυμφεύσει τάχα ... which gives some prominence to the idea

which Vergil alludes in his simile, Pallas 'castum amisit polluto corpore florem'.

When the narrator says at 10.503 f., in response to Turnus' killing of Pallas, that there will come a day when Turnus will 'wish Pallas untouched bought at great price', 'intactum Pallanta', we can now see that there is a hint of ambiguity, a glance at Pallas' eventual deflowering by death in the word 'intactum' (he will wish a *virgin* Pallas).[38] We can if we like rephrase 10.503 f. in terms implied by the poet: Turnus will regret that Pallas 'castum amisit polluto corpore florem'.

2. primitiae

There are two occurrences of the word 'primitiae' in all Vergil. Both occur in book 11 of the *Aeneid*. The basic use of 'primitiae' is in reference to the first-fruits of agricultural produce that were offered to an appropriate deity.[39] This basic agricultural sense is exploited by Vergil. 'Primitiae' is another detail which he puts to service in 'perversion of agriculture' imagery.

Allecto sows the seeds of war; Pallas is part of the harvest (section 1). Evander sees it more particularly: he sees his dead son in terms of *first-fruits*. He reasons that his son's youth yielded, not something productive (say, fame and glory) which might naturally be termed 'first-fruits', but *death* which is so termed bitterly and perversely. To express his sense of the outrageous perversion of things he apostrophizes Pallas accordingly, referring to his death thus (11.156):

of loss of virginity, *AP* 7.13 (Leonidas XCVIII GP), 182 (Meleager CXXIII GP), Peek, op. cit. 658.8 (Roman III / IV cent.), Gow and Page on Meleager loc. cit. In some, perhaps indeterminate, relation to this topos stands the myth of Persephone.

[38] 'Intactus', 'uninjured': *TLL* VII.1.2068.29 ff.; as a technical term of virgins: 2068.64 ff., e.g. Catull. 62.45, Verg. *Aen.* 1.345.

[39] See *OLD* s.v. But the word is surprisingly rare overall, and its literary register hard to define. I give some more exact information to complement the *OLD*. No examples in Enn., Cic. *poet*, Lucr., Catull., Prop., Tib., Hor.; nor in Cato *Rust.* or Varro *Rust.*, but there is one in Cato's *Origines* (in the basic sense), if Macrobius quoted below reflects Varro's own wording; no examples of the word in Caesar *Civ.* and *Gall.*, or Sall., or Cic.; one in Livy, in the basic sense, 26.11.9 'frugum'; four in Ovid, also in the basic sense, *Fast.* 2.520, 3.730, *Met.* 8.274, 10.433. See further the very useful note of Bömer on *Met.* 8.274. It is plausibly suggested that the word should be restored to accompany 'frugum' at *CIL* VI.32323.11 (Aug. age). Colum. uses the word twice (4.10.2, 10.147) of the first shoots of a plant. Other extended and metphorical uses, some of them prompted by Vergil, are cited in *OLD*.

> primitiae iuuenis miserae ...

Wretched first-fruits of your youth ...'

Pallas' death was a ghastly parody, the nightmare version of what might have been. So Evander expresses, acutely and pathetically, with 'primitiae'.

There is incitement to see if this novel use reverberates. It does. At 11.15 f. Aeneas dedicates his trophy to Mars, constructed out of the 'spolia' taken from Mezentius, with these words:

> haec sunt spolia et de rege superbo
> primitiae

These are the spoils and first-fruits from an arrogant king.

Aeneas exploits 'perversion of agriculture' imagery in bitter, one might say, cynical recognition of the destructiveness of what he has been doing. Spoils for Mars are termed first-*agricultural* fruits; offerings that issue from destruction and war are clothed in language of productiveness and peace. Aeneas recognizes his action to be a ghastly parody of a might-have-been and labels it accordingly, in a grimly exultant irony.

Evander sees the death of Pallas pathetically, as the perversion of what might have been. He suffers from this perversion. Meanwhile the death of Pallas and other such events have so embittered Aeneas that he can glory in perpetrating such a perversion. The harvester (section 1) now dedicates his first-fruits. Brutality breeds brutality, and so on (cf. above p. 155). The point is there once more to be taken, if we are responsive to 'primitiae' and to incitement.

There is an additional point to notice, perhaps mitigating Aeneas' grimness of tone. He may (in addition to what I have said above) be alluding in 'primitiae' to an impiety of Mezentius': Macrobius 3.5.10 explains Mezentius' title 'contemptor diuum' (7.648, etc.) by referring to Cato's *Origines* (fr. 12 Peter): 'ait enim Mezentium Rutulis imperasse, ut sibi offerrent quas dis primitias offerebant ...', 'Cato says that Mezentius commanded the Rutulians to render to him the first-fruits which they used to offer to the gods.' Aeneas may intend by an irony to signal the close of such an epoch. But there is no other reference to the story that I know in the *Aeneid*. And if it is in Vergil's / Aeneas' mind, it partially explains why Aeneas should adopt the word and tone that he does, but it does not remove the interpretation above.

3. praedo, latro

Aen. 7.361–4:

> nec matris miseret, quam primo Aquilone relinquet
> perfidus alta petens abducta uirgine praedo?
> at non sic Phrygius penetrat Lacedaemona pastor,
> Ledaeamque Helenam Troianas uexit ad urbes?

Have you no pity for the mother, whom the treacherous robber will leave as soon as the first North wind blows, heading for the deep and carrying off the girl with him? Was it not thus that the Phrygian herdsman entered Lacedaemon and bore off Ledaean Helen to the city of Troy?

Thus Amata, in reference to Aeneas (the 'praedo', robber or pirate, in her view).[40]. The comparison to Paris is damaging, if unfair. The label 'praedo', designed among other things to anticipate that comparison,[41] is worse.

'Praedo' is a forceful insult[42]—as is 'perfidus'.[43] 'Praedo' not only directly impugns Aeneas' motives, suggesting he is going to steal Lavinia. It is a prosaic word,[44] and its stylistic register has implications for its connotations. It will be prosaic presumably because it referred to the type of everyday robber who actually infested the reality of the Mediterranean world—or to real, everyday people who might be insultingly assimilated to such a class—and not to a buccaneer who had the resonance, let us say

---

[40] And in other people's views too. As well as the refs. below, cf. Iarbas at 4.215–7. It was an accusation that a wandering people might be prone to: note the careful *praemunitio* of Ilioneus at 1.526–9. See further R. C. Monti, *The Dido Episode and the Aeneid, Roman Social and Political Values in the Epic* (Leiden, 1981), 16–17.

[41] Paris too was represented as a robber or plunderer. Hdt. repeatedly uses ἁρπάζω, ἁρπάγη of his snatching of Helen in *Hist.* 1.3; and Paris himself at *Il.* 3.444 uses the same term. Thetis at Stat. *Ach.* 1.45 calls Paris the 'incesti praedonis'. His acquisition of κτήματα along with Helen (*Il.* 3.70, 91, etc.) made him especially vulnerable.

[42] Further discussion in Monti, loc. cit.

[43] 'Perfidus' picks up Dido's refrain: 4.305, 366, 421.

[44] Enn. 0, Lucr. 0, Cic. *poet* 0, Catull. 0, Hor. 1 (*Serm.* 1.2.43), Prop. 0, Tib. 0, Verg. 3, Ov. 4, Luc. 2, Val. 4, Sil. 0, Stat. 3 (some sign of the 'legitimizing effect'), Caes. *Gall.* and *Civ.* 5, Liv. 17, Cic. prose 115. Cicero found the power of the word as an insult, a *Schimpfwort* (see below), very useful.

glamour, to qualify for heroic poetry (cf. pp. 15 f.).[45] Amata therefore not only impugns Aeneas' motives, she denies him the resonant role that in English we might describe with the word 'buccaneer'. In a sense she belittles him (he is an everyday thief)—as she belittles Paris with the label 'pastor'.[46]

An example like this of a prosaic word being exploited is a potential incitement to pursue a sequence. And there is a sequence to pursue. Vergil has two more examples of the word, and both refer to Aeneas again. At 10.774 ff. Mezentius vows thus:

> uoueo praedonis corpore raptis
> indutum spoliis ipsum te, Lause, tropaeum
> Aeneae.

I vow you, Lausus, your very self clad in spoils seized from the robber's body, as my trophy of Aeneas.

At 11.484 the Latin matrons beg Minerva,

> frange manu telum Phrygii praedonis

Break with your hand the spear of the Phrygian robber.

Vergil therefore has three examples of the eye-catching word, and on each occasion he refers it to his hero. The sequence is designed and controlled. It raises a question. I say that *Vergil* refers the word to his hero. In fact, on each occasion the word occurs in direct speech, the product of partisan speakers. The question is: does Vergil have any sympathy with this derogatory view? There is a certain incitement to pursue the sequence further. There are however no further examples of 'praedo'. There is something else.

The opening of book 12 is marked by a striking simile for Turnus. He is compared to a wounded lion, 12.4–8:

---

[45] Not, I think, that Latin possesses a glamorous single word for a robber or pirate. If one wished to refer to someone as a robber glamorously, or in a way suited to poetry, one had to paraphrase his action in innocuous or resonant terms. Thus an act of what seems to be armed robbery on the part of Aeneas is described innocuously at 9.264 'pocula, deuicta genitor quae cepit Arisba'.

[46] Cf. Paris the βουκόλος at Eur. *IA* 180, 574, 1292. Outside epic similes and Homer, 'pastor' and βουκόλος were quite easily pejorative, since these roles were commonly filled by slaves.

Poenorum qualis in aruis
saucius ille graui uenantum uulnere pectus
tum demum mouet arma leo, gaudetque comantis
excutiens ceruice toros fixumque latronis
impauidus frangit telum et fremit ore cruento

As in Carthaginian fields the lion, smitten with a grievous wound in the breast by hunters then finally goes into battle, and rejoices as he tosses his rippling mane on his neck, and undaunted breaks the robber's spear that is fixed in him, roaring with bloody mouth ...

This is a most expressive simile. One thing it does is link to Dido's wounded hind simile at 4.69 ff. (quoted above p. 77): Turnus 'wounded' in imagery links to Dido 'wounded' in imagery, 12.4 ff. to 4.69 ff.[47] (Dido's wound is love; Turnus' is, we should infer, love, grievances in love, and so on).[48] There are patent correspondences of detail between the two similes, bringing the link to our notice; and our perception of it is forcefully assisted by Vergil's specification 'Poenorum' at 12.4 which takes us straight back to Carthage and Book 4.

It is important to see and to interpret this link. Turnus, the formidable and furious opponent,[49] the *lion*, is associated with an image in which the wound is uppermost, Dido's *wounded* hind. This reminds us that Turnus is also the *wounded* lion, a victim,[50] like the wounded hind which is patently a victim. And in fact the linked imagery connects him to a most pathetic victim: Dido. Turnus the formidable enemy may also, as someone injured, be deserving of sympathy—like Dido, to whom he is linked. All this the imagery, the linked imagery, suggests to us.

In 12.4 ff. as well as as 4.69 ff. the simile narrates an agent who has inflicted the injury. In 4.69 ff. it is a 'pastor': Aeneas, we infer.[51] In 12.4 ff. Vergil first of all talks of hunters, 'uenantes'. Then he talks of a 'latro', a word which in his time will mean 'robber', 'brigand', 'thief'.[52]

---

[47] Also 4.2 and 67.

[48] Cf. Otis, 372–3, also Lyne, *Further Voices*, 120.

[49] The simile even contains a suggestion that Turnus is a personification of 'Furor': 'fremit ore cruento' repeats a phrase in the description of 'Furor' at 1.296.

[50] Otis, 373, feels the need to make the opposite emphasis: 'But Turnus—and this is the difference between him and the amorous Dido—is no doe, but a lion.'

[51] Cf. Lyne, *Further Voices*, 195.

[52] The meaning of the word in early Latin (Plaut., Enn.) seems to have been different ('mercenary soldier', probably too 'bodyguard'): see Skutsch on Enn. *Ann*.

'Latro' stands out and catches the eye for two reasons.[53] (1) It is prosaic;[54] it is prosaic presumably for much the same reason as was suggested for 'praedo' above. (2) Its denotation is unexpected. Why should a *robber* as well as (or among?) hunters have injured the lion? The difficulty here is exposed by the desperate attempts of lexicographers and commentators to avoid it.[55] But the proper inference to make from the difficulty is not that it does not exist but that Vergil wants thereby to attract our attention. A 'latro' is comprehensible in the context, but not expected or natural: he is extrinsic to the scene. Vergil inserts an extrinsic sense and agent because he wants us to ponder on it—rather as he wanted us to ponder on the sense of 'demessum' which was slightly extrinsic in its context (cf. section 1 above). Unexpected stylistic register ('latro' is a prosaism) reinforces the invitation to consider this agent. Who is he? Who is this thief who has injured the lion, standing for Turnus?

There is a third point to notice about 'latro'. It is the partner in crime of 'praedo'. Both words are prosaic, both literally denote for a large part of their semantic range much the same thing ('robber', 'brigand'),[56] and the two are closely related *Schimpfwörter*, insults.[57]

Our eye has been caught by 'latro'. The question presented

---

57. By Cicero's time it means 'robber', 'brigand', i.e. much the same as 'praedo'. For figures on the word's occurrence see note 54.

[53] Cf. the ways in which Vergil makes 'demessum' stand out, section 1 above.

[54] *TLL* s.v. 'legitur inde a Plauto, Enn., Cic.' Some exact figures: Enn. 2, Cic. *poet.* 0, Lucr. 0, Catull. 0, Prop. 0, Tib. 0, Hor. 6 (*Serm.* 4, *Epist.* 1, *Epod.* 1), Verg. 1, Ov. 4, Luc. 0, Val. 0, Sil. 0, Stat. 0, Caes. *Gall.* and *Civ.* 4, Cic. prose 95, Sall. 5, Liv. 20. Ennius' two uses are really irrelevant, since in Ennius' time the word had a different sense (see note 52); note that Horace's examples cluster in his lower genres. As with 'praedo', so with 'latro', Cicero found the power of the word as an insult (see below) very useful in his prose works.

[55] Servius on 12.7 'modo uenatoris. et est Graecum: nam λατρεύειν dicunt obsequi et seruire mercede, unde latrones uocantur conducti milites ['mercenary' is, it is true, apparently an old sense of 'latro': see above n. 52] ... unde nunc dicit latronis telo fixum leonem, quia etiam uenatores operas suas locare consuerunt'; the latter explanation strikes me as most unlikely. *TLL* 'latro' says of our passage 'audacius de uenatore'; *OLD* effectively creates a special subsection for it (=huntsman). R. D. Williams on 12.7 says ' "the huntsman", an unusual sense of the word, which normally means "brigand" '. Quite so. Brigand, robber is the sense that Vergil would have to suppose his readers would understand, and is the one he must be exploiting.

[56] Cf. e.g. Cic. *Tull.* 50 furem, hoc est praedonem et latronem.

[57] As *Schimpfwörter* they are often in close proximity, and often virtually interchangeable. See Opelt index s.vv., and esp. 133 f., 179, 182, 209.

itself: With whom are we to identify this 'robber'? Amata, Mezentius, and the 'matronae' would have no difficulty in answering this: it is Aeneas, whom they term a 'praedo', virtually the same thing. And we might say, what *other* candidate does Vergil's text suggest? Parallels between the 'latro' of 12.7 and the 'pastor' (= Aeneas) of 4.71 make the identification the more irresistible.

If it is hard to think of anybody else to identify with the 'latro', then there is another and important point to be taken. A voice distinct from the partisan opinion of characters (Amata, etc.) in direct speech is confirming these characters' view of Aeneas. They saw him as a 'praedo', this voice terms him a 'latro', 'praedo's' partner in crime. Whose voice is it? We might choose to talk of characters' feelings affecting the narrative style here,[58] and see, say, Turnus' views as obtruding. On the other hand, it is hard to dissociate the voice that utters 'latro' from the narrator's, hard to dissociate it in fact from Vergil's.

'Latronis' at 12.7 is the last stage in the sequence which we were incited to pursue at 7.362. It affects those examples of 'praedo' by delivering an interesting and disconcerting conclusion: it validates them.

The simile at 12.4 ff. is an example where Vergil exploits the guileful medium of 'narrative through imagery' to add clandestine views (pp. 76, 82).

4. caducus

The adjective 'caducus' was used of leaves, fruits, etc. that had literally fallen or were literally liable to fall: cf. Cato, talking of windfall olives at *Rust.* 23, 58, 64, 146, Columella 12.52.22, also of dropped olives, Varr. *Rust.* 2.2.12 talking of dropped corn, 'oues ... caduca spica saturantur', Lucr. 5.1363 of acorns, Verg. *Georg.* 1.368 of fallen leaves, 'frondes uolitare caducas', Cic. *Sen.* 52 of the vine liable to fall, 'uitis ... natura caduca est, et, nisi fulta est, fertur ad terram', Prop. 2.32.40 of 'poma' (by conjecture); see *TLL* III.33.76 ff.; Vergil's 'frondes caducae' recurs several times, in Ovid and others, *TLL* III.34.2 f. The use in connection with leaves and fruits by 'business' agricultural prose

[58] Cf. *Further Voices*, 227 ff.

might suggest that, in this sense, the word was something of a technical term. By or in Vergil's time we also find other sorts of literal 'falling' designated by 'caducus': e.g. overflowing water at Varr. *Rust.* 3.5.2; Hor. *Carm.* 2.13.11 'te triste lignum, te caducum in domini caput immerentis', 3.4.44 'fulmine ... caduco'. By Vergil's time too the word had acquired a well-established, largely metaphorical sense 'infirm', 'uncertain', of things, circumstances, conditions, and this becomes common in Cicero and others: e.g. Cic. *Amic.* 102 'res humanae fragiles caducaeque sunt', *TLL* III.34.83 ff. Among the poets, the word achieves popularity with Ovid; if we are to give the word an overall label in Vergil's time, I suppose we should term it prosaic.[59]

Vergil uses the word two more times besides *Georg.* 1.368. At 6.481 the heroic Trojan dead in the Underworld are described as fallen, 'caduci', in war:

> multum fleti ad superos belloque caduci
> Dardanidae.

The descendants of Dardanus, those who had fallen in war, much bewailed in the world above.

There is no parallel for Vergil's use of the word in this way of the dead, either before him or contemporary with him; and there is hardly more than one after him (section 6). At least part of what Vergil means to convey must simply be that the heroes have fallen literally, i.e. to the ground; but, applied to men who have in any circumstances literally fallen (or are falling, etc.), 'caducus' is hard to parallel.[60]

So Vergil's use of 'caducus' is special (and 'caducus' is eye-catching by virtue of its stylistic register). The use is also puzzling. Why does Vergil transfer the word to the dead? To what end? We may sense or assume the contrivance of some

---

[59] Ovid indulges in 'caducus', but the word is very little used by poets before him, and he has less influence with his successors than one might expect. Note, as well as the figures below, that Seneca uses the word eighteen times in his prose works, only once in his tragedies. Enn. 0, Lucr. 1, Cic. *poet.* 0, Catull. 0, Prop. 2, Tib. 0, Hor. 2, Verg. 3, Ov. 15 (plus one in *Ep. Sapph.*, one in *Ib.*), Luc. 0, Val. 0, Sil. 1, Stat. 2; Cato *Rust.* 4, Varro *Rust.* 2; Caes. *Gall.* and *Civ.* 0, Sall. 0, Cicero prose 17, Livy 0.

[60] We might compare some rather odd uses in connection with epileptics, *sim.*, *OLD* s.v. 1b, *TLL* 3.34.41 ff.

effect. But scrutiny of the immediate context supplies no obvious or sufficient explanation of what that effect is. We are incited to search further abroad for the solution. If no local combination explains a use, a larger perspective may enlighten us. Nothing in Vergil is without purpose or explanation.

'Caduci' should bring to mind (by processes I shall precisely identify in a moment) the simile for the dead souls at 6.309 f.:

> quam multa in siluis autumni frigore primo
> lapsa cadunt folia ...

As many as the leaves that at the first chill of autumn drop and fall ...

The ancestors of this image lie in Homer, similes implying the impermanence and unimportance of living men: *Il.* 6.146 ff., 21.464 ff.[61] When Bacchylides (5.65 ff.) applied[62] the image to souls of the dead in the Underworld, those implications followed it. In Bacchylides' image the reader thinks of the insubstantiality both of the souls and, if he remembers Homer, of the men they once were; the poem is as much a reflection on the transitory condition of life as it is on the Underworld itself. The same thing happens emphatically at *Aen.* 6.309 f.[63] The illustrative function of the simile is simply number ('quam *multa*'); its 'narrative' function is to inform us about the insubstantiality and unimportance of these souls and of the human beings they once were— saddening and troublesome thoughts at this time.[64]

'Caduci' at 6.481 should bring to mind the simile at 6.309 f. because, unusual in its application to fallen heroes, it would be usual of the leaves of the simile (as documented above; note especially *Georg.* 1.368). To put it another way, 'caduci' has

---

[61] Cf. too *Il.* 2.468, 800. See Fränkel, 40–1; the simile is more developed in 6.146 ff. (Glaucus), perhaps more in place in 21.464 ff. (Apollo).

[62] It is not likely that he was the first so to apply it: see the next note.

[63] But it is perhaps unlikely that Bacchylides himself was Vergil's source. Sources are a tangled story. Norden on *Aeneid* 6.309–12 conjectured that a lost epic account of the Descent of Heracles to the Underworld had first transferred Homer's image to the souls of the dead. There is now a lyric papyrus to reckon with (POxy 2622), which probably applied the leaf comparison to souls, is likely to be by Pindar, and may have been Vergil's source: thus Lloyd-Jones, esp. 215, and 228–9; on this question see further Clark, esp. 247 and Thaniel.

[64] There is good comment on the expressive value of the simile in Thaniel, 244 f. The eschatology of *Aen.* VI is on the face of it (I suppose) optimistic. This simile is part of a campaign to undermine that appearance. (The simile is one of pair. See VI.4b on the other one.)

trespassed from the simile,[65] and therefore should remind us of it: it is a reverberation of the simile's 'lapsa *cadunt* folia'. So there is its explanation and function: it is a word designed to maintain the imagery of the simile quasi-*metaphorically* in the narrative. This is an example of trespass in which the trespassing term has ventured much farther afield than in the examples I have considered hitherto, but in many other respects it is comparable to them. We are particularly able to make the connection between 6.309 f. and 481, between trespass source and (distant) destination, because 'caduci' is eye-catching but under-explained in its immediate context, and incites us to find an explanation for it in a larger context.

'Caduci' applied to the heroes at 6.481 is thus quasi-metaphor-ical, maintaining, perhaps better to say reintroducing, the image of 6.309 f. from which it has trespassed. Much sense is thus being extorted from it in the processes of incitement and trespass. And the sense thus gained is effective, and disconcerting. The heroic souls who occupy the 'arua ultima' are in many respects still vivid and impressive ('bello clari ... inclutus armis ... etiam currus, etiam arma tenentem,' 6.478–85, but note 'Adrasti pallentis imago', 480). It seems that heroes, some of these heroes anyway, maintain their vigour and their heroism even beyond death. 'Caduci' pushes in the opposite direction. Literally record-ing the fact simply that these are the 'fallen' in war, it also represents them as the generations of leaves: it reminds us that they are and always were insubstantial and relatively unimpor-tant. Incitement and trespass extort troubling sense from 'ca-duci'.

5. Interlude: the soul's appearance of lifelikeness

In the above passage of Vergil, *Aen.* 6.478 ff., the souls seem convincingly lifelike. So initially they are presented. But then their actual insubstantiality obtrudes, torpedoing that appear-ance, reducing it to the pathetic reality. (This, as much else, undermines the surface, life-after-death optimism of *Aen.* 6.) Vergil here ubobtrusively re-creates an effect that had been pursued before: the soul's seeming lifelikeness is juxtaposed with

---

[65] On the topic of trespass see IV.5.

its actual lifelessness, and the latter demonstrates the former to have been a mere appearance.

Here is Apollonius, describing the shade of Sthenelus emerging from his tomb to see the Argonauts, *Arg.* 2.918–20:[66]

> τύμβου δὲ στεφάνης ἐπιβὰς σκοπιάζετο νῆα,
> τοῖος ἐὼν οἷος πόλεμόνδ᾽ ἴεν· ἀμφὶ δὲ καλὴ
> τετράφαλος φοίνικι λόφῳ ἀπελάμπετο πήληξ.

And mounting on the edge of the barrow he gazed at the ship, even as he was when he went to war; and his beautiful, four-horned helmet with its blood-red crest cast forth its light around.

Sthenelus seems convincingly lifelike. But then a μέν and δέ clause obtrudes the difference between the appearance and the real thing, between Sthenelus and the living Argonauts; and Sthenelus' mere appearance of lifelikeness is revealed for what it is. 921–2:[67]

> καί ῥ᾽ ὁ μὲν αὖτις ἔδυ μέλανα ζόφον· οἱ δ᾽ ἐσιδόντες
> θάμβησαν. τοὺς δ᾽ ὦρσε ...

And Sthenelus again entered the black darkness. But they [the Argonauts] looked and marvelled. And Mopsus urged them ...

Sthenelus himself was acutely aware of the difference. He made his dramatic entry into the upper world because he desired for a few seconds to see the real thing, men 'of character like himself', but *men* not ψυχή. 915–17:

> ἦκε γὰρ αὐτή
> Φερσεφόνη ψυχὴν πολυδάκρυον Ἀκτορίδαο,
> λισσομένην τυτθόν περ ὁμήθεας ἄνδρας ἰδέσθαι.

Persephone herself sent forth the soul of Actor's son (Sthenelus) which with many tears begged to see men of character like himself, even for a moment.

Cf. how the Trojan souls are so eager to see, and to talk to, Aeneas in 6.478 ff. They are aware, we may infer, of their status as 'caduci', that they are as insubstantial as dead leaves despite appearances; and part of their eagerness may be due to the fact

---

[66] ἀπ[ελάμπετο] in 920 is the reading of POxy. 2694 (ἐπ- the reading of the MSS). The editor of the pap. argues for its restoration.
[67] POxy 2694 confirms Bywater's ἔδυ μέλανα.

that they simply delight in the chance to see the real thing again.
6.486–8:

> circumstant animae dextra laeuaque frequentes,
> nec uidisse semel satis est; iuuat usque morari
> et conferre gradum et ueniendi discere causas.

On right and left the souls stand round in throngs. To have seen him
once is not enough; they delight to linger continually, to walk with him,
to learn the causes of his coming.

Homer achieves a similar effect at *Iliad* 23.65 ff. Patroclus' soul
appears to the sleeping Achilles (65–7):

> ἦλθε δ᾽ ἐπὶ ψυχὴ Πατροκλῆος δειλοῖο,
> πάντ᾽ αὐτῷ μέγεθός τε καὶ ὄμματα κάλ᾽ ἐϊκυῖα,
> καὶ φωνήν, καὶ τοῖα περὶ χροῒ εἵματα ἔστο.

There came to him the soul of wretched Patroclus, in all respects like his
very self, in stature, fair eyes and voice, and he was dressed in like
raiments.

Patroclus seems convincingly lifelike, at least to Achilles.[68] Lines
99–101 then certainly and spectacularly torpedo the impression,
for everyone:

> ὠρέξατο χερσὶ φίλῃσιν,
> οὐδ᾽ ἔλαβε· ψυχὴ δὲ κατὰ χθονὸς ἠΰτε καπνὸς
> ᾤχετο τετριγυῖα

Achilles reached out with his hands [for Patroclus], but could not grasp
him. Like smoke the soul went beneath the earth, twittering.

The sham of Patroclus' lifelikeness is ruthless exposed by, in
particular, the inhuman 'twittering' of the soul (the verb is used
of bats and various kinds of birds, *inter alia*).

Interestingly this effect of real insubstantiality torpedoing
apparent lifelikeness is not one pursued at *Odyssey* 11.387 ff.
(Agamemnon); nor at 471 ff. (Achilles), unless 539 φοίτα μακρὰ
βιβᾶσα κατ᾽ ἀσφοδελὸν λειμῶνα, 'he (i.e. the soul) departed with
great strides through the meadow of asphodel', has some such
impact; nor at 543 ff. (Ajax).

---

[68] The phrase in all respects *like* his very *self*, αὐτῷ, may herald the real
insubstantiality for us the readers. Cf. the significance of ψυχάς and αὐτούς at
Iliad 1.3–4 with Leaf ad loc.

6. caducus, continued

The use of 'caducus' at 6.481 is a signal one. Vergil's other use is at 10.622, again of a person. Jupiter refers to Turnus as 'caduco ... iuueni', 'the young man who will fall'. His primary meaning is that Turnus will soon literally fall in battle. But I imagine that he and Vergil also have in mind the imagery of book 6. Turnus is as sure to fall as the leaves that wither on the branch; Jupiter sees him as as insubstantial and ultimately unimportant as Apollo saw mortals at *Iliad* 21.464–6. I would argue that 'caducus' acquires the potential to deliver these sorts of implications in the rest of the text of the *Aeneid* because of that signal use in book 6. Vergil banks on our memory of what his incitement and extended trespass in book 6 produced. It is interesting to see that Tiberius Claudius Donatus cottoned on to some of it.[69] On the question of *acquisition* see the next chapter.

It is perhaps surprising that neither Lucan nor the Flavian epicists repeat such an effect; perhaps they did not understand it. Lucan and Valerius do not use the word at all. Silius' one use and Statius' two uses are identical to, or related to, the more conventional uses mentioned above (pp. 165 f.).[70] Of Ovid's many uses *Pont.* 2.8.47 f. 'sic, quem dira tibi rapuit Germania Drusum, / pars fuerit partus sola caduca tui' is perhaps relevant to our discussion. He may mean to exploit imagery from nature, in the Vergilian manner, and intend 'partus' to cohere. One other passage is interesting to note, Cicero *Sen.* 5. Talking of old age Cicero (or rather Cato)[71] says,

sed tamen necesse fuit esse aliquid extremum et, tamquam in arborum bacis terraeque fructibus, maturitate tempestiua quasi uietum et caducum, quod ferendum est molliter sapienti.

---

[69] Tiberius Claudius Donatus' comment on 10.622 evidences correct association of ideas; whether he is right to see a suggestion of *untimely* death in the word, I do not know: 'caducum dicitur quicquid immaturo tempore cadit ac perit, ut sunt arborum fructus, quorum pars appellatur caduca quae in usus hominum non uenit, propterea quod non adepta sui maturitatem prosternitur ac perit. inde translatum est ut caduci dicantur homines qui in pueritia aut iuuenta moriuntur.'

[70] At Stat. *Silv.* 2.2.129 'nos, uilis turba, caducis / deseruire bonis ... parati' and Sil. 7.57 the sense is the metaphorical 'infirm' of things, etc., paralleled e.g. at Cic. *Amic.* 102; at Stat. *Silv.* 2.1.212 'plebisque caducae / quis fleat interitus' it is the same sense transferred to people (*TLL* 'translate, i.q. infirmus de animantibus', III.34.71 ff.).

[71] J. G. F. Powell on 'arborum bacis' raises the possibility that the use of agricultural imagery is to fit with Cato's character and interests.

There had to be something final, and, as in the case of orchard fruits and agricultural crops, something as it were wilted and prone to fall at the season of ripeness; this must be borne by the wise man calmly.

Here 'uietum' and 'caducum' are (I would say) *tentatively* trespassing out of the simile and *almost* used metaphorically ('as it were') of human old age. Cicero in short is on the way to a use like Vergil's.

7. tacitum uulnus

I return us to Dido's wound of love, 4.67. It is described thus:

> tacitum uiuit sub pectore uulnus

A silent wound lives beneath her breast.

I concentrate now on the epithet. The wound is described as 'silent', or, if we take 'tacitum' predicatively, as adverbial in force, it lives 'silently'.

A psychological wound like love is aptly and comprehensibly described as 'hidden', as 'escaping notice' or 'working stealthily' (cf. Call. *Epigr*. 43.1Pf., Apoll. Rhod. 3.296, and Pease on *Aen*. 4.67). Such descriptions draw a contrast between the nature and manner of an emotional wound and the nature and manner, perspicuous to all, of a physical wound. A psychological wound is likewise well described as 'unseen', 'caecus', Lucr. 4.1120 'tabescunt uulnere caeco' (cf. *Aen*. 4.2 'caeco ... igni', with Pease), as opposed to the visible wound caused by, say, a sword. But is it comprehensibly described as *silent*? Compared with what? Are physical wounds noisy and garrulous? It seems a puzzle.[72] 'Tacitum', a neutral word, here produces an eye-catching effect whose function is not wholly explained by the immediate context. All we can say is that it is a puzzle—and perhaps ominous. We are, if past experience counts, incited to search further abroad for the whole solution.

We find it. A wound *can* in fact be envisaged as noisy—if for

---

[72] DServius flounders instructively: 'TACITVM de quo tacuerit etiam nunc apud alios. an apud Aeneam tacitum, quia sorori iam confessa est? aut tacitum tacendum et pudore plenum.'

example a chest wound punctures a lung.[73] And this is how Vergil envisages the wound for which Dido is destined, 4.689:

> infixum *stridit* sub pectore uulnus.

The wound *grates* fixed beneath her breast.

This provides the solution to the apparent puzzle in 'tacitum'. There is something to which the silence of Dido's emotional wound may be meaningfully compared and opposed: the behaviour of the literal wound with which she is eventually afflicted. 'Tacitum' links to 'stridit' in a clearly significant manner, with implications to be drawn from the connection. I think that Vergil wishes us to infer that the one wound *is preparing for* the other: the wound is silent at 4.67 but (we should now see) *it is biding its time, waiting to make its noise*, a ghastly and deathly noise. Ominous silence becomes the noise of death; the love wound becomes the death wound. In other words, love leads to Dido's death, love is the basic cause of her death.[74]

8. Saturnia Iuno

5.606–8

> Irim de caelo misit *Saturnia* Iuno
> Iliacam ad classem uentosque aspirat eunti,
> multa mouens necdum antiquum *saturata* dolorem.

Saturnian Juno sent Iris down from heaven to the Trojan fleet, and breathed fair winds for her as she went, plotting many things, her ancient grudge not yet *sated*.

'Saturo', to 'sate physically', was already established in a metaphorical use (Cic. *Planc.* 21 'hominibus iam saturatis honoribus', Catull. 64.220 'nondum / lumina sunt nati cara saturata figura'), and is not itself (used in respect of 'dolorem') especially conspic-

---

[73] Pease *ad loc.* cites Celsus 5.26.9 'pulmone uero icto spirandi difficultas est ... spiritus cum sono fertur.' No noise is mentioned in connection with two other famous wounds that he cites (Soph. *Ajax* 918 f., *Antig.* 1238 f.).

[74] Other factors show that love is the basic cause of Dido's death—which is a conclusion not obvious to all, and not without important implications: see Lyne, *Further Voices*, 173. On the remorseless progress of Dido's love-wound to death-wound see VIII.1, also *FV* 120 n. 31, Otis 70 ff., Pöschl 103 ff.

uous.[75] But one should notice that it is exploited for another effect in our context: it points to an etymology for 'Saturnia' ('Saturnian', 'daughter of Saturn'), to which it is in close proximity; 'Saturnia ... saturata' may be classed as *figura etymologica*. Cic. *N. D.* 2.64 derives the name of Juno's father 'Saturnus' as follows: 'Saturnus [presented as a Time God] autem est appellatus quod saturaretur annis', 'Saturn was so called because he was sated with years'; similarly, 3.62.[76] Presumably something like this is brought to mind by our *figura etymologica*. But this—any thought that the root of 'Saturnia' might be 'saturare'—is in our context surprising and eye-catching. For the point being referred to in 608 is precisely the *in*satiability of Juno the 'Saturnia' ('*necdum* ...')—a topic which has in one form or other been central since the beginning of the poem (1.25 ff.). Why does Vergil introduce the *figura*? Is he simply alluding to an etymology for Saturn the father (from 'sating') at a time which is piquantly paradoxical considering the daughter's mood? Or is he suggesting an etymology for the daughter, the Saturnian, in the manner of 'lucus a non lucendo'?[77] Or what? One thing we may infer is that the *figura etymologica* puts emphasis—by paradox or whatever—on the idea of Juno's insatiability. But we are still left puzzled as to the full or exact intention. Experience suggests that a solution will be found if we search further abroad. Our puzzlement in the local context is an incitement so to proceed.

A little later in the plot Venus seeks Neptune's assistance against Juno. She opens by remarking on Juno's insatiability (5.781–2):

> Iunonis grauis ira neque exsaturabile pectus
> cogunt me, Neptune, preces descendere in omnis.

Juno's grievous anger, her breast insatiable, compel me, Neptune, to stoop to every prayer.

'Exsaturabile' is a very eye-catching word; it does not occur elsewhere in surviving Latin except at Stat. *Theb.* 1.214. Here we

[75] If we are to produce an overall label for the word, it should probably be neutral.
[76] Cf. Anderson 'Juno and Saturn', 523–4. Differently, Varro *Ling.* 5.64: 'ab satu', 'sowing'.
[77] Cf. Quint. 1.6.34. There are thus various ways of countering Higham's objection to positing this etymology, 145 n.87.

have therefore further and noticeable insistence on the theme of
Juno's (emotional) insatiability; in particular, 'necdum saturata'
(5.608) may be seen as picked up by 'neque exsaturabile' (5.781).[78]
But still there is no full explanation of what is going on. Further
incitement to proceed therefore.

The theme of Juno's insatiability then quickly takes an unexpected direction. At 5.785 ff. Venus continues her speech to
Neptune thus:

> non media de gente Phrygum *exedisse* nefandis
> urbem odiis satis est nec poenam traxe per omnem
> reliquias Troiae.

It is not enough that from the midst of the Phrygian people she has
eaten their city in her unspeakable hate and dragged through utmost
retribution the remnants of Troy.

'Exedo' is a common word[79] of literal eating, and other analogous physical actions. Employed metaphorically it is much less
common; and Vergil's use here, assumed by *TLL* to be metaphorical, finds itself out on a limb (V.2.1318.22 ff. and 35). But is
it right to term Vergil's use metaphorical? Not entirely, for, as
Knauer confirms, Vergil alludes in 5.785 to Homer, *Il.* 4.35:

> εἰ δὲ σύ ...
> ὠμὸν βεβρώθοις Πρίαμον Πριάμοιό τε παῖδας (35)
> ἄλλους τε Τρῶας, τότε κὲν χόλον ἐξακέσοιο

If you were to eat Priam raw, and Priam's sons, and the other Trojans,
then would you heal your anger.

Here Zeus says that Hera would be satisfied by, and only by,
physically eating Priam and his sons; Homer touches on a theme
(divine cannibalism) perhaps more enthusiastically treated by the
cyclic epics.[80] So Venus, as the allusion shows us, does not mean
'exedo' merely metaphorically. She may be letting hyperbole and
emotion run away with her, but she wishes us to think of Juno
actually *eating* the Trojan city. Some such sense is assured by the
Homeric allusion. In addition the striking word of 'satiation',
'exsaturabilis', at 781 and the predominantly literal 'exedo' must

---

[78] It is picked up again in the notable word 'exsaturata' at 7.298.
[79] More common in prose than poetry; if forced to label it, I would call it neutral.
[80] Cf. J. Griffin, *JHS* 97 (1977), 46 with n. 46a.

combine to assert the basic sense common to both: eating. The sense we could say is extorted from the context, by combination as well as allusion.

So, the theme of Juno's insatiability has indeed taken an unexpected turn: a literal one. The insatiability of the 'Saturnia' is evidenced, according to Venus' colourful suggestion, in her having found Troy insufficient *food*. She makes a point related to Zeus' in the *Iliad*, implying cannibalism or anthropophagy. Now cannibalistic behaviour is in fact no stranger to Juno–Hera's family. Juno–Hera's father, Kronos–Saturn, devoured his children (Hesiod *Theog*. 459 ff.). This is presumably in Zeus' and Venus' minds, for it lends punch to their jibes about the daughter's putative eating habits. And we can now see what Vergil is getting at in the etymological play 'Saturnia ... saturare' at 5.606–8. He is making a point like the one which may be presumed to be in Venus' mind. He is getting at the cannibalistic predilections of Juno's family. For 'Saturnia' of 606 develops, via the recurrent theme of Juno's insatiability, into the quasi-literal and striking 'exedisse', '*eat*'. This retrojects an etymology for 'Saturnia' of *physical* 'saturare'. Both author and character are making similar jibes. Vergil's at 5.606 is that Juno is the daughter of, or she herself is, the devourer, the physical self-satisfier (in fact the same etymology for 'Saturnus' can be inferred in Cic. *N. D.* 2.64 referred to above).[81] Vergil means of course to be paradoxical, given the actual *in*satiability of Juno. But far more important are his imputations of cannibalism or anthropophagy.

So: Vergil creates a slight puzzle in his text, incites us to find a solution, and supplies it at a later point in the text: 5.785 f. explains 606–8. And the solution is a surprise.

The sequence is not ended. When Neptune replies to Venus (799) he is most unexpectedly termed 'Saturnius'. Though he too is a child of Saturn, this is the only time he receives the epithet in

---

[81] Cic. *N. D.* 2.64 quoted above goes on to refer to the myth of Saturn's cannibalism. The text continues: 'ex se enim natos comesse fingitur solitus, quia consumit aetas temporum spatia annisque praeteritis insaturabiliter expletur', 'the story is that he was in the habit of devouring his sons, because in fact time consumes the ages and fills itself insatiably with the passing years'. This rationalizes the myth, but also suggests another way of etymologizing 'Saturnus': from physical 'saturare': Saturn, mythologizers would argue (and Cicero argues against them), is the devourer, the physical self-satisfier.

the *Aeneid*; and it is emphasized in this line by the unusual pause after it.[82] Given what we have just established, it must here be sinister in tone. This is apt: Neptune is just about to act in a sinister, arguably self-satisfying way, requiring the death of the blameless Palinurus, 'unum pro multis'.

'Saturnius' is almost exclusively and very frequently Juno's epithet; the only other god to receive it besides Neptune at 5.799 is Jupiter (once, in a speech of Dido's at 4.372). Most obviously the epithet would have Golden Age associations (this is what is in Dido's mind?): the implied definition of Saturn's Golden Age shifts somewhat from *Eclogues* to *Aeneid*, but Saturn and Golden Age are still linked: cf. *Ecl.* 4.6 ff., *Georg.* 2.538 and context, *Aen.* 6.792–4, 7.203 f., 8.357 f. and context.[83] This, given the fearsome and violent nature of Juno, would mean that 'Saturnia Iuno' had an ironic potential. In 5.606–799 Vergil extorts quite other and sinister connotations from 'Saturnius' (and from 'saturo' cognates like 'exsaturata'). From then on 'Saturnia (etc.) Iuno' has acquired the potential to bring to mind a cannabilistic self-satisfier. Vergil may utilize one or both of these potentials—and others.[84]

---

[82] Diaeresis after 2nd foot without caesura in 2nd foot: see R. D. Williams *ad loc*.

[83] Cf. Anderson, 'Saturn and Juno', 520.

[84] The question why Vergil so frequently applies 'Saturnia' to Juno has of course been frequently studied. Servius had an idea, interesting but perhaps implausible: DServ. on 4.92 'ubi nocituram Iunonem poeta uult ostendere, Saturniam dicit; scit enim Saturni stellam nocendi potestatem habere', similarly on 1.23. See further the stimulating article of Anderson, 'Juno and Saturn', also P. A. Johnston, 'Vergil's Conception of Saturnus', *CSCA* 10 (1977), 57–70, Highet 145 and n. 87 with bibliography, R. D. Williams on 5.606. I have added to the possibilities. I do not think the whole story has yet been told.

VIII

Acquisition

At 10.622 f. Jupiter refers to Turnus as 'caduco ... iuueni', the young man who will fall. I suggested above (VII.6) that Jupiter implies much else by the epithet 'caducus': that Turnus is as insubstantial and ultimately unimportant as the leaves. I argued that 'caducus' had *acquired* the potential to deliver such implications by virtue of a signal use in book 6. Likewise I argued that 'Saturnius', owing to the way it is used in 5.606 ff., acquires the potential to connote sinister things in the rest of the *Aeneid* (VII.8). These are I think less certain examples of acquisition than the ones which I shall proceed to adduce now.

The technique I have in mind is not essentially a mysterious one. Characteristic of Vergil, but not confined to Vergil, it takes various forms, which I now schematically outline.

(1) If a poet uses a word on one occasion in some particularly striking way, if he organizes a combination which imparts some signal novelty of sense to it, that use will stick in our memory and affect or potentially affect our response to later occurrences of the word in the same text. It has *acquired* for the duration of this poet's text the potential to mean something special. The poet can then cash in this special value when he pleases; and he can do so more or less patently, depending on the combination he organizes at the time of encashment. 'Caducus' and 'Saturnius' (after 5.606 ff.) arguably acquire special value in this way. A more familiar example might be 'furor'. This word is given a striking political resonance[1] in its first use in the *Aeneid* (1.150), and acquires thereby the potential to bring to mind *political* madness

---

[1] Political uses of 'furor' etc. are not of course in other contexts remarkable (cf. J. Hellegouarc'h, *Le vocabulaire latin des relations et des partis politiques sous la république* (Paris 1972), 558, 569); I mean that in a mythological epic such strong contemporary-political colouring is striking.

from that point on. So do its cognates. This value is cashed in often enough, and especially at 12.946.[2]

(2) A poet may use a word repeatedly in a way which is not necessarily striking, but which is *exclusive*. Throughout his text or over a definable stretch of his text, he will always use the word in substantially the same way, where others might be lax or inventive. In this way, and in this piece of text, the word acquires a value which is not striking but very particular. The poet can then at a chosen moment cash in this acquired particularity for a special effect; again he can do this more or less patently, depending on the combination at the time of encashment. An example of this is Vergil's use of 'pinguis' and cognates in *Georgics* book 1.[3] The acquired value is cashed in at *Georg.* 1.492.

(3) A poet may do both of these things. He may during his text or a definable stretch of text use a word repeatedly and exclusively in a particular and striking way, and then cash in this strongly acquired and very striking sense at a climactic moment. An example of this last might be Vergil's use of 'uulnus' in the stretch of text that comprises the story of Dido.

1. uulnus

The story of Dido is told in book 1.494–end, book 4, and 6.450–76.[4] I shall now list all examples of 'uulnus' in this stretch of text. There are none in 1.494 ff. Use of the word starts eye-catchingly at the beginning of book 4. At 4.2 Dido's love is strikingly described as a wound:

> uulnus alit uenis

She nurtures a wound in her veins.

The same use is made of the word at 4.67. This is that notable trespass from simile to narrative to which I have referred (ch. IV, pp. 77 f.):

---

[2] The context here is, among many other things, *political*: ever since Anchises' instructions at 6.852–3, the issue of revenge and clemency has been necessarily a political one. The context therefore facilitates the encashment of a sense *political* madness in 'furiis' at 12.946.

[3] See Lyne in Woodman and West, 60.

[4] The narration of book 2 affects Dido herself, but is not directly concerned with her story.

tacitum uiuit sub pectore uulnus

'A silent wound lives beneath her breast.'

The wound here is *silent*: it bides its time, waiting to make its noise (see VII.7). The love-wound becomes the death-wound, and (4.689):

infixum stridit sub pectore uulnus

The wound grates fixed beneath her breast.

This wound, the death-wound that the love-wound has resulted in, is also referred to by Anna at 4.683:

date, uulnera lymphis
abluam

Grant me, let me wash her wounds with water.

This is the total of uses of 'uulnus' in the first two portions of the Dido story. Vergil presents to us a tragic *Liebestod*, the remorseless progress of love to death. The 'uulnus' sequence is one of his key means of showing the tragic inevitability of the story. Love-wound leads to death-wound, produces it and merges into it. The love-wound already *is* the death-wound, incipiently but inescapably. From the beginning of book 4 Dido is as good as dead: the 'uulnus' that will kill her is already there.[5]

The continuity of the 'uulnus' sequence is thus one of Vergil's key means of delineating tragic inevitability. But the fact that he exclusively uses the word in reference to Dido's love and death, her love that is death, means that the word (essentially a neutral word)[6] acquires a strong and particular sense. By the end of book 4 it is fixed in our minds as a complex of significance evocative of Dido's tragic fate. The word has been the crux of Dido's tragedy, and has had no other use.

This special acquired value is cashed in book 6, in the first line of Vergil's resumption of the Dido story. This is the final, and climactic, use. In the 'Lugentes campi' are those who have died of love, 'among whom' (6.450):

[5] Cf. VII.7, *Further Voices*, 193–4.

[6] There are signs, however, that its role in the spoken tongue is being eroded by 'plaga' (cf. Italian *piaga*).

> inter quas Phoenissa recens a uulnere Dido
> errabat ...

Among whom wandered Phoenician Dido, fresh from her wound ...

Because of the complex and special value that 'uulnus' has acquired, the phrase 'recens a uulnere' is sufficient to recall Dido's whole tragic story, her love and death, her love that was death; the stage is set for Dido's last appearance with the utmost economy. And the encashment is patent, rendered so by the combination 'uulnere *Dido*'. The reintroduction of Dido alerts us to the value acquired by 'uulnus' during the Dido story.

2. laetus

Vergil's use of 'laetus' (a neutral word) is closer to the first form of the technique mentioned above. I think that on a couple of occasions Vergil organizes a combination, we should perhaps rather say a context, which imparts a novel and special value to the word. The very first occurrence of the word in the *Aeneid* is one of these formative occasions. In therefore what is arguably the word's most commanding appearance it acquires a special value which is then available to the poet for the duration of the poem. And we see it cashed in.

The action of the poem starts abruptly, with the Trojans happy (1.34–7):

> uix e conspectu Siculae telluris in altum
> uela dabant *laeti* et spumas salis aere ruebant,
> cum Iuno aeternum seruans sub pectore uulnus
> haec secum: ...

Scarcely out of sight of Sicilian land, they were *happily* setting sail out onto the deep and churning up the sea-foam with their bronze prows, when Juno, preserving an eternal wound beneath her breast, said this to herself ...'

Juno then delivers a great monologue on her hatred of the Trojans, and sets about organizing the disastrous storm which rapidly dispels Trojan happiness. The trials of the Trojans in the first six books begin.

What we should notice is the immediate reversal besetting Trojan 'laetitia'. The impact of the reversal is heightened by a surprise, organized by syntax. The inverted 'cum' construction allows no hint of the imminent *peripeteia*. Given a conventional construction ('when the Trojans were happily setting sail, Juno ...'), we should have been alerted to the fact that Trojan felicity was contingent upon something. As it is, we hear of happiness unalloyed; then, immediately and out of the blue, trouble.

This surprise *peripeteia* at this conspicuous moment—at 1.34 Vergil sweeps us 'in medias res'—might make us ponder on the stability of 'laetitia' in the world of the *Aeneid*. At its first and commanding occurrence happiness is revealed to be strikingly vulnerable. It attracts immediate retribution. We may in consequence greet other manifestations of 'laetitia' with caution. 'Laetus' and cognates have acquired an unusual semantic potential: something like, *disaster-prone* happiness.

The opening of the Iliadic *Aeneid* has many parallels of structure and theme with book 1. Not least, we see the Trojans 'happy' again. So does Juno. And again she promptly delivers a great monologue of hate, sets about organizing trouble, this time a war; and the trials of the Trojans in 7–12 begin. The happiness is here specifically Aeneas' and is phrased thus (7.286–93):

> ecce autem Inachiis sese referebat ab Argis
> saeua Iouis coniunx aurasque inuecta tenebat,
> et *laetum* Aenean classemque ex aethere longe
> Dardaniam Siculo prospexit ab usque Pachyno.
> moliri iam tecta uidet ...
> ...
> tum quassans caput haec effundit pectore dicta:
> 'heu stirpem inuisam ...

But, look, the savage consort of Jupiter was returning from Inachian Argos, borne through the air on her way; and from the heavens afar, right from Sicilian Pachynus, she spied the *happy* Aeneas and the Dardan fleet. She saw them already building houses ... Then, shaking her head, she poured forth these words from her breast: 'Ah, hated stock ...'

And war and suffering ensue. So, in a parallel context and at a structurally parallel point in the poem, 'laetitia' attracts immediate retribution. Vergil does not repeat the inverted 'cum' effect (we would hardly be fooled again), but this must be regarded as an important reinforcement of the acquired value of 'laetus': in the *Aeneid* it connotes, or may connote, *disaster-prone* happiness. At the beginning of the Iliadic *Aeneid*, as at the beginning of the Odyssean, 'laetitia' untrammelled is of momentary duration.

These are the two contexts which I think most signally impart Vergilian novelty of sense to 'laetus', and which should most stick in our memory. We could say that 1.35 establishes a value for 'laetus' which may be cashed in the first half of the poem, and 7.288 performs the same function for the second half; and the latter retrospectively confirms the value we should have perceived in 1–6. Other passages reinforce this value.

Consider the dove at 5.512 ff.:

> illa Notos atque atra uolans in nubila fugit.
> ...
> iam uacuo *laetam* caelo speculatus et alis
> plaudentem nigra figit sub nube columbam.

The dove winged her flight to the south winds and black clouds ... [Eurytion] spied her now *happy* in the free sky, and, as she flapped her wings under a black cloud, transfixed her.

The dove's 'laetitia' is premature, disaster-prone we might say, of momentary duration. (Note the parallels in sentence construction with 7.288: 'iam laetam speculatus figit' > 'laetum prospexit; moliri iam uidet, effundit'.)

Consider too Aeneas addressing the dead Lausus at 10.827:

> arma, quibus *laetatus*, habe tua

Keep those arms of yours, in which you were *happy*.

Lausus' happiness has clearly proved disaster-prone. Similarly 'laetatus' at 6.568. Note also the Trojans donning Greek armour at 2.394 f., described as 'laeta iuuentus'. That happy idea soon backfires.

More such passages could be adduced. On the other hand it should be admitted that 'laetus' and cognates are common in the *Aeneid*, and it might be hard to argue that all examples either reinforce the acquired Vergilian value or cash it in. But let me show occasions where I think it is cashed in, one in particular.

To sum up my argument so far: Vergil organizes combinations or contexts, two in particular, which impart to 'laetus' and cognates the potential special value '*disaster-prone* happiness' in the *Aeneid*. Doom dogs 'laetitia'. Dido's first entry is described thus (1.496 ff.):

> regina ad templum, forma pulcherrima Dido,
> incessit ...
> qualis [Diana] ...
> ...
> talis erat Dido, talem se *laeta* ferebat (503)
> per medios instans operi regnisque futuris ...
> ...
> iura dabat legesque uiris ...
> ...
> cum subito Aeneas ...

The queen, Dido fairest in beauty, moved towards the temple. Even as Diana ... So was Dido, so she *happily* moved through their midst pressing on the work of her future realm ... Laws and justice she dispensed to her citizens ... when suddenly Aeneas...

Vergil introduces the queen with leisurely homage. He does his utmost to present her as the dignified, glorious, and felicitous monarch that she is. It is dramatically important that he should do so. The tragic story of Dido is based upon the overturning of all this grandness and felicity into misery and disaster: the great queen becomes the distraught and defeated suicide, a catastrophic *peripeteia*. So the initial sublimity needs to be stressed, and it is. And Dido's position and stature as a generous, admirable, and happy queen continue to be elaborated for another 150 lines and more. The first hint of impending disaster is the entrance of the ominous Venus at 1.657.

Not quite the first hint. It is subtle dramatic technique to forbode *peripeteia* even at the peak of well-being. Thus Vergil 'Laetus' has acquired for the duration of the *Aeneid* a potential novelty of value: it may connote *disaster-prone* happiness, happiness which retribution awaits. This value is cashed in now, at 1.503. Dido's 'laeta' discreetly forebodes the disaster that will come. And Vergil organizes a combination that should help us see the encashment. The syntactical structure of 1.496 ff. repeats that of 1.35 ff., the passage seminal for the new value of 'laetus'. In both 'laetitia' is presented, apparently unalloyed, in main clauses. Then comes, in both, an inverted 'cum' (as it were, the real main clause). In 1.35 ff. the 'cum' clause introduces the start of an explicit *peripeteia*; in 1.496 ff. the 'cum' clause also introduces (I would argue) the start of the *peripeteia*. And Aeneas repeats the role of the disaster-bringing Juno.[7]

I would argue that the acquired value of 'laetus' also intrudes at, say, the 'limina laeta' of 1.707, and, most ironically, in Aeneas' 'quae te tam laeta tulerunt / saecula?' at 1.605 f. The tragic, disaster-prone quality of Dido's 'laetitia' is more or less explicit in 11.73 'uestis ... quas illi laeta laborum / ipsa suis quondam manibus Sidonia Dido / fecerat', confirming our intuitions in those earlier examples.

I leave the scrutiny of further passages for others. I would remark that there is a lot of happiness in book 5 which, in consequence of this acquisition by 'laetus', is darkened. I think too that at some point 'laetus' and cognates acquire a refinement of value. They may connote a subject's happiness which has disastrous implications for others.

3. 'geminus', and the 'uestes' of Dido

To illustrate the second form of the technique of acquisition mentioned at the beginning of the chapter, I take the word 'geminus'. 'Geminus' acquires a value which is not striking, but it is exclusive. This is then strikingly cashed in.

'Geminus' is used no less than 41 times in the *Aeneid*. On all occasions except, apparently, the last two, Vergil uses it in the following unstriking but exclusive manner. He uses it to convey the notion 'twin', 'double' or 'two' when such a notion is good sense, demanded by or readily explicable in the context: twin gates, rocks, Atridae, snakes, etc. The context wants, requires, or well accommodates 'twin' gates, rocks, Atridae, snakes, and so on, and Vergil expresses 'twin' by 'geminus'. This is the word's function, established over dozens of uses. This is the value the word acquires: to signify 'two' where two is explicable.

On a couple of occasions—which are *not* the two apparent exceptions that I refer to—Vergil uses the word a trifle deviously: at 6.779 and 788. Anchises seems studiously to ignore Romulus' famous twin brother Remus in his references at 6.778 ff. to

---

[7] Cf. how Vergil indicates his disaster-bringing role by comparing him to Apollo the plaguebringer at 4.149: Lyne, *Further Voices*, 123–5.

Romulus, Rome, and the auspices (which some might remember
was a contest between the two brothers); he appears a little chary
of the brother who might bring to mind the unwelcome topic of
fratricide.[8] Vergil in a characteristic manner seems tactlessly
keen to mention 'twin' objects at this time: the 'geminae cristae'
on Romulus' head, the 'twin eyes' with which he is invited to
look at the Roman people, 6.779 and 788. What Anchises seems
anxious to obscure, Vergil insinuates. It is what on another
occasion I might have called a 'further voice'. These two uses
then may be thought slightly devious—devious, but they do not
flout the normal practice. The context well enough accommodates two eyes, and for that matter two crests—though these
crests are more of a puzzle.[9]

'Geminus' therefore acquires a value, undramatic but particular and exclusive: 'two', demanded by, or at least explicable in,
context. The two apparent exceptions are *the last two* occurrences of the word in the poem (11.72 and 12.845). The apparent
exceptions have therefore been organized at most conspicuous
occasions, at the time when we should be most sensitive to any
deviation. But deviate is what Vergil appears to do. At both
11.72 and 12.845 he seems to use 'geminus' in a most odd and
redundant manner, where 'two' or 'twin' is not demanded by
context, nor well accommodated in it. First, 11.72.

At 11.72 ff. Aeneas takes out two garments made by Dido:

> tum geminas uestis auroque ostroque rigentis
> extulit Aeneas, quas illi laeta laborum
> ipsa suis quondam manibus Sidonia Dido
> fecerat et tenui telas discreuerat auro.

Then Aeneas brought out two garments stiff with gold and purple,
which Sidonian Dido, happy in her work, had once upon a time made
for him with her own hands, interweaving the web with threads of gold.

---

[8] At 1.292 Jupiter passes over the quarrel and murder, and (if we think of this)
implies the brothers' reconciliation in heaven.

[9] Romulus' twin 'cristae' are perhaps an allusion to Mars. Val. Max. 1.8.6
mentions an apparition thought to be Mars whose 'galea' was 'duabus distincta
pennis' (Austin, Henry). The specification 'twin' eyes was not necessarily felt as
tautologous. Cf. Catull. 51.11 where the text is either 'gemina teguntur lumina nocte'
with 'gemina' (abl.) transferred from 'lumina', or 'aures geminae'; also 63.75 where
the MSS 'geminas ... aures' has been challenged by some on extrinsic grounds. See
further Fordyce on this latter passage.

And he uses *one* to veil the head of Pallas:

> *harum unam* iuueni supremum maestus honorem
> induit arsurasque comas obnubit amictu...

Of these he sadly put *one* on the young man as a last honour, and veiled[10] the hair that would burn with the raiment

It is an ineffably dense, troubled, and troubling gesture to grace Pallas with Dido's gift: expressive of Aeneas' love for Pallas, of Aeneas' and Vergil's sense of the kinship of Dido and Pallas as victims, and so on. But the point I am after at the moment is another.

Why 'two', 'geminas'? We note that of the second, the one that Aeneas does not use for Pallas, we hear nothing. The pair of 'uestes', and thus the word 'geminas', seem not demanded by nor readily explicable in this context, introduced solely to be immediately adjusted: 'harum *unam*'. The context—Aeneas veiling Pallas—requires one not two 'uestes', and it accommodates the two only—it seems—artificially: it has immediately to eliminate one of them. So why does Vergil make Aeneas produce two and choose one in this cumbersome periphrasis?[11] Why has Vergil varied his normal practice with 'geminus', which is to use it only when context wants, requires, or well accommodates 'two' of something? It seems a puzzle.

A likely answer is that Vergil is only *apparently* doing something different: in fact he is employing the significance that 'geminus' has acquired in an *unobvious* way—hence we initially assume he is doing something different. It would after all be a curious moment to depart from normal practice, it is rather exactly the time to *cash in* the acquired value: when 'geminus' has had maximum opportunity to acquire it, in the penultimate (and ultimate) example. This then is the likely supposition: that he is cashing in the value of 'geminus'; the apparent redundance of the word in its acquired sense should be regarded as a designed puzzle, a combination organized to make us pause—and, having paused, to find a discreet encashment.

Our inference should therefore be that the value 'two', seem-

---

[10] On 'obnubit' see VII. p. 157.
[11] Some might answer: because of Homeric precedent. I deal with this point below.

ingly redundant, is in fact most important. Vergil is cashing in
the value of 'geminus' to make us think of *two*: in 11.72 ff., of
two 'uestes' made by Dido. *Two* 'uestes' are important in this
context. We know what the function of one of them is: to veil
Pallas. The question therefore remains: *what about the other one?*
Vergil cashes in the value of 'geminus' to make us ask this
question.

First, we must make a point about the 'uestis' with which
Aeneas veils Pallas. Why does he choose one *made by Dido* for
this purpose? Besides the points I make above, we must appreci-
ate that it is a sign of the importance that Aeneas attaches to
Dido if he uses something made by her to grace the beloved
Pallas. One uses something that one prizes to cover the dead.[12]

Well: *what about the other one?*—the other one, which, so
Vergil's use of 'geminus' decrees, is in some way necessary or
desirable in the context? The other one remains. Vergil tells us a
simple but eloquent fact. Aeneas has hitherto kept two garments
lovingly made by the hand of Dido, and will now, since he only
uses *one* of *two*, continue to keep *one*: Aeneas has hitherto kept
two garments made by Dido *which he prized* and will continue to
keep one, and, we infer, *prize it*, a garment that Dido lovingly
made, 'laeta laborum'. These facts indicate Aeneas' continuing
emotional contact with the episode of Dido and Carthage, with
the history behind the carefully wrought cloth. When a love-
affair is absolutely over, one does not keep the love-letters, nor
prize the beloved's presents. For Aeneas the importance of Dido
is not over. From book 4 to book 11 he kept and prized the
beloved's presents. From book 11 to the end he will still be in
possession of a prized present from Dido, still in contact with the
emotional story of Carthage.

In a sense, too, we see here a slight rejoinder by Aeneas the
lover—to Mercury, Jupiter, and the claims of public duty:
Aeneas' little protest. We remember the scene when Mercury
came to send Aeneas on his way in book 4. He found him
disgracefully 'fundantem arces', 'founding the citadels' of Carthage, a dreadful sight. He delivered a stingingly contemptuous
speech, an aspect of which I discussed in III.2 ('uxorius'). Part of

---

[12] Cf. for example the coverings used to wrap the dead in the Homeric passages
adduced in the *Addendum* below.

the reason why Aeneas appeared so offensive to Mercury, part of
the reason why Mercury reckoned he deserved the jibe 'uxorius',
was the cloak he wore. It was (a) obviously foreign,[13] and (b) it
was made for him and bestowed upon him by the foreign queen,
the lover who (so the *boni* would think) shamed him. In fact
Aeneas cut a figure unhappily like Antony, who wore unRoman
clothes at Cleopatra's court.[14] All in all, it is not surprising that
Mercury felt moved to imply that Aeneas was the 'property of
his wife'.

The description of Aeneas in his shocking cloak is as follows,
4.262 ff.:

> Tyrioque ardebat murice laena
> demissa ex umeris, diues quae munera Dido
> fecerat, et tenui telas discreuerat auro.

Hanging from his shoulders was a cloak blazing with Tyrian purple, a
gift which wealthy Dido had made for him, interweaving the web with
threads of gold.

We should note that the cloak in question seems identical to the
ones produced in book 11, and is, I would presume, to be
actually identified with one of them:[15] note in particular the
exact repetition of the phrase 'tenui telas discreuerat auro'.

I think there is a question to be asked in connection with
Aeneas in book 4. Called to his senses by Mercury while he is
dressed in his flashy and shaming cloak, he has a decision to
make in connection with that cloak, and with any others he may
possess like it. He has three basic choices. He can brazenly carry
on wearing this sort of stuff; or he can abandon it in restored
Roman horror at such kit, at such gifts from such a woman; or
he may do neither of these two extremes, and he may put it away
in his suitcase. Vergil has discreetly shown that Aeneas chose the
third option at Carthage and will continue with that policy from

---

[13] Roman taste disliked the wearing of foreign clothes by Romans. Even items of
Greek dress attracted criticism: cf. Cic. *Pis*. 92 'crepidatus', with Nisbet ad loc. citing
other instances. Cic. *Rab. Post*. 27 shows that the practice could be defended; equally
the passage shows that the practice needed to be defended. Cf. further the next note.

[14] Pöschl, 52, Florus 2.21.3 (the passage well illustrates the feeling against foreign
clothes) 'patriae nominis *togae* fascium oblitus ... aureum in manu baculum, in latere
acinaces (cf. Aeneas's sword given to him by Dido, 4.261), *purpurea uestis ingentibus
obstricta gemmis*.' Note the purple (cf. Aeneas' 'Tyrio ... murice').

[15] Thus e.g. Sparrow, 67.

now (book 11) on. Vergil cashes in the acquired value of
'geminus' to show us Aeneas' small protest against Rome and
duty, as well as his continuing adherence to the emotional story
of Dido.

Addendum: Homer, *Iliad* 24.578 ff. and Vergil *Aen.* 11.72 ff.
A clear source for Aeneas' veiling of Pallas in *Aeneid* 11 is the
scene in which Achilles covers the dead body of Hector with
clothes brought as ransom by Priam. What I have argued above
is, in sum, that the presence of *two* 'uestes' is initially a puzzle.
Vergil's stylistic practice (the use of 'geminus') suggests that the
two 'uestes' are important, but the context only seems to require
one. It is a puzzle, so I argue, designed by Vergil to lead us
eventually to the question: *what about the other one?*

Many might retort: there is no puzzle. Vergil introduces *two*
'uestes' followed by a reference to *one* because Homer introduces
two 'cloaks', φάρεα, followed by a reference to *one* at the
corresponding moment in the source scene. So, if we think
Homer's twosome explicable, we should assume the same explanation in Vergil; alternatively, if we find Homer's twosome
not well motivated, then we should not be surprised at a
corresponding lack of motivation in the imitator. Either way
there is no need for subtle explanation of Vergil's 'geminas'.

The relevant portion of Homer's text runs as follows
(24.578–81 and 587–9):

> ἐϋξέστου δ' ἀπ' ἀπήνης
> ᾕρεον Ἑκτορέης κεφαλῆς ἀπερείσι' ἄποινα.
> κὰδ δ' ἔλιπον δύο φάρε' ἐϋννητόν τε χιτῶνα,
> ὄφρα νέκυν πυκάσας δοίη οἶκόνδε φέρεσθαι.
> ...
> τὸν δ' ἐπεὶ οὖν δμῳαὶ λοῦσαν καὶ χρῖσαν ἐλαίῳ,
> ἀμφὶ δέ μιν φᾶρος καλὸν βάλον ἠδὲ χιτῶνα,
> αὐτὸς τόν γ' Ἀχιλεὺς λεχέων ἐπέθηκεν ἀείρας ...

From the well-planed waggon they took the countless ransom for
Hector's head. But they left there two cloaks and a well-woven tunic, so
that Achilles might wrap the corpse and give it to be carried home ...
When the slave girls had washed the body and anointed it with oil, and
had cast round it a beautiful cloak and a tunic, then Achilles himself
lifted it and set it upon the bier...'

We note that two cloaks and a tunic are left to wrap Hector, but only one cloak and a tunic are explicitly employed for the purpose. C. W. Macleod, who thinks the twosome explicable, comments at 24.580 as follows:[16] 'The χιτών is worn next to the skin, and of the φάρεα, one is wrapped round him and one spread beneath him.' And he compares a fifth century Cean inscription[17] which translates: 'he buried the dead man in this way: in three white garments (ἱμάτια), one spread underneath (στρώματι), one put on him (ἐνδύματι), one put over him (ἐπιβλέματι).' Macleod also compares *Iliad* 18.352–3, and he continues: 'In 588 only one φᾶρος is mentioned because the other is not put 'round' Hector, but under him on the bier (cf. στρώματι ...).' That is, while we are explicitly told that one φᾶρος is put round Hector by the slave girls, we must infer that the other one is put under him when Achilles places him on the bier: so that, with the χιτών, we have a three-fold wrapping (φᾶρος under, χιτών on, and φᾶρος over) in the manner of the Cean inscription.

I doubt whether Homer is being so exact. The reference to *Iliad* 18.352–3 is evidence against rather than for the situation that Macleod envisages. In these lines the body of Patroclus is shrouded thus:

ἐν λεχέεσσι δὲ θέντες ἑανῷ λιτὶ κάλυψαν
ἐς πόδας ἐκ κεφαλῆς, καθύπερθε δὲ φάρεϊ λευκῷ.

They placed him on the bed, and covered him with a fine linen cloth from head to foot, and above that with a white cloak.

Patroclus is first covered in a linen cloth, then in a cloak. This is evidence to support the view that at 24.588 Hector is first covered by the χιτών ('next to the skin'), then, over that, by the φᾶρος. But it is no evidence that Homer envisaged the second φᾶρος being put under him. Rather it is evidence that Homer need suppose no underlay at all. So: what of the other φᾶρος mentioned at 24.580? I think that it is not easy to explain: we should accept that the text presents a slight puzzle. It may simply be that the two φάρεα became laxly merged as one. Or it may be as Macleod argues. But I think we have finally to conclude: there is a puzzle.

[16] He follows the scholia. ΣA on 24.588 ὅτι ἔδει χιτῶνα, εἶτα φᾶρος, ΣT on 580 ἔθος τοὺς νεκροὺς δυσὶν κατακαλύπτειν ἐσθῆσιν, ὅπως τὸ μὲν ἄνω, τὸ δὲ κάτω ...
[17] F. Sokolowski, *Lois sacrées des cités grecques* , (Paris, 1969), 97 A1–4.

What I would stress is that the slight Homeric puzzle, far from being eliminated by Vergil, is accentuated by him. He calls attention to the apparent non-functionality of his second 'uestis': 'tum geminas uestis ... harum *unam*'. He so calls attention to it that we must assume, as I said, that he designs a puzzle. His text emphasizes the question which Homer's leaves muted: what about the other one? There is another point. Macleod's explanation of Homer's second φᾶρος, that it was spread underneath Hector, that it acted as (in the words of the Cean inscription) a στρῶμα, will not fit Vergil's text. Pallas is already equipped with a στρῶμα, a 'stramen', a significantly rural under-'blanket' of (it seems) leaves[18] and so on, 11.64–7:

> haud segnes alii cratis et molle feretrum
> arbuteis texunt uirgis et uimine querno
> extructosque toros obtentu frondis inumbrant.
> hic iuuenem agresti sublimem stramine ponunt.

Others are quick to plait the wicker-frame of a soft bier from arbute twigs and oak withies, and to shade the couch that they had made with a covering of leaves. Here they place the young man aloft on his rural bedding ...

So the question emphatically remains: what about the other 'uestis'? And for this, the Vergilian question, there is a Vergilian answer.

4. 'geminus' (cont.) and Jupiter's Furies

At 12.845 ff. Jupiter dispatches a Fury to bring the conflict in Italy to a close. We have a similar adjusted use of 'geminus' to the one we had at 11.72 ff. 12.845 ff.:

> dicuntur geminae pestes cognomine Dirae,
> quas et Tartaream Nox intempesta Megaeram
> uno eodemque tulit partu ...
> hae Iouis ad solium saeuique in limine regis
> apparent ...

---

[18] Conington–Nettleship understand 'obtentus frondis' in the passage quoted to be a covering layer on the bier, and I am inclined to agree. Others think that a canopy is being referred to, and the language does indeed lend itself to this interpretation. Either way the essential point remains, that Pallas is already equipped with some sort of 'stramen', στρῶμα, when Aeneas comes to apply the 'uestes'.

> *harum unam* celerem demisit ab aethere summo
> Iuppiter ....

Two pestilences called the Dread Ones are talked of, whom Night bore in one parturition with Tartarean Megaera ... These appear at the throne and on the threshold of the savage king Jupiter ... Of *these* Jupiter sent *one* swiftly down from high heaven ...

The context here would seem to require only one Fury: only one is gainfully employed. The second Fury is accommodated by the context with, it seems, difficulty: the poet must immediately eliminate it ('harum unam'). But Vergil only uses 'geminus' when *two* of something are wanted, required, or can be well accommodated by the context. So the second Fury's function, apparently non-existent, should be explicable. Indeed we have much reason to think it will be important. This is the ultimate example of 'geminus' in the poem: it is a time to cash in a lengthily acquired value, not to ignore it. And in the previous and penultimate example, when Vergil used 'geminus' with identical apparent redundance ('harum unam'), that apparent redundance was shown to be a designed puzzle, a combination organized to make us pause—and to see acquired value being importantly encashed. Two 'uestes' were seen to be important at 11.72 ff. It should follow that two Furies have a role to play here. We could ask the same question here as before: what about the other one? Or, *why two*, when only one has a visible function in context?

Two Furies, we are told, customarily serve Jupiter. We are told something else. Neither is Megaera. If we now remember that in the tradition which Vergil uses there are *three* Furies in all, Megaera, Tisiphone and *Allecto*,[19] then we must conclude that of Jupiter's two agents, one *is* Allecto. The other and apparently unemployed Fury does not so much (I think) have a *dramatic* function, as the other 'uestis' did, as an *authorial* function. Her appearance here, which permits us to know that Jupiter uses the *two* Furies who are not Megaera, is Vergil's devious means of signalling the fact that Jupiter must sometimes employ the same evil monster that Juno employed in Book 7. He

---

[19] 6.555, 571, 7.324, 10.761, 12.846; cf. R. D. Williams on 12.845. The fixing of the total at *three* Furies is as early as Euripides, *Or.* 408, 1650, *Tro.* 457 (but a larger number at *IT.* 968 ff.). For the trio named as Allecto, Tisiphone, and Megaera, cf., besides Vergil, Apollodorus 1.1.4, Orphic Hymn 69 (to the Erinyes). 2 Τισιφόνη τε καὶ Ἀλληκτὼ καὶ δῖα Μέγαιρα.

may be employing her at this very moment. This is why we are
told of two Furies. Vergil cashes in acquired value to dark effect
at the conclusion of our Augustan poem.

Bibliography

The works listed below will be referred to by author's name, or author's name and abbreviated title. Other items will occasionally be cited in full in the footnotes. Standard commentaries on Vergilian and other classical texts are cited by the author's name; I have thought it unnecessary to list them all here.

ADAMS, J. N., *The Latin Sexual Vocabulary* (London, 1982).

ANDERSON, W. S., 'Juno and Saturn in the *Aeneid*', *Studies in Philology* 55 (1958), 519–32.

ANDERSON, W. S., '*Pastor Aeneas*: On Pastoral Themes in the *Aeneid*', *TAPA* 99 (1968), 1–17.

AXELSON, B., *Unpoetische Wörter, ein Beitrag zur Kenntnis der lateinischen Dichtersprache* (Lund, 1945).

BARFIELD, O., *Poetic Diction*, 3rd edn. (Middletown, Conn., 1973).

BASSETT, S. E., 'The Function of the Homeric Simile', *TAPA* 52 (1921), 132–47.

BELL, A. J., *The Latin Dual and Poetic Diction, Studies in Numbers and Figures* (Toronto, 1923).

BÖMER, F., 'Beiträge zum Verständnis der augusteischen Dichtersprache', *Gymnasium* 64 (1957), 1–21.

BONFANTI, M., *Punto di vista e modi della narrazione nell' Eneide* (Pisa, 1985).

BOOTH, W. C., *The Rhetoric of Fiction*, 2nd edn. (Chicago/London, 1983).

BOWRA, C. M., *Tradition and Design in the Iliad* (Oxford, 1930).

CAMPS, W. A., *An Introduction to Virgil's Aeneid* (Oxford, 1969).

CLARK, R. J., 'Two Virgilian Similes and the Ἡρακλέους κατάβασις', *Phoenix* 24 (1970), 244–55.

CLAUSING, A., *Kritik und Exegese der homerischen Gleichnisse im Altertum* (Parchim, 1913).

CONTE, G. B., *Memoria dei poeti e sistema letterario* (Torino, 1974).

——*Virgilio: Il genere e i suoi confini* (Milano, 1984).

——*The Rhetoric of Imitation, Genre and Poetic Memory in Virgil and Other Latin Poets* (Ithaca/London, 1986). (This includes an English translation of most of the above two books.)

CORDIER, A., *Etudes sur le vocabulaire épique dans l''éneide'* (Paris, 1939).

COUISSIN, P., *Les armes romaines. Essai sur les origines et l'évolution des armes individuelles du légionnaire romain* (Paris, 1926).

——'Virgile et l'Italie primitive: VII Les armes', *Revue des Cours et Conférences* 33 (1931–2), II.557–76.

COURTNEY, E., 'Valeriana Tertia', *CR* 79 (1965), 151–5.

ERNOUT, A., Review of Axelson: *Rev. Phil.* 21 (1947), 55–70.

——*Aspects du vocabulaire latin* (Paris, 1954).

FOWLER, D., 'Vergil on Killing Virgins', in *Homo Viator, Classical Essays for John Bramble*, ed. M. Whitby, P. Hardie, M. Whitby (Bristol, 1987), pp. 185–98.

FRÄNKEL, H., *Die homerischen Gleichnisse* (Göttingen, 1921).

GALINSKY, G. K., 'The Hercules-Cacus Episode in *Aeneid* viii', *AJP* 87 (1966), 18–51.

GENETTE, G., *Narrative Discourse* (translated by J. E. Lewin) (Oxford, Blackwell, 1980).

GÖRLER, W., 'Ex verbis communibus κακοζηλία *Die augusteischen "Klassiker" und die griechischen Theoretiker des Klassizismus, Entretiens Fondation Hardt* XXV' (Vandoeuvres-Genève, 1979), 175–202.

HAPP, H., 'Die lateinische Umgangssprache und die Kunstsprache des Plautus', *Glotta* 45 (1967), 60–104.

HARDIE, P. R., *Virgil's Aeneid: Cosmos and Imperium* (Oxford 1986).

HEINZE, R., *Virgils epische Technik*, 3rd edn. (Leipzig/Berlin, 1915).

HIGHET, G., *The Speeches in Vergil's Aeneid* (Princeton, 1972).

HOFMANN, J. B., *Lateinische Umgangssprache*, 3rd edn. (Heidelberg, 1951).

JACKSON KNIGHT, W. F., *Roman Vergil*, Revised edn. (London, 1966).

JANSSEN, H. H., *De kenmerken der Romeinsche dichtertaal* (Nijmegen-Utrecht, 1941), reprinted (in Italian) in Lunelli, pp. 67–130.

JOCELYN, H. D., '*Vergilius Cacozelus* (Donatus *Vita Vergilii* 44)', *Papers of the Liverpool Latin Seminar* 2 (1979), 67–142.

KNAUER, G., *Die Aeneis und Homer* (Göttingen, 1964).

KROLL, W., *Studien zum Verständnis der römischen Literatur* (Stuttgart 1924). Pages 247–79 (= 'Die Dichtersprache') are reprinted (in Italian) in Lunelli, pp. 1–66.

LEEMAN, A. D., *Orationis Ratio, The Stylistic Theories and Practice of the Roman Orators, Historians, and Philosophers* (Amsterdam, 1963).

LEUMANN, M., 'Die lateinische Dichtersprache', *Mus. Helv.* 4 (1947), 116–39 (= *Kleine Schriften* 131–156), reprinted (in Italian) in Lunelli, pp. 131–78.

LLOYD-JONES, H., 'Heracles at Eleusis: P. Oxy. 2622 and P. S. I. 1391', *Maia* 19 (1967), 206–29.

LÖFSTEDT, E., *Philologischer Kommentar zur Peregrinatio Aetheriae, Untersuchungen zur Geschichte der lateinischen Sprache* (Uppsala, 1911).

——*Syntactica, Studien und Beiträge zur historischen Syntax des Lateins*, 2nd edn. (Lund, 1956).

LUNELLI, A. (ed.), *La Lingua Poetica Latina*, 2nd edn. (Bologna, 1980): contains essays by W. Kroll, H. H. Janssen, and M. Leumann, translated into Italian and with updated bibliography.

LYNE, R. O. A. M., *The Latin Love Poets, from Catullus to Horace* (Oxford, 1980).

——'Diction and Poetry in Vergil's *Aeneid*', *Atti del Convegno mondiale scientifico di Studi su Virgilio* (Milano 1984), 2.64–88.

——*Further Voices in Vergil's Aeneid* (Oxford, 1987).

MACLEOD, C., *Collected Essays* (Oxford, 1983).

MAROUZEAU, J., *Traité de stylistique latine*, 2nd edn. (Paris, 1946).

——*Quelques aspects de la formation du latin littéraire* (Paris, 1949).

MOULTON, C., *Similes in the Homeric Poems* (Göttingen, 1977).

NISBET, R. G. M., '*Aeneas Imperator*: Roman Generalship in an Epic Context', *PVS* 18 (1978–80), 50–60.

ONIANS, R. B., *The Origins of European Thought, About the Body, the Mind, the Soul, the World, Time, and Fate*, 2nd edn. (Cambridge, 1954).

OPELT, I., *Die lateinischen Schimpfwörter und verwandte sprachliche Erscheinungen, Eine Typologie* (Heidelberg 1965).

OTIS, B., *Virgil: A Study in Civilized Poetry* (Oxford, 1963).

PALMER, L. R., *The Latin Language* (London, 1954).

PICHON, R., *De sermone amatorio apud Latinos elegiarum scriptores* (Paris, 1902). Pp. 75–303 republished as *Index Verborum Amatoriorum*, (Hildesheim, 1966).

PÖSCHL, V., *Die Dichtkunst Virgils: Bild und Symbol in der Aeneis*, 3rd edn. (Berlin/New York, 1977).

PORTER, D. H., 'Violent Juxtaposition in the Similes of the *Iliad*', *CJ* 68 (1972), 11–21.

PUTNAM, M. C. J., 'Possessiveness, Sexuality and Heroism in the *Aeneid*', *Vergilius* 31 (1985), 1–21.

QUINN, K., *Virgil's Aeneid: A Critical Description*, 2nd edn. (London, 1969).

RENGER, C., *Aeneas und Turnus, Analyse einer Feindschaft* (Frankfurt am Main, 1985).

RICHARDSON, N. J., 'Literary Criticism in the Exegetical Scholia to the *Iliad*: A Sketch', *CQ* NS 30 (1980), 265–87.

RIMMON-KENAN, S., *Narrative Fiction: Contemporary Poetics* (London/New York, 1983).

SENFTER, R., 'Vergil, *Aen.* 8, 589–91: Konnotationsraum und Funktionalisierung eines Vergleichs', *MD* 2 (1979), 171–4.

SILK, M. S., *Interaction in Poetic Imagery, with special reference to early Greek poetry* (Cambridge, 1974).

SPARROW, J., *Half-Lines and Repetitions in Virgil* (Oxford 1931).

STANDFORD, W. B., *Greek Metaphor, Studies in Theory and Practice* (Oxford, Blackwell, 1936).

THANIEL, G., 'Vergil's Leaf- and Bird-Similes of Ghosts', *Phoenix* 25 (1971), 237–45.

TILLOTSON, G., *Augustan Poetic Diction* (London, 1964) (= a corrected reprint of ch. I-IV of his *Augustan Studies*, London, 1961).

TRÄNKLE, H., *Die Sprachkunst des Properz und die Tradition der lateinischen Dichtersprache* (Wiesbaden, 1960).

WATSON, P., 'Axelson revisited: the selection of vocabulary in Latin poetry', *CQ* NS 35 (1985), 430–48.

WEST, D., 'Multiple-Correspondence Similes in the *Aeneid*', *JRS* 59 (1969), 40–9.

——'Virgilian Multiple-Correspondence Similes and their Antecedents', *Philologus* 114 (1970), 262–75.

WILKINSON, L. P., 'The Language of Virgil and Horace', *CQ* NS 9 (1959), 181–92.

——*Golden Latin Artistry* (Cambridge, 1963).

WILLIAMS, G., *Tradition and Originality in Roman Poetry* (Oxford, 1968).

——*Figures of Thought in Roman Poetry* (New Haven/London, 1980).

WOODMAN, T., and WEST, D. (eds.), *Quality and Pleasure in Latin Poetry* (Cambridge, 1974).

Index

Index of Passages Discussed